CONTENTS

STRUCTURING PARAGRAPHS

A Guide to Effective Writing

fourth edition

STRUCTURING PARAGRAPHS

A Guide to Effective Writing

A. Franklin Parks

FROSTBURG STATE UNIVERSITY

James A. Levernier

UNIVERSITY OF ARKANSAS AT LITTLE ROCK

Ida Masters Hollowell

UNIVERSITY OF ARKANSAS AT LITTLE ROCK

 ST. MARTIN'S PRESS • New York

EDITOR: Nancy Lyman
MANAGER, PUBLISHING SERVICES: Emily Berleth
ASSOCIATE, PUBLISHING SERVICES: Meryl Perrin
PROJECT MANAGEMENT: Omega Publishing Services, Inc.
PRODUCTION SUPERVISOR: Melissa Kaprelian
TEXT DESIGN: Anna George
COVER DESIGN: Kay Petronio

Library of Congress Catalog Number 95-67057

Manufactured in the United States of America
0 9 8 7 6
f e d c b a

For information write:
St. Martin's Press, Inc.
175 Fifth Ave.
New York, N.Y. 10010

ISBN: 0-312-11513-X

PREFACE

Like its previous editions, this fourth edition of *Structuring Paragraphs: A Guide to Effective Writing* grows out of the basic premise that as students learn and understand the form of the paragraph they will also learn most of the principles of good writing. As we stated in the preface of the first edition, "Our experience has been that the student who can write a paragraph that is purposeful, coherently developed, and free of grammatical and usage errors is more than ready to tackle the essay when the time comes." *Structuring Paragraphs* both presents the elements of effective paragraph writing and transfers those principles to the writing of the short essay.

Structuring Paragraphs: A Guide to Effective Writing guides students through the process of writing, introducing them sequentially and logically to the principles of good prose, leading them through the writing and revising of paragraphs and short essays. At each stage in the writing process, we try to give the student a great deal of practical, down-to-earth advice on how to write clearly and effectively. The presentation of each topic includes

1. a clear explanation of the concept;
2. a variety of good, representative models and examples that are exclusively student-written;
3. a concise but thorough summary; and
4. a carefully sequenced series of exercises and writing activities, interspersed throughout, that promote mastery of basic skills and the transition to independent writing.

In addition to presenting the basics of paragraph unity and development, *Structuring Paragraphs* also provides lessons in sentence-combining (in Chapter 6) and devotes full attention to the revision stage of the writing process (Chapter 9). It is this practical, clear approach to the writing process that many of the instructors and students who worked with the previous editions of *Structuring Paragraphs* found most useful about the book. It also emphasizes helping students to understand concepts rather than simply asking them to mimic the models. Instructors have told us that their students both learned and enjoyed learning from *Structuring Paragraphs*.

NEW TO THIS EDITION

The improvements to the fourth edition of *Structuring Paragraphs* are substantial and were guided by our own experiences, those of our colleagues, and the suggestions made by users of the third edition.

- First, we have added many new models on topics that are fresh and likely to be of interest to students. We have also revised a number of the exercises to make them more workable for student writers.

- Second, we have added a new chapter on answering discussion questions on quizzes and examinations (Chapter 8), which provides the student with a useful application of the writing skills taught in the text.

- Thirdly, we have introduced collaborative and portfolio activities to the chapters, enriching the writing experiences for students and increasing the number of exercise options for their instructors.

- Finally, we have expanded "A Concise Guide to Editing Sentences," which provides students with quick answers to questions regarding grammar, punctuation, and usage.

We believe that these additions strengthen the text significantly for a wide variety of paragraph-to-essay writing courses.

ACKNOWLEDGMENTS

In preparing this fourth edition of *Structuring Paragraphs,* we are again in debt to those who have assisted us. We wish, in particular, to extend our gratitude to our editor, Sam Potts; to Karen Allanson, for encouraging this edition; and to Edward Hutchinson for his thoughtful revision work. In addition, we thank Constance Chapman, Georgia State University; Martha French, Fairmont State College; David K. Himber, St. Petersburg Junior College; Rosemary Hunkeler, University of Wisconsin—Parkside; J. C. B. Kinch,

Edinboro University of Pennsylvania; Kate Mele, Roger Williams University; Linda C. Pelzer, Wesley College; and Judith Stanford, Rivier College, for their helpful comments on the third edition of *Structuring Paragraphs* and their guidance in the creation of the fourth edition.

Finally, we thank our students, whose work in the classroom has shaped and inspired this book since its first edition.

THE GENERAL-TO-SPECIFIC PARAGRAPH

Much of the writing you will do, in college and throughout your career, is *expository,* and the quality of your work will depend on how well you have mastered the skills and concepts that are basic to good expository prose. Expository prose is writing that *explains:* your purpose may be to describe a process, define a term, or discuss an idea or a point of view. In college, you will frequently be asked to write essays, research papers, or reports. On the job, you may be required to prepare letters, briefs, memorandums, or other written material. The writing skills you will need to accomplish such assignments successfully include the ability to select a topic and limit it, to organize and unify your material, to develop your topic adequately, and to connect your ideas logically and smoothly.

One good way to acquire these basic writing skills is to start on the level of the paragraph, where the demands of length do not overshadow the need to improve the *quality* of your writing. Concentrating on the paragraph will provide valuable practice on a relatively small scale. In this book, therefore, we will examine the expository paragraph. In particular, we will study the *general-to-specific* expository paragraph—the paragraph that opens with a general statement and goes on to support that statement with appropriate examples and details. Learning to write an effective paragraph of this kind means learning the skills and concepts that are essential to good writing in general. Moreover, because this type of paragraph is, in a sense, an essay in miniature, mastering its form should help you to master longer forms of writing as well. There is no better way to learn the skills of effective writing than practice, and the form of the general-to-specific expository paragraph provides a controlled and effective structure for gaining that practice.

BASIC STRUCTURE AND PURPOSE

The general-to-specific expository paragraph, like most paragraphs, is a group of sentences that work together to present a single, unified topic or idea. The first line is indented to signal the reader that a new grouping of sentences is beginning.

The length of this kind of paragraph usually ranges from about one hundred to three hundred words. This is not to say that shorter or longer paragraphs are unacceptable. Essays may even have one-sentence paragraphs, used for emphasis; and thousand-word paragraphs can provide valuable exposition in all types of writing. But we are not concerned here with very short or very long paragraphs. Rather, it is our intention to examine and construct paragraphs that are useful as practice because they are long enough to require careful development but not so long as to be unmanageable. For this purpose, the expository paragraph of about one hundred to three hundred words is the best kind to undertake.

THE IMPORTANCE OF SPECIFICS

The general-to-specific expository paragraph, as we have said, moves from a general opening statement that stands in need of support to the specifics—examples and factual details—that support the general statement. The purpose of writing an expository paragraph is usually to state a general proposition that you want your reader to accept as true. A general statement requires support, or development, if readers are to find it convincing. The details the writer furnishes enable readers to understand and evaluate the point the writer is making. For example, the following sentence is a general statement:

> Despite its brashness and humor, the long-running television sitcom *Roseanne* presents realistically many of the pressures confronting the American family.

Unless you have particular confidence in the writer's judgment, you would need to see some evidence in support of this statement. The writer should provide you with more specific information if he or she wants to convince you that the statement is valid. In the following paragraph, written by a student, a series of specific statements supports and explains the writer's point of view:

> (1) Despite its brashness and humor, the long-running television sitcom *Roseanne* presents realistically many of the pressures confronting the American family. (2) Constantly faced with a pile of bills they cannot pay, Dan and Rose-

anne Connor embody the unrelenting economic struggle of the American family breadwinners. (3) Dan pursues his dream of owning a small business but fails in his attempt to jump start a motorcycle repair shop and ultimately must settle for a job as manager of a city maintenance facility. (4) Meanwhile, to buffer the family's economic woes, Roseanne takes what jobs she can get, including telephone soliciting, waiting tables at a lunch counter, and cleaning up at a beauty parlor. (5) As the economic pressures on the family mount, so do the emotional. (6) Roseanne's having to leave the home and her children in order to supplement the family income yields for her feelings of guilt and anger and results in additional friction between her and Dan. (7) The Connors's home is further immersed in turmoil by the elopement of daughter Becky with her unacceptable boyfriend Mark. (8) If economic and emotional pressures were not enough, the family has to wage the class struggle on a daily basis as well. (9) The issue of their low social status surfaces most clearly with the appearance of a condescending next door neighbor from Chicago who looks down her nose at the community and Roseanne. (10) Ultimately, however, Roseanne and the Connor family succeed in humorously sloughing off the pretension of the neighbor and others they encounter by simply outlasting them and finding strength in their family bonds.

This paragraph provides the reader with several reasons for seriously considering its opening statement. By developing that general statement, the writer has taken steps to satisfy the curiosity and skepticism it may have aroused in the reader.

LEVELS OF GENERALITY

An effective general-to-specific expository paragraph usually has at least three levels of generality. The first and most general level is the opening statement. The second level consists of more specific statements that directly support the opening statement. These, in turn, may be supported by statements that are even more specific—the third level of generality—and so on.

The following outline demonstrates how the example paragraph uses the general-to-specific structure:

General Statement: Despite its brashness and humor, the long-running television sitcom *Roseanne* presents realistically many of the pressures confronting the American family.

Specific 1: Constantly faced with a pile of bills they cannot pay, Dan and Roseanne Connor embody the unrelenting economic struggle of the American family breadwinners.

Specific 1a: Dan pursues his dream of owning a small business but fails in his attempt to jump start a motorcycle repair shop and ultimately must settle for a job as manager of a city maintenance facility.

Specific 1b: Meanwhile, to buffer the family's economic woes, Roseanne takes what jobs she can get, including telephone soliciting, waiting tables at a lunch counter, and cleaning up at a beauty parlor.

Specific 2: As the economic pressures on the family mount, so do the emotional.

> *Specific 2a:* Roseanne's having to leave the home and her children in order to supplement the family income yields for her feelings of guilt and anger and results in additional friction between her and Dan.

> *Specific 2b:* The Connors's home is further immersed in turmoil by the elopement of daughter Becky with her unacceptable boyfriend Mark.

Specific 3: If economic and emotional pressures were not enough, the family has to wage the class struggle on a daily basis as well.

> *Specific 3a:* The issue of their low social status surfaces most clearly with the appearance of a condescending next door neighbor from Chicago who looks down her nose at the community and Roseanne.

> *Specific 3b:* Ultimately, however, Roseanne and the Connor family succeed in humorously sloughing off the pretension of the neighbor and others they encounter by simply outlasting them and finding strength in their family bonds.

As the outline indicates, the most general statement in the paragraph is the first sentence. The sentences at the next level of generality are labeled specifics 1, 2, and 3. These three sentences furnish major points of support, but they become more effective when pinned down even further by the details presented in sentences 1a and 1b, 2a and 2b, and 3a and 3b. (We discuss the movements of paragraph development through levels of supporting statements in more depth in Chapter 3.)

Note that, because the paragraph moves from general to specific, there is no place in it for a second statement as general as "Despite its brashness and humor, the long-running television sitcom *Roseanne* presents realistically many of the pressures confronting the American family." For instance, if a new statement—"The private lives of the stars of the television sitcom *Roseanne* have often attracted more attention than the long-running show"— were inserted in the paragraph, the focus of the paragraph would shift. The new statement, because it has little to do with the content of the rest of the paragraph, cannot function as support in the paragraph. Furthermore, the new statement, because of its level of generality, is broad enough to require a whole paragraph of specific explanation in itself.

■ SUMMARY

1. To understand the basics of clear writing, it is useful to examine first the general-to-specific expository paragraph.

2. A general-to-specific expository paragraph is a group of sentences, set apart from preceding material by indentation, that present a unified topic or idea.

3. Most general-to-specific expository paragraphs range in length from one hundred to three hundred words.

4. The general-to-specific expository paragraph moves from a general opening statement to specific supporting statements.

5. The general-to-specific expository paragraph is usually built with three levels of generality: the general opening statement, less general supporting statements, and further details that elaborate on the supporting statements.

6. No other sentence of the same level of generality as the opening statement should appear in the paragraph.

■ EXERCISES

I. In this chapter you have seen that a general-to-specific expository paragraph moves from a general opening statement to specific supporting statements and details. This exercise will give you practice in distinguishing the general from the specific. Examine the following sentences and decide whether each sentence, if used in a general-to-specific expository paragraph, would serve as a general statement requiring further support or a specific statement requiring no further support.

A. There are several stages of alcoholism.
B. The Berlin Wall fell in 1989.
C. Chunks of interstellar debris hit Jupiter.
D. It is difficult to be married to the Prince of Wales.
E. Education should do more than merely teach skills.
F. The car accident occurred on the south exit ramp of the highway.
G. Being a member of a social club has definite advantages for a college student.
H. Boston has a number of famous buildings that date back to the American Revolution.

II. The following paragraphs, taken from student writing, move successfully through varying levels of generality. Read the paragraphs carefully and then indicate in the space before each sentence its level of generality. Use GS (general statement) to indicate a sentence that is at the first level of generality and that the other sentences support. Use Arabic numerals (1,2,3) to indicate sentences that are at the second level of generality, and use lowercase letters (a,b,c) to indicate sentences that are at the third level of generality.

MODEL:

  _GS_ Scientists are uncovering new facts that challenge their long held beliefs about dinosaurs. _1_ First of all, dinosaurs were most likely not cold blooded. _1a_ Unlike cold blooded animals, they could travel briskly in cool weather. _1b_ Also, many lived above the Arctic Circle, where there is no sun during the winter. _2_ Secondly, dinosaurs may not have been a uniform dull green in color. _2a_ Rather, evidence points to the possibility of their being striped, spotted, and even brilliantly colored. _3_ Thirdly, dinosaurs were not the loners that scientists previously believed them to be. _3a_ For instance, the herbivore Triceratops, often perceived as solitary, traveled in herds and went on annual migrations. _3b_ What is more, the predatory Tyrannosaurus Rex hunted in packs. _4_ Finally, and perhaps most significantly, scientists have discovered that not all dinosaurs are extinct. _4a_ In fact, one line is flourishing today. _4b_ That line of resilient descendants is birds.

A. _____ Many popular sayings are based on historical situations and customs that have for the most part been forgotten. _____ To give someone the "cold shoulder," for example, today means intentionally to shun or ignore that person. _____ The origin of this term is believed to go back to the ancient Scottish custom of offering guests who overstayed their welcome a "cold shoulder" of mutton instead of a warm meal for dinner. _____ The phrase "flash in the pan" has an equally interesting origin. _____ While today it refers to an overnight sensation whose popularity quickly fades because it fails to live up to expectations, the term originally referred either to a "flash in the pan" of a musket that exploded but failed to fire a bullet or to a speck of fools' gold in a miner's pan that brought immediate but false expectations of a large and valuable find. _____ The popular phrase "knock on wood" has several possible origins. _____Today we "knock on wood" for good luck. _____ One explanation for this curious custom was the reverence early Christians showed for the wood of the cross. _____ Another tradition says that the practice of knocking on wood for luck began in medieval times, when accused criminals received sanctuary from the law as soon as they knocked on the wooden doors of a church. _____ Still another possible origin for this custom may be the worship of trees and shrubs by the prehistoric inhabitants of Great Britain.

B. _____ Many questions linger today concerning the 1963 assassination of President John Fitzgerald Kennedy in Dallas, Texas. _____ One major question that is often debated is the number of shots fired at the president's motorcade. _____ Initially, investigators concluded that three shots were fired. _____ However, subsequent evidence has pointed to four and even six. _____ Another nagging question concerns the direction from which the shots were fired. _____ The official investigation concluded that the three shots came from the Texas School Book Depository. _____ But eyewitnesses have claimed that the president was fired upon from a nearby grassy knoll and from directly in front of the motorcade. _____ Perhaps the most controversial question concerns the number of assassins involved. _____ The investigation conducted by the Warren Commission concluded that a lone assassin, Lee Harvey Oswald, was solely responsible for the act. _____ But since the time of the commission report, evidence has surfaced suggesting that three or more teams of assassins were responsible.

C. _____ Walking has recently become extremely popular among people of all ages. _____ One important reason is the physical benefit of added strength and stamina that walking provides. _____ In their off-seasons, professional athletes often walk or hike when they are not exercising more rigorously. _____ Young people are now walking where they used to ride so that they can stay healthy and participate in physical activities. _____ A second reason for the popularity of walking is that a brisk walk can burn off calories and fat. _____ Dieters and people who have jobs that do not require a great deal of physical activity often walk because of this benefit. _____ Lastly, walking is especially popular among older people who find other forms of exercise too strenuous. _____ On the advice of a doctor, an older person can walk many blocks or even many miles a day without running the risk of a heart attack.

D. _____ The inability of alcoholics to control their drinking often seriously affects the members of their families. _____ For example, alcoholics often abuse their spouses both mentally and physically. _____ An alcoholic may go into a rage over the smallest of irritations and argue, shout, insult, curse, or even hit a spouse. _____ Likewise, the uncertainty of never knowing what to expect when an alcoholic comes home at the end of a day is often more than some spouses can bear. _____ Life for the child of an alcoholic is often full of fear, tension, and insecurity. _____ Yesterday's permitted behavior incurs severe punishments today. _____ The child of an alcoholic never knows what to expect because rules for bedtime, curfews, and television hours are always changing. _____ Evidence of psychological and emotional damage may not appear in the child until years later. _____ Younger children living in families with an alcoholic parent frequently think that they deserve to be punished for something that they haven't really done and in later life continue wanting to punish themselves, sometimes by becoming alcoholics. _____ Similarly, adolescents who must endure the trauma of living with an alcoholic parent often feel embarrassed and ashamed to bring friends or dates to their homes, and this embarrassment in turn generates guilt for them in later life.

III. Write a general statement on a topic of your choosing. Then exchange statements with another student in your class. As you examine your classmate's general statement, think about possible specifics that could be used to develop that sentence into an expository paragraph. Are there many possibilities for development? Or does the sentence require no further support? After you have had time to think about the general statement, share your reactions with your classmate.

2

HOW TO BEGIN
WRITING
PARAGRAPHS

For some writing assignments, you may be given a topic to write about or be asked to choose from among several topics. For other assignments, you may be allowed complete freedom to write on a topic of your own choosing. Either way, you will often have to decide what aspect of your topic to focus on in your paragraph. The suggestions in this chapter will help you both when you select a topic of your own and when you write on a topic chosen for you.

SELECTING A SUITABLE TOPIC

If your assignment is to write a paragraph on a topic of your own choice, you may end up spending more time selecting a suitable topic than you do actually writing the paragraph. Many students have difficulty deciding what to write about and find themselves staring at a blank page while time for completing the assignment dwindles. It is true that words and ideas do not usually flow from the end of a pen or from the keys of a word processor, but words will come more easily if you approach your writing systematically and follow certain guidelines.

You must, of course, write on a topic about which you have enough information to put together a convincing paragraph. You may draw on information you have gathered from such sources as television, newspapers, magazines, movies, talks with friends, or school courses. You may also draw on your own experiences. *Don't underestimate your interests and activities as sources of topics for your writing or assume that others would find them boring to read about.* For example, if you work part-time in a supermarket, you may be able to write a more interesting paragraph on how to pack a grocery bag than on a complex subject like inflation, foreign policy, or the morality of abortion.

The following paragraph is on a topic with which the student writer had little familiarity but which he chose because he thought it would be "interesting to the reader":

> Mexico is a land of extremes. A friend told me that during the day temperatures get very high, but at night you have to wear a coat. The streets of cities like Acapulco are crowded with square stone haciendas, green trees, and gorgeous flowers; but these cities contrast sharply with Mexico's deserts, which are populated only by lizards and cactus plants. A television commercial once showed someone diving from one of the high cliffs near Acapulco. These cliffs are spectacular. The Aztecs who used to dive from these cliffs had developed an advanced civilization. They knew a great deal about building and about astronomy. In fact, they had cities and temples and art long before the United States was ever thought of.

Obviously the writer had never been to Mexico and had not acquired enough knowledge of the topic to provide support for the opening sentence. What the writer knows about Mexico as a "land of extremes" is exhausted after a few sentences, so he fills out the paragraph with sketchy bits of information, drifting from a discussion of a modern diver, to Aztec divers, to Aztec civilization. None of this information provides specifics that support his description of Mexico as a "land of extremes."

The next paragraph, on a topic about which the student writer clearly had first-hand experience, is more satisfactory:

> Taking a test is a nerve-racking experience for me. Even if I have done well in homework assignments and have studied hard, when the test questions are handed out, my hands become sweaty, my heart begins to pound, and my hands shake so much I can hardly hold my pencil. All during the test, I am afraid that I am failing it. Even the simplest questions become very difficult for me. If anyone coughs, my attention is instantly diverted. The time seems to pass too quickly. Each time the instructor announces the time remaining for completion of the test, I become more nervous. When the instructor says that we have only a few minutes to finish, I panic even if I have already finished and am going back to check my answers.

The writer has given us valid reasons to accept her general opening statement. The more specific statements that follow the opening statement convince us that taking a test is, for her, an ordeal.

The following is a successful paragraph that contains information derived from reading rather than from personal experience. The student writer satisfied her curiosity about Mexico by taking some time to read about it in the library. From her research, she gained enough information on the topic she chose, "Mexican foods," to write a successful general-to-specific paragraph. Her opening statement is followed by specifics that develop her general idea:

Some of the principal foods of Mexico have come down from the days of the Aztecs. For example, the Aztecs used corn as the foundation for their cooking, and corn remains the basic item of Mexican cooking today. Tortillas made from corn flour, for instance, form a staple of the Mexican diet, and tamales, steamed in corn husks according to the same process once used in ancient Mexico, regularly appear on the tables of modern Mexico. Also served with modern Mexican dinners is a corn soup called *pozole,* an item that has retained its popularity among the people of Mexico for centuries. Other popular Mexican dishes whose origins date back to Aztec times are largely made from *frijoles,* or beans. Most commonly eaten boiled, beans are also served fried, refried, and occasionally even refried again. Similarly, the same kinds of fowl that graced Aztec tables hundreds of years ago please Mexican palates today. Chicken is, or course, quite popular, and the fact that Mexicans value turkey as a delicacy probably derives from the ancient Aztec religious ritual of sacrificing turkey meat to the gods. In addition, many of the fruits harvested and eaten by the Aztecs can still be found in Mexican markets today. Just as the Aztecs did in ancient times, Mexican shoppers walk through open markets where they purchase avocados, mangoes, and papayas. Finally, beverages the Aztecs liked still continue in favor. Hot chocolate is eagerly enjoyed, and mescal and tequila buoy up the spirits of the Mexicans of today just as they did those of the Aztecs of more than a thousand years ago.

Topic Ideas

If you are asked to write on a topic of your own choice and have trouble thinking of one, you may find consideration of the following list of broad subject areas helpful:

advertisements	diets	movies
aging	diseases	music
automobiles	dormitory life	pets
books	enemies	politics
careers	exercise	poverty
clothes	fears	prejudice
compulsions	heroes	sports
computers	hobbies	status symbols
dancing	holidays	study habits
dating	hunting	success
day care	lifestyles	television
depression	money	travel

These subject areas may suggest more specific topics on which you could write an effective paragraph. Each of the following topics, for example, is derived from a subject on the list and might be suitable for the type of writing you will be doing:

day care for the elderly (aging)

how to pick a used car (automobiles)

popular dances from another decade (dancing)

television dating programs (dating)

when to break a diet (diets)

symptoms of Lyme's Disease (diseases)

dormitory laundry facilities (dormitory life)

a hobby that would terrify me (hobbies)

ways to finance a college education (money)

movies on Sunday afternoon television (movies)

women and job promotions (prejudice)

favorite bass lures (sports)

frequently overlooked monuments to visit in Washington, D.C. (travel)

In exploring a subject area for potential topics, writers often find it useful to ask questions about the subjects that interest them. The following simple questions, when asked in reference to a subject, are likely to provide several related topics that are suitably focused for development into a paragraph: *Who?*, *What?*, *When?*, *Where?*, and *Why?* Take, for example, the general subject area of *fears*. In itself, *fears* is probably too general a subject to become the topic for a paragraph. The diagram that follows, however, illustrates several potential topics that emerge when the subject of *fears* is analyzed in terms of the above questions:

Subject: fears

Question:	*Topic:*
Who?	terroristic military fanatics
What?	poisonous insects
When?	common childhood anxieties
Where?	falling from bridges and high places
Why?	common causes of agoraphobia (fear of crowds)

Considering Audience

Another strategy that writers use to explore a topic is to consider the situation and the immediate audience's needs. The information that a particular circumstance or reader requires may dictate the focus of a paragraph. For instance, a writer may be called upon to write a paragraph on the topic of Acquired Immune Deficiency Syndrome (AIDS) to be included in a manual for disease prevention. In that case the writer will have to focus on the audience's need for preventive strategies. In another situation, that writer may want to write a paragraph on AIDS for inclusion in a term paper focusing on worldwide health problems. In this case, the writer will want to include, for the reader's sake, statistics that demonstrate the threat that AIDS poses. Yet another situation, an oral presentation to a class of future medical professionals, might result in the need to describe the process of the disease. In this case, the writer preparing the text would need to include the stages in the development of the disease and information about each stage. Given then the influence of situation and audience on the appropriateness of a topic, the writer can benefit from exploring these areas when arriving at a topic for a paragraph.

■ EXERCISES

I. Choosing from the list of thirty-six broad subject areas, make a list of ten specific topics, other than those in the lists above, on which you might write a paragraph. Try exploring your subject areas by means of the questions *Who?*, *What?*, *When?*, *Where?*, and *Why?* to determine your topics. Remember that a good topic is one that you know enough about, through personal experience or through reading, to write an effective paragraph.

II. Discuss with a classmate your reasons for selecting the ten topics you chose in Exercise I. Then ask the classmate to narrow down your selections to two, indicating why he or she feels those would be your best bets. Provide the same opportunity for your classmate to narrow down his or her topics.

III. Choose one topic area from the thirty-six broad subject areas. Discuss with a classmate the possible situations and audiences that might require you to write about an aspect of that subject. From your discussion, identify five different approaches you might take to the subject given changes in situation and audience.

THE TOPIC SENTENCE AND THE CONTROLLING IDEA

Whether you select a topic yourself or are assigned one by your instructor, once you have a topic, you are ready to think about constructing a paragraph. In the general-to-specific paragraph, the first sentence announces your topic and makes a general statement about it that the rest of the paragraph will explain or justify. This sentence is known as the *topic sentence*. The remaining sentences in the paragraph are subordinate to it and, as we have seen, provide specific supporting ideas. Because the entire paragraph is constructed around the topic sentence, this sentence is the most important one in the paragraph.

Not only does the topic sentence announce what the paragraph is about, but, even more important, it also conveys the *controlling idea*. To understand this concept, consider the second paragraph on Mexico (p. 11). It is clear from the opening sentence that the topic of the paragraph is "Mexican foods." But besides identifying the topic, the topic sentence signals to the reader what *point* about the topic the writer will focus on. Here we learn that the author will show that many modern Mexican foods *have come down from the days of the Aztecs.* This idea—the aspect of the topic that will be focused on in the paragraph—is the controlling idea. As in this example, the controlling idea is expressed in certain words or phrases that appear in the topic sentence.

Understanding the difference between a topic and a controlling idea, both of which are essential to the topic sentence, is an important step toward writing successful paragraphs. A topic alone cannot give your paragraph the needed focus and direction. For example, look at the following items:

1. The Middle East conflict
2. The Middle East conflict altered the lives of a generation of Americans.
3. There are several important lessons to be learned from the Middle East conflict.
4. The Middle East conflict is responsible for many changes in American foreign policy.

Item 1 is simply a topic. By itself it does not suggest any one aspect of the Middle East conflict for the writer to focus on. But item 1 can be more narrowly focused in several ways; items 2, 3, and 4 suggest three possibilities. Item 2 can be used as a topic sentence, conveying the controlling idea that the Middle East conflict "altered the lives of a generation of Americans." The sentence communicates both the topic of the paragraph—"the Middle East conflict"—and the focus of the paragraph, signaled by the words *altered the lives of a generation of Americans.* Item 3 is also suitable for use as a topic sentence. Here, the topic is stated at the end of the sentence, and the words signaling the focus are *several important lessons.* In item 4, the topic is again at the beginning of the sentence and the words indicating the focus are *many changes in American foreign policy.* Unlike 1, either 2, 3, or 4 can be used as a topic sentence expressing a controlling idea, and any one of the three, when so used, will provide a good beginning for a general-to-specific expository paragraph.

■ **EXERCISES**

I. In each of the following sentences, identify (1) the topic and (2) the focusing words or phrases that state the point about the topic (controlling idea) the writers will focus on.

MODEL: First-year college English is a time-consuming course.

TOPIC: First-year college English

FOCUSING WORD: time-consuming

A. A student who works full-time and also runs a household has busy evenings.
B. A good wine is easily identified by three traits.
C. Drop/add policies at this school are too lenient.

D. Planting a vegetable garden yields many rewards.
E. College registration can be a frustrating experience.
F. During the past several years, the protective ozone layer surrounding the earth has shown definite signs of deterioration.
G. The crusade to save the great whales from extinction is a crucial ecological last stand.
H. To annoy the viewer seems to be the only purpose behind some television commercials.
I. *Self-destructive* is a term that can be applied to the lives of some of Hollywood's greatest stars.
J. A number of stand-up comics have made self-deprecation the basis for successful careers.

II. For each of the following topics, construct a good topic sentence that expresses a controlling idea.

MODEL:

TOPIC: cooking

TOPIC SENTENCE: Cooking today involves the use of many timesaving devices.
A. designing a living room
B. a recent election (national, local, or campus)
C. television talk shows
D. dieting
E. single-sex colleges
F. cycling
G. "The Far Side" (or any other comic strip)
H. being a secretary (or student)
I. the Information Superhighway
J. relics of the lost Mayan Civilization
K. Vitamin E

III. Construct six topic sentences of your own, and underline the controlling idea in each. Be able to identify (1) the topic and (2) the focusing words in each.

IV. Exchange one of the topic sentences that you constructed for Exercise III with a classmate. As you look over each other's sentence, jot down notes on how the sentence could be developed with specifics. Then discuss with your classmate what you have discovered as well as any suggestions each of you might have for improvement.

DECIDING ON A CONTROLLING IDEA

Because the controlling idea is crucial to the success of a paragraph, don't start to write a paragraph until you have decided on *both* your topic and your controlling idea. If you simply start writing about a topic with no controlling idea in mind, you may wander off in different directions and deal with a number of ideas, each of which could be better developed in a separate paragraph.

The controlling idea expressed in the topic sentence of an expository paragraph, of course, requires development; otherwise, you would have no reason for writing. Consider, for example, this sentence:

John was born in Chicago.

Such a sentence would not be a good topic sentence for a general-to-specific paragraph because it would be difficult to develop; it is a statement of fact that does not need explanation or expansion. Consider, on the other hand, the following sentence:

The fact that John was born in Chicago had a profound effect on his life.

This sentence can be used as a topic sentence because it expresses an idea that can be developed in the paragraph: you would go on to explain how being born in Chicago affected John's life.

One mark of a workable controlling idea—here, that John's being born in Chicago affected his life profoundly—is that it raises a question or a series of questions that you, as the writer, are expected to discuss in your paragraph. In this case, the questions raised might include the following: Was John's career determined by the place of his birth? Did Chicago shape his character? Did it affect his health? Were his family life and education in any way influenced by the city? Answering such questions is your responsibility, and the skill with which you answer them will determine the effectiveness of your writing.

At the same time, you should avoid using a topic sentence with a controlling idea that is too vague for effective discussion. For example:

Colorado is a great place.

This sentence is just as difficult to develop as the topic sentence "John was born in Chicago," but for a different reason. The "Chicago" sentence provides no controlling idea to develop into a general-to-specific paragraph; the "Colorado" sentence, because its idea is not narrow enough, fails to indicate a particular direction for development. A sentence such as the following calls for expansion:

Colorado is a vacationer's paradise twelve months of the year.

This sentence is an effective topic sentence because it indicates a need for development and points to the road that the writer will take: he or she will reveal the facilities and assets that Colorado offers vacationers at different times throughout the year.

The strengths of the topic sentence "Some of the principal foods of Mexico have come down from the days of the Aztecs" (p. 11) are not only that it announces the topic and commits the writer to developing it but also that it requires the writer to discuss *nothing but* the similarities in diet and cooking between present-day Mexicans and the ancient Aztecs. Having settled on this particular topic sentence, the writer could not go on to compare

Mexican foods and American foods, nor consider the cost of food to the consumer today.

THE TOPIC SENTENCE AS CONTRACT

You may find it helpful to think of a topic sentence as a *contract*. In effect, with the choice of a topic and a controlling idea and the expression of both in the topic sentence, writers establish a contract between themselves and their readers. The responsibility of the writer is to convince the reader that the topic sentence is explainable. The degree to which the writer succeeds in fulfilling the terms of the contract determines how effective the paragraph will be.

Again, look at the paragraph on Mexican foods (p. 11). The writer's topic sentence, "Some of the principal foods of Mexico have come down from the days of the Aztecs," establishes a definite contract. The remaining sentences in the paragraph must explain the idea that the people of Mexico are still eating foods which the ancient Aztecs ate and thus carry out the contract established between the writer and the reader in the topic sentence. The writer of the paragraph on p. 10, whose topic sentence is "Mexico is a land of extremes," also establishes a contract. But instead of supporting his idea by demonstrating the extremes to be found in Mexico, he wanders off to other subjects, so that by the end of the paragraph the reader has little evidence that Mexico indeed is "a land of extremes." The paragraph is unsuccessful because the writer has not fulfilled the contract.

▪ SUMMARY

1. The writer's first concern is to find an appropriate topic on which to write a paragraph.

2. The writer should be familiar enough with the topic, either through experience or research, to develop it effectively in the paragraph.

3. Two strategies for exploring a subject area for a suitable topic include asking simple questions (*Who?, What?, When?, Where?,* and *Why?*) and considering the situation and audience.

4. The topic sentence is the first sentence in a general-to-specific paragraph and expresses the topic and the controlling idea of the paragraph. The rest of the paragraph explains or justifies the topic sentence.

5. The controlling idea limits the topic by focusing on one aspect of it and thus determines the direction that the rest of the paragraph will take. The aspect to be focused on is signaled by certain significant words or phrases in the topic sentence.

6. The topic sentence establishes a contract between the writer and the reader. The writer's obligation is to fulfill that contract by developing clearly the aspect

of the topic that is expressed by the controlling idea. The writer also has an obligation to avoid including in the paragraph any material that is *not* related to the controlling idea.

■ EXERCISES

I. Supply topic sentences for the following paragraphs. Be certain that each topic sentence conveys a clear controlling idea.

MODEL: *Successfully transplanting a tree requires careful attention to details.*

> Before planting, check to see if the tree's roots are moist; if they are not, soak them in water for two or more hours until they appear soggy. While the roots are soaking, find a sunny spot in which to plant the tree. The soil should be a dark brown color—indicating that it is rich in nutrients. If the soil is in poor condition, mix in peat moss or potting soil. Next, dig a hole big enough to allow the tree's roots room to spread out. Place the tree in the hole and, while holding the tree straight, fill in the hole with dirt; pack the dirt lightly. Water the tree every day for a week so that the roots can take hold in the ground.

A. _____

> Home computers can perform tedious bookkeeping tasks that most families never seem to have time to do properly. They can balance checkbooks in seconds, endearing themselves immediately to those of us who are always overdrawing our accounts. They can easily keep track of family budgets and aid in the filling out of income tax forms. In addition, home computers can provide entertainment for the whole family. There are, of course, many computer games on the market that can be enjoyed by children and adults. And with a little study of programming techniques, buyers can learn to program their own games. There are many other applications for home computers as well. Computers can be programmed to control heating systems, to function as security systems, or to act as efficient memo pads for important messages and dates.

B. _____

> One tell-tale sign of depression is a feeling of sadness or helplessness that lasts for more than a few weeks. Depressed individuals tend to feel that their problems are hopeless and that no solutions exist for the difficulties in their lives. Another sign of depression is a constant feeling of fatigue, especially if accompanied by difficulties in getting to sleep. People who suffer from serious depression usually complain of being tired, and yet they tend to lie awake at night and often experience extended bouts of insomnia. In addition, depressed individuals tend to lose interest in sex, and they have problems in concentrating. Perhaps the most significant sign of depression, however, is recurring thoughts of suicide. Because depressed people feel overwhelmed by a sense of hopelessness, they often think that suicide is the only answer to their suffering.

C. _____

Documentaries, particularly those that deal with nature, are often shown on television. *The Undersea World of Jacques Cousteau,* the *National Geographic Specials,* and *Nature* fit into this category. Sophisticated news broadcasts and commentaries such as *The MacNeil/Lehrer NewsHour* and *Washington Week in Review* enjoy widespread popularity. Programs like these familiarize viewers with real situations and raise important questions concerning the outcome and lasting effects of political and historical events as they unfold. While ballets, operas, concerts, and plays appear infrequently on commercial television, they are often aired on educational networks. Specifically, several national acting companies, the Metropolitan Opera, the New York Philharmonic, the Boston Pops, and even the Bolshoi Ballet can, at the flick of a switch, entertain viewers in their living rooms. Finally, television for children has made great advances, moving away from the Saturday morning cartoons and toward such educationally oriented programs as *Sesame Street* and *Mister Rogers' Neighborhood.*

II. Consider each of the following sentences as possible topic sentences. Rewrite any sentences that you consider too specific or too vague:

A. Raleigh is the capital of North Carolina.
B. The World Series of 1993 offered baseball fans some real surprises.
C. General George Washington was president of the United States for two terms.
D. NASA has several exciting space projects planned for the next few decades.
E. Bread frequently costs a dollar or more a loaf today.
F. Many people love ice skating.
G. Jewelry serves more purposes than just ornamentation.
H. Communication is a crucial part of every relationship.

III. Write a paragraph for one of the following topic sentences. Feel free to alter the topic sentence according to your preferences, opinions, and experiences. For example, if you have never thought of buying a home but are an avid automobile enthusiast, you might alter sentence C to read, "An antique automobile is a worthwhile investment."

A. Commuting to school has its advantages and its disadvantages.
B. A habitually slow driver is as dangerous as a speedster.
C. A home is a worthwhile investment.
D. Final exams are an outdated custom.
E. Quiet people make better friends than do talkative people.
F. Instructors who grade leniently are not always the best teachers.
G. Shaquille O'Neal [or any other athlete] is an outstanding athlete and individual.
H. American women are currently obtaining positions of leadership in fields of the work force once dominated by males.

IV. Write a paragraph for a topic sentence of your own choice.

V. Exchange rough drafts of the paragraphs you and a classmate are writing for Exercise IV. Read the paragraphs, focusing on the role of the topic sentence as well as the quality of the information that is being used to support the topic sentence. After you have read and thought about each other's paragraphs, share reactions and constructive suggestions with your classmate.

VI. Start a portfolio. Locate a folder where you can keep the paragraphs and essays that you write during the semester. Accumulating your work in a folder will enable you to have a record of your development. Your folder will also provide you and your instructor with specifics to discuss when you meet to talk about your writing. Throughout this text, you will be asked to draw from your portfolio and to reflect on your progress. You can begin your collection of writings with the paragraphs you wrote in response to Exercises III and IV.

PARAGRAPH UNITY
AND STRUCTURE

In Chapters 1 and 2 you learned what a general-to-specific expository paragraph is and how to begin writing one. In this chapter you will learn how to put a paragraph together so that it will be unified. You will recall from Chapter 2 that the general-to-specific paragraph begins with a topic sentence that establishes the *topic* and conveys a *controlling idea,* the idea that is to be explained in the paragraph. The statement of the controlling idea in the topic sentence focuses the paragraph on one aspect of the topic.

WHAT IS PARAGRAPH UNITY?

As you learned in Chapter 2, the topic sentence has a special relationship to the other sentences in the paragraph. It is a contract that you as writer establish with your reader. To fulfill the contract and satisfy the reader that your topic sentence is valid, you must see to it that every sentence in the paragraph supports the controlling idea expressed in the topic sentence. If any does not, your paragraph will not be unified and will not communicate effectively. On the other hand, if every sentence in the paragraph provides direct or indirect support for the controlling idea, your paragraph will be unified. Every expository paragraph, no matter how short or how long, must be unified to be effective.

An important point must be made here: not all sentences that relate in some way to the *topic* of a paragraph *necessarily* help to unify the paragraph.

A sentence may be related to the topic of the paragraph and provide information that is accurate and interesting, but a sentence that doesn't develop or support the *controlling idea* of the paragraph will destroy the paragraph's unity.

To understand the importance of unity, examine the following paragraph, which is *not* unified:

> (1) Pilots are the primary cause of many aircraft accidents. (2) Ignoring their responsibilities, many pilots fail to perform their duties efficiently, and tragedy has too often been the needless result. (3) History records that many fatal accidents have occurred, for example, because pilots failed to listen to the advice of air traffic controllers who were in a position to warn them about impending disasters. (4) To become an air traffic controller, one must be extremely intelligent. (5) Sometimes pilots are overtired, and they neglect to take the precautions necessary to avoid accidents. (6) They may even be taking drugs which slow down their physical reactions. (7) As we all know, statistics indicate that many college students abuse drugs, and these students should realize that if they continue to use drugs they will never enter careers such as aviation. (8) Sometimes accidents occur through a malfunction in the plane's equipment. (9) A door may open during flight, or a tire may blow out as the plane takes off. (10) Pilots, of course, aren't responsible for accidents such as these. (11) Perhaps most startling is the fact that every year one or two air traffic accidents are caused by student pilots who attempt journeys beyond their capabilities and end up producing catastrophes that destroy life and property. (12) Because they don't employ student pilots, commercial airlines are the safest form of air transportation. (13) The next time you take a commercial flight, you should be sure to ask yourself the following questions: Does the pilot look happy and healthy? What are the weather conditions outside? Do there seem to be any cracks in the wings or tail of the plane?

You probably had difficulty following the writer's reasoning in this paragraph. While all of the sentences in the paragraph relate at least in some way to the *topic,* "aircraft accidents," the paragraph is not unified because not every sentence supports the *controlling idea* that "*pilots are the primary cause* of many aircraft accidents."

If we look at each of the sentences in this paragraph individually, we find that the following sentences do not belong because they do not lend support to the controlling idea:

(4) To become an air traffic controller, one must be extremely intelligent.

(7) As we all know, statistics indicate that many college students abuse drugs, and these students should realize that if they continue to use drugs they will never enter careers such as aviation.

(8) Sometimes accidents occur through a malfunction in the plane's equipment.

(9) A door may open during flight, or a tire may blow out as the plane takes off.

(10) Pilots, of course, aren't responsible for accidents such as these.

(12) Because they don't employ student pilots, commercial airlines are the safest form of air transportation.

(13) The next time you take a commercial flight, you should be sure to ask yourself the following questions: Does the pilot look happy and healthy? What are the weather conditions outside? Do there seem to be any cracks in the wings or tail of the plane?

In these sentences the writer discusses qualifications for air traffic controllers, drug abuse among students who might wish to become pilots, mechanical malfunctions, and commercial airline safety; the writer even provides a list of precautionary questions for the commercial airline passenger. But since none of these sentences supports the controlling idea that "*pilots are the primary cause* of many aircraft accidents," they detract from the unity of the paragraph. With each sentence we wonder what the writer is saying and why; we may even stop reading as we lose track of the idea we thought we were following.

The other sentences in the paragraph do support the controlling idea. If the writer had included only those sentences, the result would have been a more compact and unified paragraph, as we can see by reading through the list below:

(1) Pilots are the primary cause of many aircraft accidents. (topic sentence)

(2) Ignoring their responsibilities, many pilots fail to perform their duties efficiently, and tragedy has too often been the needless result.

(3) History records that many fatal accidents have occurred, for example, because pilots failed to listen to the advice of air traffic controllers who were in a position to warn them about impending disasters.

(5) Sometimes pilots are overtired, and they neglect to take the precautions necessary to avoid accidents.

(6) They may even be taking drugs which slow down their physical reactions.

(11) Perhaps most startling is the fact that every year one or two air traffic accidents are caused by student pilots who attempt journeys beyond their capabilities and end up producing catastrophes that destroy life and property.

■ SUMMARY

1. Every expository paragraph, no matter how short or how long, must be unified.

2. In a unified general-to-specific paragraph, every sentence supports the controlling idea expressed in the paragraph's topic sentence.

3. In general, the more unified a paragraph is, the clearer and more effective it will be.

■ EXERCISES

I. Read each of the following paragraphs carefully. Collaborate with a partner to specify the controlling idea expressed in the topic sentence and then examine the paragraph for unity. Identify by number any sentence that does not develop or support the paragraph's controlling idea.

A. (1) Two methods that horse owners use to make their horses fit for riding are "gentle breaking" and "bronco busting." (2) To "gentle break" a horse means simply to train it, through coaxing and reward, to submit willingly to its owner's commands. (3) Horses trained through the gentle-breaking method usually retain their free spirit but allow themselves to be handled and ridden by their owners because of the mutual trust that develops between the rider and the animal. (4) The "gentling" technique, as it is also called, was learned from the Plains Indians, who needed well-trained and obedient horses. (5) As we all know, the Plains Indians lived in the West, so they depended on horses for transportation. (6) Sitting Bull was a Plains Indian. (7) He fought at Wounded Knee, possibly on a horse that had been trained through the gentle-breaking method. (8) In the bronco-busting method, on the other hand, the rider forces the horse into submission by attempting to stay mounted on the animal until it stops bucking, running, or rearing. (9) The bronco-busting method also originated in the Old West and is most often seen today in rodeo games. (10) Because the bronco method is more forceful than the gentle method, horses trained by it are usually less spirited and more submissive than are horses that undergo the gentle treatment.

B. (1) A successful rummage sale requires advance preparation. (2) Approximately two weeks before the sale, a location should be selected. (3) The location should be easy for people to find and large enough to accommodate anticipated crowds and provide areas for the items for sale. (4) For the rummage sale to be a success, moreover, advance advertising is essential. (5) Local and regional papers and magazines should carry notices about the sale. (6) Well in advance of the day of the sale, signs should be made that will direct prospective buyers to the sale. (7) Posters announcing the sale should be displayed in churches, stores, and other public places. (8) During the week preceding the sale, the merchandise to be sold should be categorized and priced. (9) Clothing, for example, should be separated from appliances and tools. (10) Most clothing purchased at rummage sales is a good buy. (11) Many people come just to get a bargain on the price of clothes. (12) Because most purchases range from five to seventy-five cents, a plentiful supply of nickels, dimes, and quarters is a necessity at a rummage sale.

II. Read each of the following paragraphs carefully. Working on your own, specify the controlling idea expressed in the topic sentence and then examine the paragraph for unity. Identify by number any sentence that does not develop or support the paragraph's controlling idea.

A. (1) The living conditions in many city jails are appalling. (2) Many of the jail cells aren't fit for human habitation. (3) They are often filthy and unsanitary. (4) Disinfectant and cleaning agents are rarely used. (5) Roaches and rats scuttle across the floors looking for crumbs of food. (6) Roaches, of course, are difficult to get rid of even in clean places. (7) Scientists say that roaches have changed little since prehistoric times and that if the world were to experience an atomic holocaust, roaches would be one of the few living creatures to survive. (8) Scientists also estimate that there is one rat for every person on the earth. (9) In addition, many city jails are overcrowded. (10) As many as three or four inmates sleep in cells that are only twelve feet wide and twelve feet long. (11) Finally, because the pay is limited, there aren't always enough guards in the jails. (12) When violence arises, guards, fearing for their own safety, are afraid to take proper action. (13) In some city jails, murders and suicides have occurred because guards were occupied in other parts of the building and were unable to arrive in time to prevent them.

B. (1) Many unusual parallels exist between Abraham Lincoln, assassinated in the nineteenth century, and John Fitzgerald Kennedy, assassinated in the twentieth. (2) Both presidents were shot on Friday, and both died of head wounds received in full view of their wives. (3) Kennedy had a secretary named Lincoln, and Lincoln had a secretary named Kennedy. (4) Every president since Washington has employed a secretary, and some presidents have hired several. (5) Without presidential secretaries, the business of the nation would probably come to a halt. (6) Kennedy was elected president in 1960, exactly one hundred years after Lincoln was elected to the same high office. (7) Both of their secretaries were with these presidents during their full terms in Washington. (8) Both Lincoln and Kennedy lost sons while living in the White House. (9) Their sons died of different causes. (10) Both John Wilkes Booth, who shot Lincoln, and Lee Harvey Oswald, who shot Kennedy, were themselves killed before juries could convict them for their crimes. (11) Finally, the last names of both slain leaders contain seven letters each, while the full names of their murderers contain fifteen letters each.

C. (1) The real cowboys of the American West bore little resemblance to the myth created by films and television shows of the 1940s and 1950s. (2) First of all, not all cowboys were white. (3) Indeed, a substantial number of them were black. (4) Several thousand African Americans worked as cowboys during the era of the open range, and at times as many as one in four cowboys was black. (5) Secondly, not all cowboys were heroic. (6) Many became rustlers, bank robbers, and outlaws. (7) Even working cowboys were notorious for flouting the law. (8) In fact, such Western icons as Wyatt Earp and Bat Masterson built their reputations by protecting towns from the mayhem that cowboys frequently caused at the end of cattle drives. (9) Finally, not all those who qualified to be called "cowboys" were boys at all. (10) On the contrary, many women rode the range, carried six-guns, and dressed in chaps, high boots, and the signature "cowboy hat." (11) At least two of these women, Annie Oakley and Calamity Jane, achieved celebrity status that equaled the renown of the most famous cowboy figures. (12) Calamity Jane became the hero of numerous popular novels and magazine stories, and Annie Oakley earned widespread fame as one of the best sharpshooters of the Old West.

III. Look back at the paragraph or paragraphs that you wrote in response to Chapter 2 and placed in your portfolio. Is your writing unified? That is to say, have you employed a series of supporting facts and ideas that focus on the controlling idea? If not, rewrite the paragraph(s) to improve their unity.

PLANNING AND CONSTRUCTING A UNIFIED PARAGRAPH

We have seen that paragraph unity can sometimes be improved simply by eliminating from completed paragraphs those sentences that don't develop the controlling idea. However, you cannot rely on this method alone to achieve paragraph unity. Most writers agree that *the best way to achieve unity is to plan their work carefully.* Once you have written a topic sentence, you face the task of organizing the body of your paragraph so that it effectively explains your controlling idea. To do this within the limited framework of a one-hundred- to three-hundred-word paragraph requires planning and thought. You must carefully select your evidence and clearly relate all the sentences in the paragraph to your controlling idea.

Preliminary Steps

You will find it easier to write effective paragraphs if you develop your ideas systematically. Begin this process with the following important steps:

1. *Select a topic and a controlling idea and write a topic sentence in which they are expressed.* This step was discussed in Chapter 2.
2. *Jot down the facts and ideas that you think might support your controlling idea.* Note: For this initial list, you may simply write down a word or a phrase for each thought that comes to mind. Don't hesitate to include all or most of what occurs to you; at this point you are simply accumulating material that you will sort through and examine at a later stage. You are by no means committed to using any particular fact or idea in the final paragraph, so feel free to use your imagination and let yourself go. You cannot make a mistake at this point in the writing process. The more data you gather, the easier the writing will be later on.
3. *Review your list of preliminary facts and ideas and ask yourself whether your controlling idea is a good one.* You need not examine each item in your list closely at this point. Simply scan the list to get a sense of whether or not you have enough material to explain your controlling idea effectively. If you are uncertain, you need to reexamine your topic sentence. You may have selected a controlling idea that simply isn't explainable because it isn't valid or is either too broad or too specific for sensible development (see pages 15–17). On the other hand, it may be that you don't know enough about your topic to support your controlling idea and that you need to learn more, either by searching through your own experiences or by doing further research. If you find that you have problems with your controlling idea, *now* is the time to catch and correct them. You cannot write an effective paragraph if your controlling idea is difficult or impossible to explain.

Now, let's consider how this process works. Suppose that your topic is "Washington, D.C.," and that you have decided on the controlling idea expressed in the following topic sentence:

> Washington, D.C., has many exciting places for tourists to visit.

The controlling idea in this sentence is signaled by the phrase *many exciting places for tourists to visit.*

The next step is to jot down a list of facts and ideas that you think could be used to develop or support your topic. Writers refer to this process of gathering information as "brainstorming." In completing this stage in the writing process, you might find it helpful to ask of your controlling idea the same questions that you used to focus your topic in Chapter 2 (see p. 12). *Who?, What?, When?, Where?,* and *Why?* In the case of this particular controlling idea, the questions *What?* and *Where?* are the most appropriate to ask, for these are the questions that your controlling idea invites you to explore.

In answering these questions, you would be likely to form a preliminary list that might look something like this:

Watergate Complex	Ford's Theater
Capitol	U.S. Holocaust Memorial Museum
Supreme Court	Mount Vernon
Arlington National Cemetery	Great Falls
Lincoln Memorial	Smithsonian Institution
Potomac River	National Zoo
Library of Congress	Grand Central Station
Jefferson Memorial	Reflecting Pool
Botanical Gardens	National Cathedral
National Archives	Mint
White House	Federal Bureau of Investigation
John F. Kennedy Center for the	National Gallery of Art
Performing Arts	Washington Monument
Blair House	Tidal Basin

In looking back over the information and data that have been listed as possible support for the controlling idea that Washington, D.C., has "many exciting places for tourists to visit," you can see that there are many such places mentioned. In fact, so many places are mentioned that if you were organizing this paragraph, you would have far more data and information at your disposal than you could use. This is indeed a good sign. Writers who take the time to brainstorm usually end up in the enviable position of having to eliminate potential information rather than having to wrack their brains for enough data to develop their controlling idea and thus wasting time that they could be using productively. Having thus gathered more than enough information to write an explanatory paragraph about your controlling idea, you can now proceed to the next stage of organizing your paragraph with a reasonable amount of assurance that you can develop or support your controlling idea effectively.

Primary Supports

Once you have completed the three preliminary steps, you are ready to begin piecing your paragraph together. Your first task is to reexamine carefully your list of supporting information and to identify those items that are likely to provide the most effective support for your controlling idea. Once you have identified those items, you should create sentences from them that can be used in your paragraph as major supporting statements for the controlling idea in your topic sentence. Consider these sentences *primary supports* because within the paragraph they function as the *primary* evidence that the writer provides in *support* of the validity of the topic sentence of the paragraph.

Keep the following two guidelines in mind as you begin to create, select, and write primary supports for your paragraph.

1. Limit your selection to items that are *most likely* to explain to your reader what you are trying to say in your controlling idea.
2. Choose items that will generate sentences that can function appropriately at the second level of generality in your paragraph (as we discussed on pages 3–4 of Chapter 1).

A primary support should be less general than the topic sentence (the first level of generality) and should provide details that directly support the topic sentence. And, on the other hand, primary support should still be general enough so that, if you choose, it can be further developed and explained by sentences at a third level of generality.

When selecting and writing your sentences of primary support, keep in mind that this is an important stage in the writing process, and it requires careful thought, reflection, and analysis. An item may relate to your topic but have little or no ultimate connection to your controlling idea. Another item may relate to your controlling idea yet not help to present it effectively. You may, for example, find yourself unable to develop an item further, or it may turn out to be insignificant. Still another item may contain information that you realize would be more relevant at the third level of generality—that is, in support of sentences of primary support. Finally, an item might provide the basis for effective primary support, but for one reason or another it is simply not as potentially effective, from your point of view, as another item might be.

A paragraph can, of course, be supported in any number of ways by different information. In fact, no two writers are likely to develop identical paragraphs on the same topic sentence, and yet their paragraphs can be equally successful. Both will rely on their experiences and knowledge, as well as any information they can gather, to complete their paragraphs. Therefore, at this stage in the writing process, your job is to select information that you feel will provide the most effective and convincing support for your controlling idea.

In the initial stages of planning the paragraph on Washington, D.C., for example, you would need to keep in mind the controlling idea that Washington has "many exciting places for tourists to visit." Because the brainstorming list contains more information than it is possible to use in a paragraph, you face the task of focusing on those items from the list that will provide the most effective support for the controlling idea. In deciding which ideas to use, you may find it useful to evaluate your information in terms of the now familiar questions: *Who?, What?, When?, Where?,* and *Why? Where?,* for instance, in Washington should all tourists make it a point to visit? *What* about these places makes them so important? *Why* do you feel that these places stand out as more significant than other places on your list?

As you ask yourself these questions, you will begin to see differences in the value of the information you have gathered. Some of the items will probably begin to appear inappropriate. For example, "Mount Vernon" and "Great Falls" can be eliminated because the focus of the paragraph is on places to visit *in* Washington, D.C. Mount Vernon and Great Falls, while in the vicinity of Washington, are not in the district itself. Some items on the list may be appropriate but less significant than others. The "Potomac River," the "Reflecting Pool," "Ford's Theater," and "Blair House," for example, while interesting and worthwhile places in Washington to visit, are by no means as significant or indispensable for a tourist to see as other items on the list such as the "Capitol" and the "White House." Asking the questions *Who?, What?, When?, Where?,* and *Why?* in connection with your controlling idea will help you to focus on items that will be the most useful to you as you structure your paragraph.

After a careful process of analysis and selection, several items will eventually stand out as those most suitable for primary supports for your controlling idea. For the paragraph on Washington, D.C., the "Smithsonian Institution," the "National Gallery of Art," the "Capitol," and the "White House" stand out as among those places that most tourists to Washington, especially those visiting the city for the first time, will definitely want to see. Hence, these items would provide effective primary supports for the topic sentence of the paragraph. When written out in sentences, these items might appear as follows:

1. One of the most fascinating places to see in Washington, D.C., is the Smithsonian Institution.
2. Another spot in Washington that every visitor to the city will want to see is the National Gallery of Art.
3. Finally, no trip to Washington, D.C., would be complete without stops at the Capitol and the White House.

These sentences directly and effectively support the controlling idea of the paragraph. They also leave open, if desired, the possibility for further development and discussion. As you will see in the section to follow on "Secondary Supports," you can easily continue to develop this paragraph by providing specific illustrations to show why each of the places mentioned in these sentences has been singled out as one of the most significant sights in Washington to visit. As such, the above sentences should provide a solid structural foundation for the finished paragraph. In the meantime, hold onto the other items from your list of possible supporting information. As you begin to develop your paragraph more fully, you might wish to delete one of your primary supports in favor of another item on your list, or you might wish to add still more primary support to your paragraph. In addition, some of the items on your list may be useful when you develop your primary support with secondary support, the next step in structuring your paragraph.

■ SUMMARY

1. The best way to achieve unity in your paragraph is through careful planning.

2. The first step in the planning process is to select a topic and a controlling idea and to write a topic sentence in which they are expressed.

3. Under your topic sentence, jot down facts and ideas that come to mind as possible support for your controlling idea. This process is often referred to as "brainstorming."

4. Before going on, scan your list and make sure that your controlling idea is valid and explainable.

5. The next step in the planning process is to select those items that will best serve as primary support for the controlling idea and to write sentences of primary support about them.

6. Primary support sentences directly support the controlling idea and can be further developed by other details that you have listed. Primary supports constitute the second level of generality in a paragraph, as discussed in Chapter 1.

7. In generating information for your list of potential support (i.e., brainstorming), you may find it useful to explore your controlling idea in terms of the questions *Who?*, *What?*, *When?*, *Where?*, and *Why?* These questions will also be useful in determining which of the items in your preliminary list are likely to be most appropriate and effective as primary supports for your paragraph.

■ EXERCISES

1. Working with a classmate, indicate each sentence that might serve as a primary support for the given topic sentences. Remember that primary supports must relate directly to the controlling idea and offer effective development of the point that the controlling idea expresses.

   A. *Topic Sentence:* When smokers give up their habit, they are likely to undergo a typical pattern of experiences.

      1. On the first day after they stop smoking, their enthusiasm is at a high pitch.
      2. The next few days are generally uncomfortable.
      3. Smoking is a very difficult habit to break.
      4. Part of the discomfort that they experience results from the body's elimination of various chemicals.

5. People who quit smoking are less likely to develop lung cancer than are people who continue to smoke.
6. After two or three weeks, the craving for tobacco gradually disappears, though it may return if the former smoker attends a social gathering where others are smoking.
7. As the craving for tobacco decreases, appetite begins to increase.
8. Even though the smoking habit is weakened, it is never broken.
9. One cigarette or one cigar can return the backslider to the ranks of confirmed smokers.

B. *Topic Sentence:* Women who drink alcohol during pregnancy risk harming their unborn children.

1. Babies born of alcoholic mothers are frequently retarded.
2. Pregnant women who drink often don't exercise as much as they should.
3. Doctors have compiled detailed studies on pregnant women who are heavy drinkers.
4. Studies have indicated that if a pregnant woman consumes an average of one or two ounces of alcohol per day, there is one chance in five that her baby will develop a serious disease called fetal alcohol syndrome.
5. Alcohol makes pregnant women feel sluggish.
6. Pregnancy often involves some degree of risk.
7. Pregnant women who are alcoholics frequently neglect their health and rarely maintain a proper diet.
8. Alcoholic women who are expecting a baby can easily forget important appointments with their physicians.

II. On your own, indicate each sentence that might serve as a primary support for the given topic sentences. Remember that primary supports must relate directly to the controlling idea and offer effective development of the point that the controlling idea expresses.

A. *Topic Sentence:* Night classes can prove extremely difficult for a first-year college student.

1. Competition is more intense than in daytime courses.
2. For students who commute, getting to and from the campus is often more difficult at night than during the day.
3. Typical eighteen-year-old college students who live on campus prefer to spend evenings in the dormitory with their friends.
4. Night classes are often geared to the needs of older students.
5. Attending class at night often requires students to change their study habits.
6. Night classes are frequently quite tiring.
7. Ninety percent of the students in night classes are much older than the average first-year college student, who often feels intimidated to the point at which he or she is unable to learn.
8. No one likes to finish school at ten o'clock in the evening.
9. Many of the best television programs are broadcast during the times when night classes are offered.

B. *Topic Sentence:* The electoral college is an outdated and unrepresentative way of electing the president of the United States.

1. Most Americans don't really understand how the electoral college works.
2. The reasons for the electoral college's coming into being are no longer important concerns.
3. Two states with unequal populations may cast the same number of popular votes, but the state with the greater population receives more electoral votes.
4. The voters of each state do not get fair representation in the electoral college.
5. The electoral college votes do not always reflect the desires of the voting public.
6. Even though Grover Cleveland had more popular votes, he lost the 1888 presidential election to Benjamin Harrison, who had more electoral votes.
7. In some states delegates to the college aren't bound to vote for the candidates who receive the majority of their state's popular votes.
8. Eighty-one percent of the population disapprove of the electoral college.
9. No other country in the world has an electoral college.
10. Delegates to the electoral college have too much power.

III. Identify the controlling idea in each of the following topic sentences, and then brainstorm with a partner a list of information that might become the basis for sentences of primary support for that controlling idea. From your list, construct three sentences of primary support for each topic sentence. In generating your list of information, be sure to explore your controlling idea in terms of the questions *Who?, What?, When?, Where?,* and *Why?* Be certain that each of your primary supports relates to the controlling idea expressed in the topic sentence and not just to the topic.

MODEL:

TOPIC SENTENCE: Working students have special problems.

PRIMARY SUPPORT: *Their time in the library is limited.*

PRIMARY SUPPORT: *Fewer courses are offered in the evenings.*

PRIMARY SUPPORT: *Work often causes them to miss class.*

A. *Topic Sentence:* Tragedies bring people together.
B. *Topic Sentence:* Hollywood has given us different kinds of classic movie monsters.
C. *Topic Sentence:* Stress often reveals itself in a variety of forms.
D. *Topic Sentence:* Students who pay their own way through college value their education more than students who do not have to pay their own way.
E. *Topic Sentence:* National health care reform would address a number of inequities in our society.
F. *Topic Sentence:* Many television commercials are an insult to human intelligence.
G. *Topic Sentence:* Year-round schooling would present major challenges and benefits to local school districts.

IV. Develop one of the topic sentences and primary supports from Exercise III into a paragraph. To begin, decide if each of the primary supports needs further support? If so, provide additional information where needed in a rough outline. Then, as you draft the paragraph, see if other thoughts occur to you. After you have finished the draft, examine what you have written for unity. Share your draft with your classmates and instructor. Then insert it into your developing portfolio.

Secondary Supports

Primary supports, particularly those that develop unfamiliar or complex controlling ideas, often require additional information or illustration if the reader is to understand or accept them. To supply this additional information requires additional sentences, called *secondary supports*. These sentences constitute the third level of generality discussed in Chapter 1. Instead of reinforcing the controlling idea directly, secondary supports reinforce a point or points made in a primary support by adding information or detail that helps explain a primary support. They *indirectly* support the paragraph's controlling idea.

Developing Secondary Supports   Looking again at the primary support in the paragraph on Washington, D.C., we can see how the addition of secondary support provides details that make the primary support—and indirectly the controlling idea—more understandable and convincing. In the outline that follows, each statement of primary support is reinforced by two statements of secondary support:

Topic Sentence: Washington, D.C., has many exciting places for tourists to visit.

> *Primary Support 1:* One of the most fascinating places to see in Washington, D.C., is the Smithsonian Institution.
>
> > *Secondary Support 1a:* Acclaimed throughout the world as the most outstanding museum and research institution in the United States, the Smithsonian displays thousands of items that are of incalculable significance for anyone interested in American culture and history.
> >
> > *Secondary Support 1b:* Among the many permanent displays in the Smithsonian are the plane that Charles Lindbergh flew across the Atlantic and some stones that the Apollo astronauts brought back from the moon, as well as some interesting items from America's popular culture, such as the chair that Archie Bunker immortalized on the television show *All in the Family.*
>
> *Primary Support 2:* Another spot in Washington that every visitor to the city will want to see is the National Gallery of Art.
>
> > *Secondary Support 2a:* Donated to the people of the United States by Andrew W. Mellon during the early part of the twentieth century, the National Gallery of Art contains priceless examples of the world's greatest paintings and sculpture.

Secondary Support 2b: Especially noteworthy is its collection of Renaissance masterpieces, all of which were donated, like every other work of art in the gallery, to the government by private individuals as part of a public trust.

Primary Support 3: Finally, no trip to Washington, D.C., would be complete without stops at the White House and the Capitol.

Secondary Support 3a: Located at 1600 Pennsylvania Avenue, the White House has been home to every American president since John Adams and is open to the public for daily tours.

Secondary Support 3b: Begun in 1793 and completed in the late nineteenth century, the Capitol houses the Congress of the United States and has become the world's greatest symbol of democracy and freedom.

With your outline of primary and secondary supports complete, you are ready to write the paragraph, refining your preliminary sentences as necessary. Below is a possible final product:

(1) Washington, D.C., has many exciting places for tourists to visit. (2) One of the most fascinating places to see in Washington, D.C., is the Smithsonian Institution. (3) Acclaimed throughout the world as the most outstanding museum and research institution in the United States, the Smithsonian displays thousands of items that are of incalculable significance for anyone interested in American culture and history. (4) Among the many permanent displays in the Smithsonian are the plane that Charles Lindbergh flew across the Atlantic and some stones that the Apollo astronauts brought back from the moon, as well as some interesting items from America's popular culture, such as the chair that Archie Bunker immortalized on the television show *All in the Family.* (5) Another spot in Washington that every visitor to the city will want to see is the National Gallery of Art. (6) Donated to the people of the United States by Andrew W. Mellon during the early part of the twentieth century, the National Gallery of Art contains priceless examples of the world's greatest paintings and sculpture. (7) Especially noteworthy is its collection of Renaissance masterpieces, all of which were donated, like every other work of art in the gallery, to the government by private individuals as part of a public trust. (8) Finally, no trip to Washington, D.C., would be complete without stops at the White House and the Capitol. (9) Located at 1600 Pennsylvania Avenue, the White House has been home to every American president since John Adams and is open to the public for daily tours. (10) Begun in 1793 and completed in the late nineteenth century, the Capitol houses the Congress of the United States and has become the world's greatest symbol of democracy and freedom.

The secondary supports add to the effectiveness of the paragraph by providing specifics that reinforce the primary supports. For instance, the secondary supports following primary support 1 offer specific reasons and examples to show *why* the Smithsonian Institution is a place that tourists to Washington will definitely want to visit. This specific information about the significance of the Smithsonian and its incomparable collections leads a reader to understand and accept the assertion, offered in primary support 1, that the Smithsonian is "one of the most fascinating places to see in Washington, D.C." Likewise, primary supports 2 and 3 are more effective when the significance of the National Gallery of Art (primary support 2) and of the White House and the Capitol (primary support 3) are reinforced and illustrated with specific examples.

In a carefully planned paragraph, primary and secondary supports work in a unified manner to explain the paragraph's controlling idea. Secondary support sentences provide specifics that reinforce the primary supports, and strong primary supports, in turn, lead the reader to understand and accept the paragraph's controlling idea. The finished paragraph is effective because all of its sentences are unified in their support of the paragraph's controlling idea.

A Word of Caution: Digressions at the Secondary-Support Level   Since secondary supports relate only indirectly to the controlling idea of a paragraph, most problems in unity occur on the level of secondary support. Here it is easy to lose sight of the controlling idea and introduce facts or ideas that do not add relevant support. For this reason, you should take special care not to get off the track when you are selecting secondary supports. Make sure that you select secondary supports that effectively reinforce your primary supports and that do not digress into related areas. Remember: *Primary supports reinforce the controlling idea directly. Secondary supports reinforce the primary supports and, indirectly, the controlling idea.*

As the following paragraph illustrates, a single digression on the level of secondary support can cause the writer to wander far from the topic sentence and thus destroy the unity of a paragraph.

> (1) Soap operas deal with true-to-life problems. (2) Frequently depicted on soap operas, criminal acts such as murder and rape are problems that we all fear and may face, directly or indirectly, at some time in our lives. (3) Hundreds of murders occur weekly in the United States. (4) Rape, too, is an all too frequent crime that police and citizens in every major city try to combat and prevent. (5) Soap operas also show characters suffering from serious diseases, such as cancer, heart attack, and stroke, which many people actually must face. (6) One out of every four Americans will eventually suffer from cancer. (7) Many forms of cancer are curable if discovered during their early stages. (8) Fortunately, medical science has devised several effective tests for diagnosing cancer at an early stage. (9) Unfortunately, however, most people don't take the time to receive these important tests when they should. (10) If you know people who have symptoms that may indicate cancer, be sure that they receive the proper medical attention. (11) Otherwise they may suffer the unhappy fate of some of the characters on television soap operas.

Until sentence 7, this paragraph proceeds effectively. Sentence 2 is a primary support that reinforces the controlling idea that soap operas *deal with true-to-life problems.* Sentences 3 and 4 are secondary supports that provide specific evidence in support of sentence 2. Sentence 5 brings up the next primary support dealing with disease, and it, in turn, is reinforced by the secondary support in sentence 6.

In sentence 7, however, the writer goes off track. Instead of providing additional secondary support for sentence 5, the writer wanders off into a discussion of curable forms of cancer, tests to detect cancer, and the folly of people who don't take such tests when they should. By this point the writer has wandered far from the topic sentence. In fact, by the end of the paragraph, both writer and reader have almost completely lost sight of its controlling idea. Because the writer did not structure the paragraph carefully, a single digression on the level of secondary support moves the paragraph away from the controlling idea, undermining the unity of the work.

Much more effective is the following paragraph, which has the same topic sentence:

> (1) Soap operas deal with true-to-life problems. (2) Frequently depicted on soap operas, criminal acts such as murder and rape are problems that we all fear and may face, directly or indirectly, at some time in our lives. (3) Hundreds of murders occur weekly in the United States. (4) Rape, too, is an all too frequent crime that police and citizens in every major city try to combat and prevent. (5) Soap operas also show characters suffering from serious diseases, such as cancer, heart attack, and stroke, which many people actually must face. (6) One out of every four Americans will eventually suffer from cancer. (7) An equal number of Americans experience heart attacks and strokes. (8) Divorce is another problem that soap operas frequently depict and that many people must deal with in the course of their lives. (9) Recent statistics show that for the 12 months ending in March 1994, an estimated 1,182,000 couples divorced in the United States. (10) Further, many of these people have divorced more than once, and even those who have not been divorced may contemplate the possibility.

In this paragraph, the primary and secondary supports work together to explain and support the controlling idea. Sentences 2, 5, and 8 provide primary support for the controlling idea; the other sentences (including new sentences 7, 9, and 10) are secondary supports that effectively back up the primary supports and do not digress into related areas. The result is a unified paragraph that convincingly discusses what it sets out to discuss.

So important are secondary supports to the overall unity of your paragraphs that even occasional digressions at the level of secondary support can seriously harm the unity of your writing, as in the following example:

> (1) Nashville, Tennessee, is the country-and-western-music capital of the world. (2) Most of the major country-and-western-music stars, including Minnie Pearl, Johnny Cash, and Tammy Wynette, own homes in Nashville. (3) Their homes, which have become symbols of Nashville's country-and-western heritage, are visited by thousands of admiring fans. (4) Many of these same fans also visit the home of Andrew Jackson, which is located just outside Nashville. (5) Several of Nashville's music halls boast festivals that attract country-and-western enthusiasts from around the world. (6) The internationally famous Opryland, U.S.A., set in a beautiful park, houses the Grand Ole Opry, where the

stars of country-and-western music perform every Friday and Saturday night. (7) Other Nashville monuments include a restored colonial fort and a fine arts museum. (8) Several small night spots on Nashville's famed Elliston Place offer less established country-and-western artists the opportunity to gain public notice. (9) One of these, the Exit Inn, was popularized by Robert Altman in his film *Nashville,* an epic account of the country-and-western-music industry. (10) Some other famous films by Altman are *M*A*S*H, Buffalo Bill and the Indians,* and *The Wedding.*

This paragraph is carefully planned and structured at the primary-support level. The author has chosen three primary supports that back up the controlling idea that Nashville is *the country-and-western-music capital of the world:*

> *Primary Support 1:* Most of the major country-and-western-music stars, including Minnie Pearl, Johnny Cash, and Tammy Wynette, own homes in Nashville.
>
> *Primary Support 2:* Several of Nashville's music halls boast festivals that attract country-and-western enthusiasts from around the world.
>
> *Primary Support 3:* Several small night spots on Nashville's famed Elliston Place offer less established country-and-western artists the opportunity to gain public notice.

However, some of the secondary supports the writer has supplied are unrelated to the controlling idea and have little or nothing to do with the primary supports. The reader wonders, for example, what Andrew Jackson's home has to do with Nashville as the country-and-western-music capital of the world; or why the writer chose to mention that a visitor to Nashville can see a restored colonial fort and a fine arts museum; or why the writer listed three films by Robert Altman which have nothing to do with Nashville or with country-and-western music. These digressions distract the reader and make the paragraph far less effective than it might have been had they been eliminated or replaced.

■ SUMMARY

1. Often primary supports, particularly those that develop unfamiliar or complex controlling ideas, require additional details or explanation.

2. The sentences in a paragraph that reinforce a primary support by supplying additional details or explanation are called *secondary supports.* They constitute the third level of generality (see Chapter 1).

3. Unlike primary supports, secondary supports do not reinforce the controlling idea directly. Instead, they relate directly to a sentence of primary support. By adding information that helps make a primary support believable to the reader, they *indirectly* support the paragraph's controlling idea.

4. Since secondary supports relate only indirectly to the controlling idea of a paragraph, most problems in unity occur on the level of secondary support, where it is easy to lose sight of the controlling idea.

5. When you choose the secondary supports for your paragraph, be sure that they effectively reinforce your sentences of primary support. Do not use secondary supports that simply digress into related areas.

6. Even occasional digressions on the level of secondary support can seriously harm the effectiveness of your writing.

■ **EXERCISES**

I. For each of the following paragraphs, work with a partner to identify the topic and the controlling idea expressed in the topic sentence. Then decide whether the remaining sentences offer primary support or secondary support. If any sentence fails to support the controlling idea either directly as primary support or indirectly as secondary support, delete it.

A. (1) Students who need a part-time job should consider becoming a waiter or waitress. (2) The working hours in a restaurant are ideally suited to a student's schedule. (3) Most restaurants operate between the hours of 5:00 and 10:00 P.M., after students have finished their classes and have had time to do their assignments for the following day. (4) Students should always hand in their assignments on time, or they run the risk of lowering their grades. (5) Since restaurants don't expect their help to work more than three or four days a week, students who work as waiters or waitresses have more than enough free time to complete papers and projects on their days off. (6) The salary of a waiter or waitress is usually higher than what students can earn in other part-time jobs and is normally enough to pay for living expenses. (7) Expensive restaurants pay as much as $10.00 per hour to their waiters and waitresses, who also have the opportunity to earn as much as $200.00 per night in tips. (8) Even in small, inexpensive establishments, students who work as waiters or waitresses can usually earn $6.00 to $7.00 per hour plus tips.

B. (1) Pet owners who wish to keep their dogs fit and trim need to understand the reasons why overweight dogs tend to become obese. (2) The most common reason why dogs become overweight has to do with lack of exercise. (3) If a dog consumes more calories than it burns, it gains weight. (4) Similarly, dogs that lead idle lives also tend to become bored, and bored dogs tend to become overweight. (5) Like humans, dogs often eat when they are bored as a way of indulging themselves. (6) Another factor contributing to canine obesity is neutering. (7) The exact reasons why neutered pets gain weight are uncertain, but neutered animals definitely have a greater tendency toward obesity than do their unneutered counterparts. (8) Some diseases can also contribute to a dog's gaining weight. (9) Glandular diseases, for example, tend to increase a dog's appetite. (10) Finally, puppies that are overfed tend to become overweight as adults. (11) By feeding a puppy too much food, dog fanciers inadvertently increase the number of fat cells in their pet, thus predisposing it to obesity and illness.

C. (1) London is a city of historical splendor. (2) Westminster Abbey, a Gothic structure built during the thirteenth century, is 531 feet long and almost 102 feet high. (3) Its architectural highlights include a splendid nave, special chapels, and a magnificent choir loft, all created by skilled artists and masons. (4) Many of Britain's most distinguished men—including Geoffrey Chaucer, Alfred Tennyson, Robert Browning, Isaac Newton, Charles Darwin, and Sir Laurence Olivier—are buried in Westminster Abbey. (5) Big Ben, a famous clock located on the tower of the Houses of Parliament, is a historic landmark in itself. (6) The ringing of its thirteen-and-one-half-ton bell, hung in 1858, has marked the passing of some of Britain's most historic hours. (7) Also in London is Buckingham Palace, the royal family's home for over a hundred years. (8) Within the palace are a throne room where many historic events have taken place and an impressive staircase where visiting royalty have traditionally been received by the British monarch. (9) Queen Elizabeth is, of course, unlikely to talk with tourists, but it's worth a trip to Buckingham Palace anyway.

II. For each of the following paragraphs, identify the topic and the controlling idea expressed in the topic sentence. Then decide whether the remaining sentences offer primary support or secondary support. If any sentence fails to support the controlling idea either directly as primary support or indirectly as secondary support, delete it.

A. (1) If a wooden pool cue is to remain an accurate piece of equipment, it must be properly cared for. (2) The tip, or crown, of the cue should be kept rough and well chalked. (3) Keeping the tip of the cue in good condition helps prevent it from slipping when it strikes the ball. (4) The first eight inches of the cue's shaft should be rubbed with steel wool and kept covered with a layer of baby powder. (5) This procedure keeps oil and residue from collecting at the end of the stick and producing unnecessary friction. (6) Excess friction can severely impair the speed and accuracy of a pool shot. (7) In addition, the cue stick should be kept away from extreme heat and dampness. (8) Heat and moisture cause the stick to warp, making shooting a ball on center difficult. (9) For this reason, wooden pool cues should be kept in a case when not in use. (10) Cue cases reduce exposure to heat and moisture.

B. (1) There are three popular fallacies concerning Egyptian pyramids. (2) First, they were not built by slaves but by farmers. (3) During the spring, when the Nile overflowed its banks and flooded adjacent farms, farmers who could not till their fields were hired by the pharaoh to work on the construction of the pyramids. (4) These workers were paid in food and were free to quit whenever they wished. (5) Second, the pyramids weren't, as some people think, built by ancient astronauts as landmarks for flying saucers. (6) They were built as memorials to the pharaohs who were buried within them. (7) Third, pyramids were not built as sturdily as most people imagine. (8) The reason that they have survived for so long is the lack of humidity and rainfall in the Egyptian climate. (9) If the pyramids had been built in a climate like Michigan's, they would have been a heap of decayed and scattered stones by now.

C. (1) The Zugspitze Mountain in southern Germany is an ideal place to visit for a wondrous view of the Bavarian Alps and their neighboring scenery. (2) Standing on the peak of this mountain and facing east, one has a breathtaking view of the many snow-capped mountains that form the Bavarian Alps. (3) These mountains are covered with tall pines and thick firs that stand straight and stretch up to the sunny blue sky. (4) Turning to the north, one can look down upon the picturesque village of Garmisch. (5) Its many church steeples and quaint houses surrounded by high mountains give it a look of both beauty and tranquility. (6) During World War II, some important battles were fought near Gamisch. (7) Most people, however, have put the war behind them and are more concerned with enjoying the present than with rehashing history. (8) Facing west and looking out into the distance, one can see the Neuschwanchstein Castle. (9) This giant castle, standing lonely in the mountains, has great walls and huge towers that give it a magical look all its own. (10) Turning southward, one can observe the beautiful Austrian Alps. (11) These mountains look as though they were sleeping giants covered with glistening blankets of powdered snow.

III. Supply two secondary supports for each of the following primary supports. Be certain that each secondary support reinforces its primary support and doesn't simply digress onto a related topic suggested by the primary support. Again, keep in mind that while secondary supports relate only indirectly to the controlling idea, their ultimate function is to add support to the controlling idea.

MODEL:

TOPIC SENTENCE:	Different kinds of insurance offer different kinds of protection.
PRIMARY SUPPORT 1:	Life insurance provides financial assistance to the family of the insured in the event of death.
SECONDARY SUPPORT 1A:	*The insured can provide for a sum to be paid to dependents in case of death.*
SECONDARY SUPPORT 1B:	*He or she can also plan to arrange an annuity for offspring.*
PRIMARY SUPPORT 2:	Health insurance is designed to pay medical bills if the insured becomes ill enough to require treatment.
SECONDARY SUPPORT 2A:	*Standard medical insurance covers most of a family's hospital bills.*
SECONDARY SUPPORT 2B:	*Additional medical plans can provide further coverage.*
PRIMARY SUPPORT 3:	Disability insurance supplements or pays in full the salary of the insured if he or she becomes disabled or ill and cannot work.
SECONDARY SUPPORT 3A:	*Disability insurance usually pays the worker injured on the job a percentage of income.*
SECONDARY SUPPORT 3B:	*But there are types of disability that pay a full income to the injured.*

A. *Topic Sentence:* Job applicants should always look their best for an interview. *Primary Support 1:* Job candidates should wear clothes that are pleasant and tasteful.

Primary Support 2: In addition, job candidates should make sure that they look clean and well groomed.

Primary Support 3: Above all, job candidates should appear cheerful, relaxed, and cooperative.

B. *Topic Sentence:* Americans are constantly being induced to spend their money.

Primary Support 1: Billboards and magazine ads bombard us with slogans that promise happiness and fulfillment if we buy this or that product.

Primary Support 2: Coupons and sales entice us to buy products and services that we often don't really need.

Primary Support 3: Television commercials condition us to think that we can't live without the things they advertise.

C. *Topic Sentence:* People marry for a variety of reasons.

Primary Support 1: Some people marry for companionship.

Primary Support 2: Others marry because they want children.

Primary Support 3: But the majority of people marry because they are in love.

D. *Topic Sentence:* Anyone who enters the field of politics must be prepared to face the scrutiny of the public.

Primary Support 1: Because politicians are considered celebrities, the most trivial events in their personal lives attract public attention.

Primary Support 2: Recently passed legislation requires candidates for public office to make their financial records public, and these records often become the subject of public controversy.

Primary Support 3: Even the families of politicians must sacrifice their privacy when one of their members enters politics.

E. *Topic Sentence:* Television has something for everyone.

Primary Support 1: Some programs are specially designed to provide entertainment and instruction for children of all ages.

Primary Support 2: Lighthearted comedies and action-packed dramas cater to individuals who wish to escape from their everyday problems.

Primary Support 3: For the more discriminating viewer, television offers self-help programs, artistic productions, and carefully researched documentaries and specials.

IV. Develop a paragraph based on your work in Exercise III. After creating secondary supports for one of the topic sentences and its primary supports, write the paragraph that you have planned. Share a draft with a classmate. Would your partner have chosen the same secondary supports you did? Discuss your similarities and differences of approach. After sharing your paragraph with your instructor, place it in your portfolio.

HOW MUCH SUPPORT IS ENOUGH?

A perplexing yet important problem you will encounter as you write is deciding how much supporting evidence to use in each paragraph. Once you have studied your list of potential supporting statements and focused on those which you may wish to use to develop and support your controlling idea, you face the problem of deciding how many primary supports are needed and, even more difficult, how many, if any, secondary supports should be included for each primary support.

There are no set rules to follow. As writer, you must decide for yourself how many primary and secondary supports are necessary to back up the controlling idea of your paragraph. With experience, you will learn that the number of primary and secondary supports needed varies from paragraph to paragraph. Various combinations of primary and secondary supports can produce an effective paragraph.

In deciding on the pattern of supporting statements to use in a paragraph, keep in mind that your goal in writing the paragraph is to help your reader understand and accept your controlling idea, as you contracted to do in the topic sentence. This means that you must use enough primary supports to develop your controlling idea fully and convincingly and enough secondary supports to guarantee that your reader will believe your primary supports.

How Many Primary Supports?

Your first and most important task is to decide how many primary supports are needed to develop and support your controlling idea effectively. In some instances, the controlling idea itself may dictate the appropriate number. The following topic sentences are cases in point:

> A career in psychiatry demands *patience, understanding,* and *skill.*
>
> *Four major factors* contributed to the downfall of the Roman Empire.
>
> Regular exercise *relieves tension, strengthens the muscles,* abd *reduces the risk of heart disease.*
>
> Benjamin Franklin will long be remembered for his achievements as *diplomat, inventor, printer,* and *writer.*
>
> The accidents of *Three Mile Island* in Pennsylvania and *Chernobyl* in the Soviet Union call into question what scientists and engineers have told us about the safety of nuclear reactors.
>
> Having one's wisdom teeth removed can be a *frightening* and *painful* experience.
>
> When potting chrysanthemums, one should follow *three basic steps.*
>
> *Loneliness* and *fear* are *two major reasons* that the suicide rate among college students is high.

In each of these sentences, the italicized words suggest to the reader that a certain number of primary supports will follow, and it is the writer's responsibility to organize the paragraph along those lines.

Not every paragraph you write, however, will have a topic sentence that commits you to a definite number of primary supports; for those paragraphs that don't, you must decide for yourself how many are needed. In general, when you are in doubt about how many primary supports to include, you should use at least three. One point of primary support is usually inadequate development for the controlling idea unless the information it presents, when amplified through secondary supports, leaves no question unanswered. Two points of primary support are often enough to back up an idea—but if some of your readers don't accept or fully understand one of your supports, the effectiveness of the paragraph will be weakened. Three points of primary support usually provide enough information to help readers accept what you claim in your topic sentence.

The following topic sentence and three primary supports illustrate this principle:

> *Topic Sentence:* One should think twice before moving into a mobile home.
>
> *Primary Support 1:* Most mobile homes are too cramped to provide adequate living space.
>
> *Primary Support 2:* Furthermore, many mobile-home owners discover too late that trailers lack privacy.
>
> *Primary Support 3:* Finally, even well-constructed mobile homes aren't sturdy enough to support the activities of the average occupants.

If a paragraph with this topic sentence included only one or two of the primary supports above, many readers might remain unconvinced that "one should think twice before moving into a mobile home."

Keep in mind that using three primary supports is a useful guideline but not a hard-and-fast rule. As we have mentioned, in some cases it is adequate to use two primary supports (or even one) if each is sufficiently convincing and adequately reinforced by secondary supports. In other cases, it may be appropriate to use more than three primary supports, either because you have additional points that you feel are too important to leave out or because you have little or no information to add at the level of secondary support. Be wary, however, of weighing your paragraph down with so much supporting evidence that your writing becomes dense and tedious to your reader.

How Many Secondary Supports?

For many students, knowing how many (if any) secondary supports to use is more difficult than deciding on the number of primary supports. Keep in mind this simple rule: *Secondary supports are necessary to back up any primary supports that you feel your readers are unlikely to understand or accept without additional explanation.*

If your primary support is a straightforward and specific statement of fact, you probably don't need to develop it with secondary supports. The following paragraph on Daniel Boone, for example, consists only of a topic sentence and a series of primary supports of this type:

(1) The Daniel Boone of history differs greatly from the Daniel Boone of legend. (2) The historical Daniel Boone never "kilt a b'ar" with his knife. (3) He didn't discover Kentucky, and he didn't write an autobiography. (4) Although people say that Daniel Boone was well over six feet tall, in reality he stood five feet five inches in his stocking feet. (5) The legendary Daniel Boone was motivated only by humanitarian concerns, but the real Daniel Boone was a land speculator whose get-rich-quick schemes nearly landed him in jail. (6) According to his own testimony, Boone killed only one Indian, not the hundreds legend says he did. (7) At the time of Boone's death, his neighbors did not associate the world-famous legends of his exploits with the old man of limited means and strength whom they knew, and he died lonely and neglected.

If, on the other hand, your primary support is an assumption based on facts or ideas with which your readers might be unfamiliar, or if it is a statement of fact that requires additional information before it can be properly understood, then you should buttress it with the information your readers need to know in order to accept it.

The following paragraph outline, for example, illustrates the effective use of secondary support:

Topic Sentence: Rolling a cigarette is not as easy as cowboy stars make it seem.

Primary Support 1: First, break up all lumps in the tobacco.

Secondary Support: Lumps can puncture the paper, with the result that smoke will not pass through the cigarette.

Secondary Support: Lumps also burn at a different rate from properly packed tobacco.

Primary Support 2: Next, obtain high-quality papers recommended by a friend.

Secondary Support: Poor-quality paper spoils the taste of the tobacco.

Secondary Support: Many brand-name papers are of poor quality, and friends who have used different kinds of papers are the best source of information on which paper to purchase.

Primary Support 3: Next, form a pocket in the paper by creasing up approximately one quarter of the nongummed end.

Secondary Support: The pocket keeps the tobacco from spilling out of the wrapper.

Primary Support 4: Place the tobacco in the pocket, and spread it evenly across the length of the cigarette.

Secondary Support: If the tobacco is spread unevenly, the cigarette may not burn well.

Primary Support 5: Holding the filled paper with the thumb against the index and middle finger, roll the cigarette carefully.

Secondary Support: Using more than three fingers to roll the cigarette can produce a loosely rolled product, which is difficult to smoke.

The writer of this paragraph selected secondary supports thoughtfully, never allowing them to detract from the unity of the paragraph. The secondary supports reinforce and explain the primary supports, thereby making them more comprehensible.

Let us examine the structure of this paragraph more closely. The secondary supports that follow primary support 1 explain *why* lumps should be removed from any tobacco used in the making of cigarettes. Once the reader has read the secondary supports, the reasons for following the writer's instructions become clear. The secondary supports that follow primary support 2 explain *why* friends are the best source of information on the kind of cigarette paper to purchase and why the quality of the paper is important. Primary supports 3, 4, and 5, unlike 1 and 2, are each followed by only one secondary support. In each of these instances, one sentence was adequate to explain *why* the instructions in the primary support sentences should be followed.

If you are having trouble structuring the primary and secondary supports in your paragraphs and elect to follow a pattern of three primary supports for each topic sentence, you may find it helpful to use *two* sentences of secondary support to reinforce each primary support. In this way, you will be certain of having enough primary support for your controlling idea and enough secondary support to reinforce your primary supports. The basic structure for a paragraph of this sort is as follows:

Sentence 1:	Topic Sentence
Sentence 2:	Primary Support 1
Sentence 3:	Secondary Support
Sentence 4:	Secondary Support
Sentence 5:	Primary Support 2
Sentence 6:	Secondary Support
Sentence 7:	Secondary Support
Sentence 8:	Primary Support 3
Sentence 9:	Secondary Support
Sentence 10:	Secondary Support

The paragraph on Washington, D.C. (page 34) follows this pattern. So, too, does the following version of the paragraph on mobile homes, fully developed here by the use of secondary supports:

(1) One should think twice before moving into a mobile home. (2) Most mobile homes are too cramped to provide adequate living space. (3) Normal-size furniture barely fits into the narrow confines of the mobile home. (4) Shins and ankles are easily bruised on the protruding corners of end tables and other furnishings that crowd passageways. (5) Furthermore, many mobile-home owners discover too late that trailers lack privacy. (6) Footsteps echo loudly from one end of a trailer to the other, especially during the night, when normal sounds

become amplified in the quiet. (7) Television, stereo music, and voices carry through the thinly paneled walls of the mobile home, sometimes into the home adjacent to it in the trailer park. (8) Finally, even well-constructed mobile homes aren't sturdy enough to support the activities of the average occupants. (9) Lacking a strong foundation, mobile homes gradually sink into the ground, causing doors to hang awry and furniture to shift. (10) Storms frequently ravage mobile homes, and even a washing machine on spin cycle can cause a mobile home to jump and wobble.

Without secondary supports, this paragraph would not be as convincing to the reader. The addition of secondary supports makes the primary supports more believable, thereby reinforcing the controlling idea.

As you become more confident in your writing, you may wish to experiment with different arrangements of primary and secondary supports. We by no means wish to discourage you from doing so now if you feel that you have enough understanding of paragraph unity and structure to know when and how primary and secondary supports should be used. As long as your paragraphs are unified and adequately developed, they can follow whatever arrangement of supporting statements you desire to use. The important thing is that you understand the nature and purpose of primary and secondary supports and that you realize the importance of developing your paragraphs according to a carefully planned system of support.

■ SUMMARY

1. As a writer, you must learn to decide how many primary and secondary supports are needed to reinforce the controlling idea of your paragraphs.

2. Every paragraph should contain enough primary supports to back up the controlling idea fully and convincingly, and it should have enough secondary supports to guarantee that the reader will understand and accept its primary supports.

3. Sometimes the controlling idea of a paragraph will suggest or even dictate the number of primary supports that should be used in the paragraph.

4. When you are in doubt about how many primary and secondary supports to use in a paragraph, a good rule of thumb is to use three primary supports and two secondary supports for each primary support.

■ EXERCISES

1. Write a paragraph using one of the following topic sentences. In your paragraph, use three primary supports and follow each primary support with two secondary supports. Make sure that each of your primary supports adds direct support to the paragraph's controlling idea and that your secondary supports back up the primary supports that they follow.

A. Preparing a Thanksgiving dinner involves more than just roasting a turkey.

B. Not all students want the same things from a college education.
C. Clothes often reflect the personalities of the people who wear them.
D. Deciding to have children requires serious thought.
E. The death of a favorite pet can seem as traumatic as the death of a family member.
F. History sometimes repeats itself.
G. Different kinds of cars suit the needs of different kinds of people.
H. Although rock-and-roll music is often associated with antisocial behavior, several rock stars have made significant contributions to society.

II. Share a draft of the paragraph that you have written for Exercise I with a classmate. Ask him or her to provide you with feedback on its unity. Is the controlling idea clear and appropriate? Have you focused your primary and secondary supports on the controlling idea? As your partner is in the process of evaluating your paragraph, do the same for your partner. When you get back together to share your reactions, be sure to follow some basic guidelines for giving effective feedback:

A. Summarize what you have determined to be the purpose of the paragraph.
B. Praise the aspects of the paragraph that fulfill that purpose.
C. Suggest ways that the writer can improve the paragraph.

III. Consider the topic sentence that was used for the model paragraph discussed in this chapter: "Washington, D.C., has many exciting places for tourists to visit." Substitute the name of the city where you grew up (or the name of any other city) for "Washington, D.C.," and write a paragraph on that topic sentence. For instance, if you grew up in Tecumseh, Oklahoma, your topic sentence would read as follows: "Tecumseh, Oklahoma, has many exciting places for tourists to visit." In writing your paragraph, follow the same steps and structures that were used in writing the paragraph on Washington. First, using the questions *Who?, What?, When?, Where?,* and *Why?* as your guides, brainstorm a list of information that might be used for potential supporting sentences. Second, evaluate your list of supporting information, and then construct three sentences of primary support. Third, develop each of your sentences of primary support with two sentences of secondary support.

IV. Write paragraphs on two of the following topics. Use whatever arrangement of primary and secondary supports you feel most effectively supports your controlling idea. After you have written each paragraph, underline all sentences that function as primary supports. Make certain that each of your primary supports relates directly to the controlling idea of the paragraph and helps to support that idea effectively. Then make certain that your secondary supports back up the primary supports that they follow. Feel free to alter the topics in whatever manner you see fit. Instead of "dancing," for example, you may choose to write on ballet or club dancing.

A. dancing
B. my favorite movie
C. taxes
D. video games
E. fast-food restaurants
F. slogans
G. sex symbols
H. slang
I. myths/legends
J. a pastime I absolutely cannot appreciate

V. Plan and write a unified paragraph that uses *only primary supports* to develop its controlling idea.

VI. Plan and write a unified paragraph on a topic of your own choosing. Use whatever arrangement of primary and secondary supports you feel best develops your controlling idea, and make certain that every sentence in the paragraph directly or indirectly supports the controlling idea.

VII. Don't forget your portfolio! After submitting your paragraphs from this chapter for evaluation by your instructor and receiving them back, be certain to place them in your portfolio. Look through the paragraphs as you insert them in the folder. Are you improving? Are there areas where you need work? Share your reactions and concerns with your instructor.

4

METHODS OF DEVELOPMENT

Example, Cause and Effect, and Process Analysis

In Chapter 3 you learned that all of the sentences in a paragraph must support, either directly or indirectly, the controlling idea expressed in your topic sentence. There are, however, ways to develop your controlling idea so that your readers will understand it.

In this chapter, we discuss three methods of developing an expository paragraph. You should become familiar with each so that you can organize and shape your explanation in the way that is most effective for making the point that you wish to convey. Three other methods will be explained in Chapter 5. The three to be considered here are as follows:

1. Example
2. Cause and Effect
3. Process Analysis

These three methods have been used by good writers for centuries. In fact, you will find that one or another of these methods has been used in the sample paragraphs included in this book and in many well-written paragraphs you will encounter elsewhere in your reading.

These methods of development have been widely used because they communicate ideas effectively. And they communicate effectively because they represent the ways our minds naturally work when we wish to provide information and support our views. When we state that something is true, we are likely to give examples to explain what we assert. Or we might want to show why something came about or what its effects will be. And we often need to explain how something works. In other words, you would use these methods even if you didn't study them because they represent thought processes that come naturally to all of us. But study of the methods will show you how to use each effectively and how to select the one that will best serve you in getting a particular idea across effectively.

EXAMPLE

Example is probably the simplest method of development. In using it, the writer selects examples to support the controlling idea of the paragraph. In the following paragraph, the writer has developed a controlling idea—that smoking *is hazardous to health*—by giving examples of various types of health hazards that smoking may bring about:

> According to information collected by the American Cancer Society and other health-related organizations, smoking is hazardous to health. The rate of lung and throat cancer is far greater in cigarette smokers than in nonsmokers. Men who smoke pipes have a higher incidence of lip and mouth cancer than those who have never smoked a pipe. Moreover, smokers are more likely to experience heart attacks, ulcers, bronchitis, and emphysema than are nonsmokers. Recent research has uncovered the fact that women who smoke during pregnancy are more likely to have miscarriages than are women who don't smoke. Finally, babies born of smoking mothers are usually below average in weight.

The controlling idea of this paragraph, expressed in the first sentence, makes a statement evaluating a still widespread habit. Thereafter, the writer gives explicit examples to explain the statement that smoking is hazardous to health:

1. The chance of having throat and lung cancer is greater for cigarette smokers.
2. The chance of having lip and mouth cancer is greater for pipe smokers.
3. The chance of having heart attacks, ulcers, bronchitis, or emphysema is greater for smokers.
4. The chance of having a miscarriage is greater for the smoking woman.
5. The weight of babies born of smoking mothers is usually lower than that of babies born of nonsmoking mothers.

Each of these examples effectively backs up the controlling idea of the paragraph.

When you develop a paragraph by giving examples, keep three important guidelines in mind:

1. *Be sure that your examples are appropriate*. The examples you use should clearly and directly support the controlling idea you state in your topic sentence.

2. *Be sure that your examples are specific.* Don't generalize. Don't be vague. Your examples should be concrete and clear.
3. *Use enough examples to convince the reader.* Usually three or more examples are needed. But, in the right situation, you may use one extended example that is developed in sufficient detail to provide adequate explanation.

Choosing Appropriate Examples

Be sure that every example you use illustrates your controlling idea directly and clearly. The following paragraph does not follow this advice to the fullest:

> Of the many monsters that have been "sighted" on land or sea around the world, not one has been captured and preserved by the scientists or explorers who have sought them out. For example, millions of people are convinced that the Loch Ness Monster exists in a loch, or lake, of Scotland. It is even known affectionately as "Nessie" by the people who live nearby. But no one has ever captured a "monster" in Loch Ness. According to natives in the mountains of southern Asia, the huge, shaggy yeti make large footprints in the snow, and their name is used to frighten children into obedience. But the only "evidence" of their existence anyone has ever produced was a scalp covered with long hair, which proved to be a fake. Children are familiar with a frightening man-giant that they have read about in the tale of *Jack and the Beanstalk*. But nobody has ever found this monster or discovered any of the other monsters mentioned in children's stories. And of course, King Kong of movie fame was right out of fiction.

The first two examples—Loch Ness Monster and yeti—are appropriate. Both are monsters which, according to sworn testimony, have been sighted in recent years. The other examples, though, are not suitable. According to the topic sentence, the writer is concerned with monsters that people report actually sighting. No one in sober condition has ever reported seeing the *Jack and the Beanstalk* giant or the other monsters that the writer vaguely alludes to as figuring in children's stories. And of course King Kong, as the writer says, is right out of fiction. The paragraph needs to be rewritten so that *all* the examples deal with monsters that people believe they have sighted.
Here is the paragraph as the student revised it:

> Of the many monsters that have been "sighted" on land or sea around the world, not one has been captured and preserved by the scientists or explorers who have sought it out. For example, millions of people are convinced that the Loch Ness Monster exists in a loch, or lake, of Scotland. It is even known affectionately as "Nessie" by the people who live nearby. But no one has ever captured a "monster" in Loch Ness. According to natives in the mountains of southern Asia, the huge, shaggy yeti make large footprints in the snow, and their name is used to frighten children into obedience. But the only "evidence" of their existence anyone has ever produced was a scalp covered with long hair,

which proved to be a fake. In the United States, many workers and campers have been convinced that they saw a huge, hairy man-creature that has come to be known as "Big Foot." But it has turned out that the only "specimen" of Big Foot, a weird creature preserved in ice, was skillfully manufactured to order for a promoter who made a lot of money by exhibiting it at fairs. A creature similar to Big Foot comes to us from Canada. There, the big-footed, shaggy man-giant is called Sasquatch. But although people swear that they have sighted him—or her, in many cases—and one person claims to have shot the creature, no corpse has ever been recovered. Perhaps it is just as well that all of the monsters that people fear or love still live on the borderline between truth and fiction.

In this paragraph, all of the examples develop the controlling idea that "of the many monsters that have been 'sighted' on land or sea around the world, not one has been captured and preserved. . . ." The writer unifies the paragraph by getting rid of the material about purely storybook characters, whom nobody has reported sighting. The writer strengthens the paragraph further by adding two suitable examples—about Big Foot and Sasquatch—that give further support to the controlling idea.

Including Specifics

All your examples should be made concrete and clear by the use of specifics. Not only is the following student paragraph too brief to be convincing, but the examples it contains are much too vague:

> The Bible presents a great variety of literary genres. It includes books that deal with history. It offers dramas as interesting as many dramas today. In the Bible, one can read numerous biographies. The Bible also offers poetry in many of its books.

The writer does offer some appropriate examples: she lists as literary genres what she calls "history," "drama," "biography," and "poetry." But the examples are not specific enough. The average reader may not be aware that the Bible does in fact contain many kinds of literature. Therefore, in order to provide adequate explanation for the point expressed in the topic sentence, the writer should name specific books of the Bible that contain the literary genres she has listed and supply other explanatory details.

Following is an improved version of the same paragraph:

> The Bible contains a great variety of literary genres that provide us with some very interesting reading. It gives us history in Kings, Judges, Samuel, and other books. It gives us drama in Exodus and in the Book of Job. In fact, the story in Exodus of how the Israelites escaped from Egyptian slavery became the plot for a popular movie starring Charleton Heston as Moses, and the Book of Job has been turned into a well-known modern play. Indeed, Job has become one of the best-known characters in all literature. The Bible also contains several biographies. The best known is, of course, that of Jesus. In the first four books of the New Testament, there are four versions of the life of Jesus, recounting the events

of his life from his birth and childhood to his crucifixion. The Bible also offers poetry in many of its books, but the psalms are the most famous of its poems. They have been chanted in monasteries and churches and memorized by millions of people through the ages.

Providing Enough Examples

Using Three or More Examples In developing a paragraph by the use of examples, the writer does not have to use every appropriate example that comes to mind. But the writer should use enough examples to be clear and convincing. A good rule of thumb is to use three or more examples, each of which constitutes a primary support. As can be seen in the following paragraph, written by a student, two examples are usually not enough:

> College students who need financial assistance with their education often have more options available to them than they realize. For example, loan programs, such as the Federal Perkins Loan and the Federal Stafford Loan, are available at relatively low interest rates to students who qualify for them. Both undergraduate and graduate students may be eligible for a Perkins loan, which can pay as much as $3,000 a year toward an undergraduate student's educational expenses and $5,000 a year for a graduate student's expenses. Similarly, a Stafford loan can range from $2,625 per year for a first-year, dependent undergraduate to $18,500 per year for a graduate student.

The two examples given of financial assistance programs for college students are not enough to explain in adequate detail the controlling idea that college students in need of financial assistance "have more options available to them than they realize." The writer must present more examples to develop the controlling idea effectively. The following paragraph is more effective because it includes more examples:

> College students who need financial assistance with their education often have more options available to them than they realize. For example, loan programs, such as the Federal Perkins Loan and the Federal Stafford Loan, are available at relatively low interest rates to students who qualify for them. Both undergraduate and graduate students may be eligible for a Perkins loan, which can pay as much as $3,000 a year toward an undergraduate student's educational expenses and $5,000 a year for a graduate student's expenses. Similarly, a Stafford loan can range from $2,625 per year for a first-year, dependent undergraduate to $18,500 per year for a graduate student. Students also may qualify for aid programs that do not require that the amount received be paid back. One such program is Federal Work Study, which provides a part-time job, usually on campus, for students willing to work up to twenty hours a week. Another possibility that involves an award and not a loan is the Federal Pell Grant, a program that provided a maximum of $2,300 to qualifying undergraduates in the 1993–94 academic year. A final program granting awards to college students is the Federal Supplemental Educational Opportunity Grants program, which provides as much as $4,000 per year to qualifying students.

The writer of this paragraph adds examples to make her point effective. We are given five examples of financial assistance programs and some specifics concerning the terms of each.

You should also note that while all of the examples in this particular paragraph are appropriate and specific, none is discussed in much detail. A practical guideline is that the less you develop each example, the more examples you will need to back up your controlling idea. Two or three examples must be supported by detailed secondary supports to be as effective as five examples discussed only briefly.

Using One Extended Example   There are occasions when one example very fully developed may carry the weight of many that are more briefly stated. A good illustration of the use of one extended example is the paragraph that follows:

> Although they may appear friendly, the bears in Yellowstone National Park can be extremely dangerous and destructive. I learned this lesson on a camping trip last summer. A friend of mine and I were setting up camp close to a dry river bed in a forlorn canyon when our attention was directed toward two large bears that were peacefully walking down a narrow path. Suddenly the huge animals stopped, gave us a curious look, and then turned slowly and disappeared into the forest. Unafraid, we continued our work. Afterward, we built a fire and cooked meat and eggs for supper. Being inexperienced campers, we left food scraps—an obvious attraction for wild animals—around the campsite when we retired for the night. Thirty minutes later we awoke to the sound of growls and crunches. Two bears were eating the abandoned scraps of food and tearing at our partially filled knapsacks. Seeking safety, we climbed a nearby pine tree and watched helplessly as the bears completely demolished our camp in an apparent search for more food. After this destructive action, the bears, to our surprise, walked into the forest, completely ignoring us. Had we antagonized them, though, they might very well have attacked us.

The controlling idea of this paragraph, communicated in the topic sentence, is that "the bears in Yellowstone National Park *can be extremely dangerous and destructive.*" "I learned this lesson on a camping trip last summer" serves as primary support for the opening statement. The extended example or narrative that follows is actually a secondary support, although it contains a series of events. This variation on the general-to-specific paragraph can be very effective—especially if you draw on personal experience.

■ **SUMMARY**

I. In a paragraph developed by the use of examples, all the examples should be *appropriate*—that is, they should support the controlling idea of the paragraph.

2. All examples should be *specific*.

3. The writer should use *enough* examples to make the paragraph effective. Three or more examples are usually needed, but one extended example may sometimes be sufficient.

■ EXERCISES

I. Read the following topic sentences; then think of a number of examples (preferably more than three) that you can use to support each one. Be sure that your examples are appropriate and specific. If any of the topics lends itself to development by the use of one extended example, explain how you would develop this example.

A. Some of the most popular programs on television today involve series that were first produced years ago.
B. Space exploration has given us many small miracles.
C. Citizens who report sighting an unidentified flying object risk bringing ridicule upon themselves.
D. Prejudice comes in many forms.
E. Many new job opportunities are open today as a result of the development of the computer.
F. Some people are their own worst enemies.
G. Americans have many patriotic songs.

II. From the list of topic sentences that you have developed in Exercise I, choose one for discussion with a classmate. Describe to your classmate the examples or extended example you would use to develop that topic sentence, justifying your choices according to the guidelines in this chapter. Then listen while your classmate shares his or her choices and justifications with you. After you and your partner are satisfied that you understand each other, describe to the rest of the class your partner's plan, and have your partner describe to them your plan. Consider carefully their reactions and suggestions.

III. Read each of the following paragraphs carefully. Write down each sentence that begins a new example; then list the number of examples contained in each paragraph. State whether or not each example is *appropriate* and *specific*.

A. There are many ways to cut the costs of rising grocery bills. Purchasing store brands instead of the popular brands advertised on television and in magazines saves money, since the cost of advertising does not have to be included in the cost of store-brand items. Peanut butter and canned vegetables with store-brand labels usually are of the same quality as widely advertised national brands. Another way to make pennies count is to clip money-saving coupons from newspapers and to watch for weekly specials. Buying in quantity can also cut per-item expenses. And shopping for fresh fruits and vegetables when they are in season can result in considerable savings for the shopper. Finally, shoppers who bring marketing lists and stick to them avoid the temptation of buying on impulse and thus avoid spending money that they otherwise would not spend.

B. Researchers have found in case after case that even when identical twins have been raised in completely different environments they still show an amazing number of similarities. In one such case, two female twins, Rosalie and Corinna, accidentally encountered each other when both were attending a teachers' convention in New York. They immediately recognized that they must be related and soon concluded that they were twin sisters. They had been separated when less than a year old, and they had been raised in different states. Nevertheless, the two shared a remarkable number of similarities. Not only were both women high school teachers, but both taught biology. Each had given birth to two children, and each had authored two illustrated children's books. Moreover, they liked the same foods, they had the same favorite movie, and both had a passion for collecting and restoring antique furniture. In another particularly extraordinary case, two male twins, both named Bill, found each other forty-two years after having been separated when they were five days old. The two were astounded by the things they shared in common. Both men had married women named Martha, divorced them, and then remarried women named Ann. One had named his son William Arthur, and other had named his Arthur William. Both men drove blue Jeep Cherokees, and both had worked as game wardens. They each enjoyed fly fishing, and both played the guitar.

C. Would you believe that something as small as the peanut could have hundreds of uses? Every year millions of peanuts are turned into peanut butter, one of America's favorite foods. Roasted peanuts are salted and eaten as snacks or used in candies and bakery products. Salad oils and margarines are made from peanuts. Farmers use peanut vines, hulls, and skins as feed for their animals. Other products made from the peanut are cosmetics, soap, packing oil, medicines, and even explosives. In fact, there are more than three hundred uses for the peanut plant and its fruit.

D. According to ancient superstitions, moles on the body reveal a person's character and foretell the future. Some moles reveal strengths and weaknesses of character. A mole on the back of the neck indicates that the bearer is a spendthrift. Moles on both sides of the neck reveal extreme stubbornness. A mole on the left knee is a sure indication that the bearer is unwise in business matters. In fact, a mole on any part of the leg indicates that one is both indolent and wasteful. A mole over the left eyebrow hints of laziness as well as selfishness. If one meets someone with a mole on any finger, he should hold on to his wallet: according to superstition, the person is sure to be a crook. But a friend with a mole on his nose is strong of character and will always remain a true friend. In addition to revealing character, moles are said to foretell the future. There is an old saying, "A mole on the neck, money by the peck." If the mole is on the front of the neck, good luck may come from any source. A mole on the ear also brings good luck in the form of money. A mole over the right eyebrow means success in love, money, and career. A mole on the hand, however, is the most to be desired: it forecasts the good news that one will be talented, healthy, rich, and happy.

E. Representatives in Congress really enjoy the "gravy" provided by the American tax dollar. To start with, the salary itself is impressive. In 1995, our representatives' salaries were $133,600. The leaders in the House and Senate earned $148,400, and the Speaker of the House received $171,500. In addition to their salaries, representatives receive fringe benefits galore. Available to them is a base allowance to cover expenses incurred in carrying out their duties. These expenses can range from the costs of stationery and postage to those incurred for grooming and recreation. Further advantages include numerous free round trips per year between their homes and Washington, subsidized international travel, a free furnished office in Washington, and a hefty allowance for staffing. Moreover, Congressional representatives are covered for life by generous life and health insurance programs. Finally, when they retire they do so on a substantial pension that would be the envy of most of the voters that elected them.

F. In many ways the staff at this university has given me a hard time with my education. When I first arrived here three years ago from my native China, Mr. "N," in the Office for Foreign Students, lost my visa. Since then the staff and computers have given me innumerable occasions for worry and frustration. For three years in a row, the people in the registrar's office have sent me notices saying that I was not carrying a full-time load when, in fact, I was carrying a fourteen-hour load, two more hours than is required of full-time students. The office lists my birth date as August 1, 1974, but they insist that I am forty-eight years old. They say that I am a freshman, but I am really a junior. There are many other mistakes that they have made, but the one that takes the cake is their informing me, just last week, that I am an American Eskimo from Tunisia.

IV. Write a paragraph on one of the following topics. Develop your topic sentence through the use of examples. Before you submit your paragraph for evaluation by your instructor, share it with a classmate. Ask your partner to comment on the appropriateness and specificity of the examples, as well as on whether the paragraph is engaging and convincing.

   A. body language
   B. celebrities
   C. fishing lures (or techniques)
   D. gender-biased language
   E. phobias
   F. bores
   G. villains
   H. faces
   I. unusual pets

V. Using example as your method of development, write a paragraph on a topic of your choosing. Be certain that your example or examples are appropriate and specific. And be certain that you use enough examples, or develop one example fully enough, to support your controlling idea adequately.

VI. Collect the paragraphs you have written thus far into your folder. As you look back over your work, your classmates' feedback, and your instructors' evaluations, assess your strengths as a writer. Also, identify areas where your writing could improve.

CAUSE AND EFFECT

The second method of development is *cause and effect*. It is one of the most frequently used methods in contemporary writing because it fits naturally the needs of this scientific age. As a result of the scientific approach to understanding the world and our experiences in it, we have come to assume that there is a cause (or causes) for every event and that, conversely, every event has results or effects.

Cause and effect may be said to constitute two sides of the same coin: if you can develop a paragraph using cause, you should have no trouble developing a paragraph using effect—the techniques involved in the two approaches are the same. Cause and effect are means of communicating relationships. In using the method, you examine an event in relation to other events that *precede* or *follow* it. In other words, you show *why* an event has occurred by examining its causes, or you show what happens *as a result of* the event by examining its effects.

There are two rules to follow if you want to use cause and effect competently:

1. Cite the *most important* causes or effects. This means looking for causes or effects that are clearly and directly related to the event under consideration.
2. Be sure that in using cause and effect you *do not mistake mere conditions*—that is, some related happening or background—*for active causes or effects*.

Citing Important and Convincing Causes and Effects

In developing a paragraph by cause and effect, you must be sure that what you label *effect* clearly and directly resulted from what you label *cause*. In other words, you must be convincing and accurate when you say that A was the cause or the effect of B.

In the following student paragraph, developed by an examination of causes, the writer does not accomplish the goal successfully:

> The reasons for the decline in the popularity of humanities courses in American colleges and universities today are not hard to identify. In the first place, with good jobs becoming harder to get, students opt for a practical education, which may give them skills to use in making a living, rather than for humanities courses. Further, with the increase in importance of the computer and computer science, more students have been lured into computer courses, and the pool of students furnishes fewer who are interested in the humanities. But one modern invention, the nuclear bomb, has filled people with such fear that, as a result, fewer people are interested in studying courses that humanities departments offer. Because people are becoming more obsessed with safety, they are becoming uninterested in literature, philosophy, and history, and humanities classes register fewer and fewer students.

In the paragraph above, the student was trying to bring together some of the important causes for the decline in popularity of humanities courses today. The first cause is a valid one: with first-rate jobs getting ever harder to find, students *are* having to look to technical courses in preparing for a future in which they will be employed. Also, the advance in computer science has definitely caused many students to turn their interests toward computers and computerized work, and this has naturally caused a decrease in the number of students left to take humanities courses. But the nuclear bomb cannot, by any stretch of the imagination, be called a cause of the decline in interest in the humanities. Many people are, as the writer says, filled with fear of thermonuclear disaster, but one can make a good cause for the claim that this fear makes people more interested in looking at history—with the intention of avoiding the mistakes of the past—and more interested in literature and philosophy as an escape from fear and means of spiritual guidance. The following revision omits reference to the nuclear bomb and brings out other valid reasons for the decline in prestige of humanities courses:

> The reasons for the decline in the popularity of humanities programs in American colleges and universities today are not hard to identify. In the first place, with good jobs becoming harder to get, students opt for a practical education, which may give them skills to use in making a living, rather than for humanities courses. Further, with the increase in importance of the computer and computer science, more students have been lured into computer courses, and the pool of students furnishes fewer who are interested in the humanities. The dominance of television over society today has also caused the humanities to diminish in popularity. People have become watchers rather than readers. As they get more of their facts and ideas from the TV screen rather than from books, they become less interested in studying history, philosophy, and literature via the written page. Even the decline in prestige of college and university presidents who have strongly supported the humanities in the past has weakened administrative support for the humanities departments of universities today. Thus, the humanities are drawing fewer students today than was the case a generation ago.

The student paragraph that follows also illustrates a convincing treatment of causal forces at work:

> A series of events led to the collapse of Elvis Presley's career. His wife, Priscilla, moved out of Graceland Mansion in 1972, leaving Elvis depressed and alone. Immediately after Priscilla left, Elvis's buddies moved in and involved the rock star in a series of round-the-clock parties. As a result of overindulgence in party fare and failure to exercise, Elvis found himself with a serious weight problem. By 1974 he weighed 240 pounds and was so fat that when he appeared in Las Vegas, photographers were forbidden to take pictures of him. A crash diet, which was supposed to reduce the singer's weight, instead brought on a prolonged period of depression from which he never really recovered. Appalled at his heaviness, audiences rejected the overweight entertainer, and his career rapidly deteriorated.

After finishing this paragraph, the reader feels that the writer has pointed out some valid causes of the collapse of Elvis Presley's career. The analysis proceeds through a series of events, beginning with the separation of the singing star from his wife and ending with the decline of Elvis's popularity. Each event in the series is *believably attributed to a cause,* and the final outcome is the deterioration of Presley's career—the occurrence the paragraph set out to explain.

In a paragraph developed by cause or effect, the writer must describe the causes or effects in such a way that the reader is convinced of their direct relationship to the event being discussed. The following paragraph, which describes the "serious consequences" that the death of a child can have on the relationship between the surviving parents, accomplishes this very well:

> The death of a child often has serious consequences for the marriage of the parents who survive. Because it is natural for parents to feel guilty when a child dies, many bereaved parents tend to blame themselves and one another for not having shielded their child from death. As a result, these parents can easily become withdrawn, suspicious, and uncommunicative, and their marriage is likely to experience a great deal of unanticipated stress. Another unforeseen consequence of the death of a child involves the rate at which each parent grieves. If the griefs of the spouses fail to synchronize, the spouse who grieves the longer tends to blame the other for being insensitive and uncaring. Previous tensions in the relationship become heightened, and separation frequently ensues. For such parents, accepting the end of a marriage seems easy after having adjusted to the loss of a child, and it may even seem an appropriate form of self-inflicted punishment for not having been able to keep the child alive. In addition, the death of a child tends to force grieving parents to reflect on the entirety of their lives and to reexamine many of their previous commitments. Because they have less emotional energy than before, they reassess where they wish to invest what little energy they have. If there were any problems in their marriage before their child's death, those problems can seem insurmountable, and divorce then appears inevitable. Thus, the divorce rate among bereaved parents tends to be much higher than that among parents who have not experienced the loss of a child.

Mistaking Conditions or Circumstances for Active Causes or Effects

Very often, through faulty reasoning, people assume that a state of affairs or an event causes another event, when in fact the so-called cause is not directly responsible at all. They mistake circumstances for actual causes.

In the following paragraph, for example, environmental circumstances are confused with *causes:*

> An attractive environment causes children to become emotionally stable and productive. Because of the comfortable setting, they feel confident and trusting of themselves and others. They are happier, make more friends, and enjoy school activities more. Children even earn higher grades when they study in attractive surroundings. Their parents may be happier in an attractive home,

and, if so, the children are happier because they know that their mother and father are contented. It is amazing how much better children function when they live in a beautiful and attractive environment.

An attractive environment does not *cause* a child to become emotionally stable and productive. It provides a setting that may allow a state of well-being to develop, but it does not necessarily bring about emotional development of any kind. We all know of children who live in beautiful homes but who are unhappy because their parents are incompatible, because there is serious illness in the family, or because they are neglected by busy or uncaring parents.

■ SUMMARY

1. Use cause and effect when you want to show *why* an event has occurred (by examining its causes) or when you want to show what happens *as a result of* the event (by examining its effects).

2. Be sure that you cite important causes and effects and that you present them effectively.

3. Be sure that you deal with causes or effects that are clearly and directly related to the event under consideration.

4. Do not mistake mere conditions for active causes or effects

■ EXERCISES

I. Following are seven topic sentences that may be developed by the use of cause and effect. Read each sentence and state whether it would be developed more effectively in a paragraph of cause or a paragraph of effect. List the causes or the effects that should be included in developing and supporting the topic sentence.

A. Many parents are turning to home schooling as an alternative to public education.
B. Polls show that both high school and college students are more conservative today than they were twenty-five years ago.
C. Grades sometimes fail to show what a student learns.
D. Rabies has re-emerged as a widespread problem among wild animals.
E. The baseball strike of 1994 will have a long-lasting effect on America's Pastime.
F. People lie for a variety of reasons.
G. Depletion of the ozone layer will have disastrous environmental consequences.

II. From the list of topic sentences in Exercise I, choose one for discussion with a classmate. Describe to your classmate the causes or effects that you would use to develop that topic sentence, justifying your choices according to the guidelines in this chapter. Then listen while your classmate shares his or her choices and justifications with you. After you and your partner are satisfied that you understand each other, describe to the rest of the class your partner's plan, and have your partner describe to them your plan. Consider carefully their reactions and suggestions.

III. Carefully read all the following paragraphs. Each shows a student's attempt to develop a paragraph by cause or effect. Some paragraphs use the method well; others are not so effective. After considering each paragraph, answer the following questions:

1. Has the writer of the paragraph attempted to develop it by cause or by effect?
2. Is the attempt successful or not? Give explicit reasons for your answer.
3. Which paragraphs, if any, merely show *circumstances* conducive to producing a result rather than actual *causes* of the result?

A. There are many situations that cause pressure and tension to build up inside of us. Performing in front of an audience commonly produces pressure. We suffer from fear of making an embarrassing mistake during the performance. Many of us also experience tension when we are among new people. In such situations, we become quiet out of fear that other people will label us as "loud mouths." Coaches and athletes often feel tension before big games because they do not want to commit errors that might cause their teams to lose. I feel tension right now as I write this paragraph. I want it to be the best paragraph I've written this semester, for I know that this is my last chance to better my grade in this course. Pressure and tension are common in our environment. No matter how hard we try to avoid them, there will inevitably be times when breathing becomes hard and fear gets a grip that is difficult to loosen.

B. In the past few years, higher education has become increasingly important to young people everywhere. Higher education is essential for those who wish to enter the fields of medicine, engineering, and communications. These fields are essential for the survival of the human race. In the future, successful people will undoubtedly be those who have received technical instruction in fields such as these. Without this education, humans cannot survive. The very existence of the human race depends on the ability to progress in highly technical fields.

C. Entering a hospital isn't always in one's best interest. Many doctors give a standard battery of tests to every incoming patient. Such a procedure means that some patients receive more tests than they actually need. Sometimes these tests can even be dangerous. X-rays, for example, involve radiation, and exposure to radiation can sometimes result in birth deformities or in cancer. Before many medical tests, the patient must undergo enemas, which involve the use of harsh laxatives that sometimes dehydrate the body. Most doctors feel that individually these tests do little harm to a patient; however, doctors don't seem to take into consideration the fact that the average hospital patient may receive as many as four or five tests in a single day. This many tests can weaken even a healthy person. In addition, statistics indicate that 9 percent of all hospital patients contract an illness or infection while in the hospital. So sometimes the cure is worse than the disease.

D. Transferring from a two-year college to a four-year university has proven to be very difficult for me. First of all, I lost a number of course credits during the transfer process. When I attended the community college, I took courses to fulfill the general education program there. However, when I came to the university I found that many of those courses do not count for general education credit. In fact, some of them do not even apply toward graduation. As a result I will have to spend an additional semester making up the difference. Secondly, at the university I cannot always get the courses I need to fulfill my major requirements. The competition for courses is greater here than it was at the community college because of the size of the student body. Seniors get first choice, and what is left is often not enough for the rest of us. Finally, sometimes I feel that I am a number and not a person in this environment. Lecture classes are sometimes very large, and the discussion sessions are taught by graduate assistants and not the professor. So it is difficult to determine where to go when I need help. On these occasions, I feel abandoned and look back with some relish to my time at the community college.

E. Even the most occasional cocaine users need to think very seriously about what this powerful drug is capable of doing to them. Cocaine is one of the most highly addictive of all narcotics. Laboratory animals addicted to cocaine prefer cocaine over food even if they are at the point of starving to death. Research has shown that using cocaine on only one or two occasions can result in a serious addiction. Cocaine also affects the heart. Under certain circumstances, even a small dose of cocaine is capable of producing a fatal heart attack in an otherwise healthy individual. Habitual cocaine users are likely to experience serious cardiac problems such as palpitations of the heart, angina, and various other pulmonary abnormalities. In addition, cocaine alters the neurological centers of the brain and can permanently damage the nervous system. Habitual users are likely to experience a variety of psychological disorders ranging from total sexual dysfunction to loss of memory and even lasting states of psychosis and neurosis.

IV. Using cause or effect, develop a paragraph on one of the following topics. Before you write a draft of the paragraph, share your plan with a classmate. Discuss whether the topic can be better developed by dealing with causes or by dealing with effects, and then get your partner's ideas on how to formulate effectively your topic sentence so that the purpose of the paragraph is clear. Then, if the development of the paragraph is to involve causes, jointly test that development to ensure that you are not confusing circumstances with actual causes.

A. collecting antiques (or stamps or anything else that people commonly collect)
B. term limits on Congress
C. domestic violence
D. discrimination
E. advertising
F. handguns
G. obesity
H. adult education
I. Agent Orange
J. sports injuries

V. Using cause or effect as your method of development, write a paragraph on a topic of your own choosing. Be sure that you cite causes and effects that are important and directly related and that you do not mistake circumstances for active causes or effects.

VI. Collect the paragraphs you have written thus far into your folder. Compare the cause and effect paragraphs you have just written with others that appear in your portfolio. How are they different? How are they alike? Are you improving? If you are, write a cause and effect paragraph examining the reasons for your improvement.

PROCESS ANALYSIS

Like cause and effect, *process analysis,* the third method of development, is particularly important in our technologically oriented society. Much of what we do—from assembling a model airplane to attending a political convention—requires an understanding of how things work. And much of what we observe—from how a vegetable garden grows to how Congress passes a law—arouses our interest in how things come about. Process analysis is a method of communicating such information.

Process analysis has a wide variety of uses. Instructions, for example, are usually a form of process analysis. Directions for assembling a model airplane describe a process to be followed to obtain a desired result. A recipe containing instructions for making a lemon pie describes a process, as do instructions for developing film. A slightly different use of process analysis is seen in accounts of biological processes—how leaves change color, for example, or how a caterpillar develops into a butterfly. Process analysis might also be used to describe the standard process that students go through when they register for classes at the beginning of each semester. We read of mechanical processes, biological processes, chemical processes, and processes established by human law or custom.

In developing a paragraph by process analysis, the writer is considering a series of steps, toward a specific end, which take place in a certain order. Thus, *all processes involve a series of events in time.* Further, in order to be a process, the series must be one that is, or can be, repeated. Thus, an account of a particular Civil War battle will reveal a series of events that necessarily occurred in time, but it cannot be called process analysis because no other battle would repeat that series of events.

In addition, it is important to note that you may write *about* a process, such as a school registration, but unless you treat the event *as a process*—as a series of events in time that can be repeated—you will not be using process analysis. Suppose that you do write a paragraph recounting the events of a long morning spent in registering for spring-term classes. If you treat the stages of the activity simply as events in your day, you won't be writing a process analysis; instead, you will be writing a narrative, or story, about this particular morning. But if your account of the event explains the series of steps you followed and that *every* student must follow at registration—from picking up the information kit to receiving a complete class-schedule card—then you will have developed your paragraph by process analysis.

The rules involved in developing a paragraph by process analysis are relatively simple:

1. You must be sure that you present a series of steps that are either necessarily or customarily involved in bringing about a certain result.
2. You must present all the steps in the order in which they normally occur.

In the following paragraph, the writer had intended to explain the process by which a campfire is built, but her explanation is incomplete because she did not list *all* the steps involved in the order in which they belong:

> Building a good campfire involves a routine that the serious camper learns very early. The camper must know what kind of wood to use and then must find some wood of this type. To start a fire, he needs three things: matches, dead grass, and twigs. Also desirable are some pine wood, for starting the fire, and some spruce wood, for keeping the fire going. The experienced camper takes care to add new wood to the fire stick by stick, for too many pieces added at one time may put the fire out or cause a lot of smoke. By following these steps, almost anyone can build a campfire successfully.

This paragraph gives a prospective camper helpful information about starting a campfire, but there are gaps that must be filled in for the reader to have a complete, step-by-step picture of the process. We are told, for example, that matches, dead grass, and twigs are needed to build a good campfire, but we are never told how to use these items. Moreover, the preliminary steps in the process—preparations for building a fire—are completely omitted.

The following revised paragraph is much more complete:

> Building a good campfire involves a routine that the serious camper learns very early. Before trying to start a fire, the camper prepares a site. He clears an area with a radius of about ten feet to ensure that the fire will not spread. He then gathers the following materials: dry grass, dry twigs, and some pine and spruce wood. In laying the fire, the camper first makes a small pile of grass in the center of the firesite. He then stacks twigs in a pyramidal or tepee shape around the grass. He usually starts the fire with matches, though the experienced camper can also start it by rubbing two sticks together if necessary. As the fire progresses, he adds small sticks of dry pine wood and then larger pieces as the fire spreads out and becomes hotter. When the fire is very hot and is thoroughly established, he adds spruce wood or another long-burning wood if such is available. He takes care to add new wood to the fire stick by stick, for too many pieces added at one time may put the fire out or cause a lot of smoke. By following these steps, almost anyone can build a campfire successfully.

This paragraph is carefully and properly developed. The writer has presented all the steps involved in starting a fire, in the order in which they should be taken. Readers can now understand the process of building a fire and can even repeat it if they wish.

■ SUMMARY

1. A process involves a number of events that are customarily repeated and that lead to a specific end.
2. In developing a paragraph through process analysis, the writer should include all the important steps that are either necessarily or customarily involved in the process.
3. The steps in the process should be presented in the order in which they necessarily or customarily occur.

■ EXERCISES

I. Read the following topic sentences carefully. Each sentence lends itself to development by process analysis. List the steps that are involved in the process to be described. Be sure that you do not omit any important steps. Then list the steps in the sequence in which they occur.
   A. Washing (or waxing) a car requires more thought than people may realize.
   B. Painting a room requires a good deal of planning.
   C. From being seated to giving a tip, getting a meal in a restaurant has become a ritual.
   D. Growers of houseplants should learn how to repot a plant correctly.
   E. The scientific process entails a very specific set of steps.
   F. The process of mitosis is simple in concept yet complex in reality.
   G. Psychologists often detect a pattern in the background of a prisoner whereby child abuse leads to criminal behavior.

II. From the list of topic sentences in Exercise I, choose one for discussion with a classmate. Describe to your classmate the steps that you would use to develop that topic sentence, justifying your choices according to the guidelines in this chapter. Then listen while your classmate shares his or her choices and justifications with you. After you and your partner are satisfied that you understand each other, describe to the rest of the class your partner's plan, and have your partner describe to them your plan. Consider carefully their reactions and suggestions.

III. Read each of the following paragraphs. Is the writer concerned with a process, or is the paragraph simply an account of a happening or a series of happenings? If a process is presented, has the author included all the steps in the process, or have some steps been omitted? Does the writer treat any factors that are not actually steps in the process?
   A. Some people can quit smoking as soon as they decide to stop, but for most people breaking the habit takes time and effort. When smokers decide to stop smoking, they must be determined to break the habit. At first, smokers

should keep a careful record of the times when they most desire to smoke. They should also list the number of cigarettes they smoke each day and then reduce that number each day thereafter. Depending on their willpower, they may give up those cigarettes that are most important to them or those that are least important. In any event, they will gradually begin to withdraw from the habit. During the process of withdrawal, smokers should put cigarettes and matches where they cannot be reached without effort. Cigarettes should be put in one place and matches in another, so that smokers are forced to take several steps before satisfying their urge to smoke. Smokers should avoid activities that they formerly accompanied with a smoke. If determined to smoke, smokers should try to postpone lighting up a cigarette for fifteen minutes, then for thirty minutes, and then for longer periods. They should also keep a weekly record of the total number of cigarettes smoked and allot a smaller number of cigarettes for the week to follow. Smokers whose appetite for food increases to the point where they gain weight excessively during the process of withdrawal should plan a careful schedule of exercise. Throughout the entire process, prospective nonsmokers should remember the pledge they once affirmed and hang on stubbornly to the determination that will carry them through.

B. Have you ever wondered why leaves turn color in the autumn? In late summer and early fall, a ring of corky cells grows across the base of the leaf, slowly blocking the routes that carry food and water to and from the blade. By early October, the vein system of the leaf is totally cut off from its former source of nourishment. Without water, the leaf stops making food. Green chlorophyll disappears, and a bright yellow pigment called xanthophyll, which during the summer had been masked by the green of the chlorophyll, gradually becomes visible. Leaves that contain a substance called carotene start to turn red or orange. Deep reds and purples show up in leaves that contain a chemical compound called anthocyanin. At last the transformation from summer to fall colors is complete. With its nourishment cut off, the leaf loses all its green and yellow coloring and bursts forth into a brilliant and dazzling display of beauty.

C. About a year and a half ago, when I was in one of my annual "It's time for a change" moods, I stopped eating meat. I have felt healthier and happier ever since. I had been reading with great interest about the pros and cons of low-protein diets when I began to entertain the possibility of becoming a vegetarian. At the time meat prices were soaring, as they still are, and the fact that I was living in a college dormitory and eating cafeteria food of unknown origin forced me to consider the possibility all the more seriously. To test my curiosity and willpower, I eliminated all forms of beef from my diet and gradually cut back my consumption of poultry and pork. Realizing that I was losing weight and feeling better than I had in several years, I stopped eating meat altogether. Vegetables, fruits, and dairy products began to taste better, and I knew that I had successfully replaced an old habit with a new, healthier one.

D. To make good lasagna, follow these simple instructions. First, slowly brown one pound of Italian sausage and spoon off the excess grease. Stir in the following ingredients: one clove of minced garlic, one tablespoon chopped fresh basil, one and a half teaspoons salt, one one-pound can of tomatoes, and two six-ounce cans of tomato paste. Simmer the ingredients for thirty minutes, stirring occasionally. In the meantime, cook ten ounces of lasagna noodles in boiling salted water until tender, drain the water, and rinse the noodles. Next, beat two eggs and add three cups cream-style cottage cheese. Add to the egg mixture the following ingredients: one-half cup grated Parmesan cheese, two tablespoons parsley flakes, one teaspoon salt, and one-half teaspoon pepper. Next, assemble the four items to be layered: the noodles, the cottage cheese-egg mixture, one pound of mozzarella cheese, and the meat sauce. To layer, first place one-third of the noodles in a 13×9×2-inch baking dish. Cover the noodles with some cottage cheese filling, add a layer of mozzarella cheese, and cover with meat sauce. Repeat this procedure twice until all the ingredients are used up. Bake the lasagna at 350° for about thirty minutes. When the lasagna is done, let it stand for about ten minutes before serving.

E. Out-of-shape people who want to take up jogging need to prepare themselves by following a fifteen-week program that gradually builds muscles and strengthens the heart. No one should ever begin serious exercise without first consulting a physician. Only after a thorough physical examination and the full approval of a physician should anyone attempt exercise. Once a physician's approval has been given, a potential jogger should purchase a good pair of jogging shoes and should learn stretching exercises. These exercises prepare the muscles for stress and strain and should be performed before each attempt at jogging. For the first five weeks, would-be joggers need to practice walking. During the first week, they should walk approximately twenty consecutive minutes every other day. A day of rest between walks allows the muscles to relax. For each of the next four weeks, potential joggers should add ten minutes to the time they walk until by the end of the fifth week they find themselves able to walk one full hour every other day. At this point, they should alternate ten minutes of walking with five minutes of jogging for approximately thirty minutes of exercise. Again, a day of rest should be taken between each attempt to exercise. During the weeks to follow, joggers should gradually increase the length of time that they spend jogging while gradually decreasing the intervals of walking. Even after reaching the point where it is possible to jog for thirty consecutive minutes, joggers should still walk at least two or three minutes after each half hour of jogging. And jogging should never be done on a daily basis. Even the strongest of runners needs a day between episodes of strenuous exercise for the muscles to recover from the strain that jogging inevitably entails.

F. Saddling a horse is not as difficult as it may seem. First, place the saddle blanket high on the horse's shoulders; then slide it down to the middle of the back. This operation flattens the hair under the blanket and helps prevent the formation of painful galls. Next, pick the saddle up and fold the right stirrup over the seat to keep it from catching under the saddle. Then place the saddle gently on the horse's back. To settle it, shake the saddle carefully. Then reach under the horse's belly and pull the girth toward you. Tighten the girth gradually but firmly. If the girth is too tight, it may produce sores on the horse's flesh; if it is too loose, the saddle may fall off when the rider tries to mount. It should be just tight enough to allow the rider to slip two fingers between the girth and the horse's belly. Before trying to mount, grasp the saddle by the horn and pull. If the saddle stays firm and doesn't give, the horse is ready for a rider.

IV. Write a paragraph on one of the following topics. Before you write a draft of the paragraph, share your plan for using process analysis to develop your controlling idea with a classmate. Explain to your partner each step in the process in the correct time sequence. Then ask him or her to point out where your process lacks clarity. Perform the same service for your classmate.

A. changing a flat tire
B. preparing for an exam
C. balancing a checkbook
D. conducting a successful interview
E. bathing a cat, dog, bird, or other pet
F. frying an egg (making fudge, etc.)
G. parking a car
H. the formation of a tornado
I. the mummification process
J. surfing the Internet
K. sending a fax

V. Using process analysis as your method of development, write a paragraph on a topic of your own choosing. Make sure that you include all the steps involved in the process being discussed and that you present the steps in the order in which they occur.

VI. As you place your process analysis paragraphs into your portfolio, think about the three methods of paragraph development that you have experienced in this chapter. Which method did you like the best? Which method do you think you will use the most? Are there some general challenges that writers confront no matter which method they use? If so, what are they? Share your responses to these questions with a partner or the class.

5

FURTHER METHODS OF DEVELOPMENT

Definition, Comparison and Contrast, and Classification

In working through Chapter 4, you learned to develop a paragraph by citing examples, by stating causes or effects, and by explaining a process. In this chapter we present three more methods that will prove useful as you go about the business of writing paragraphs. Like the three discussed in Chapter 4, the methods to be presented in this chapter follow and use logical modes of thinking. They were not invented as artificial schemes for your use. Rather they follow the natural ways in which your mind works. The next three methods are the following:

1. Definition
2. Comparison and Contrast
3. Classification

Often when you want to clarify a point, you will define one or two terms, or you will compare or contrast two items you are concerned with, or you will create an order out of a mass of items by classifying them. The first method we will take up is definition.

DEFINITION

A writer employs *definition* as a method of development to explain the meaning of a word, phrase, term, or concept for the reader. Definitions may be either *formal* or *informal*. We will consider each of these.

Formal Definition

Formal definitions are the kind found in dictionaries. There are two parts to a formal definition. In the first part, the word being defined is assigned to a *class,* or larger category of related concepts. For example, the formal definition of the term *semaphore* would assign it to the class "device for signaling." The second part of the definition lists the characteristics that differentiate the item from other items in the same class, such as, in this case, a telegraph. What sets a semaphore apart from other "devices for signaling" is that the signaling is achieved "by the use of an arrangement of flags or lights." A complete formal definition of *semaphore,* then, is "a device for signaling that employs special arrangements of flags or lights."

The table that follows contains five terms that have been broken down into the two elements of formal definition: *class* and *differentiating characteristic(s).*

TERM	CLASS	DIFFERENTIATING CHARACTERISTICS
chameleon	lizard	having the ability to change the color of its skin
minaret	slender tower	connected to a mosque, and the place from which a crier calls Muslims to prayer
graffiti	writing	on walls or public places
UFO	flying object	with unknown origin and identity
clone	offspring	reproduced from a cell of a single animal or plant

Any term that is placed in a class and then distinguished from other items in its class in terms of specific differences is defined by means of formal definition. In differentiating a term, you must be careful to make your definition narrow enough to ensure that it cannot cover any other terms from the same class.

In a paragraph, a formal definition may be used in one of two ways:

1. A formal definition may itself form the basis of the paragraph.
2. A formal definition may be used to clarify the controlling idea of a paragraph. In this method of paragraph development, the rest of the paragraph develops the controlling idea by showing that the definition fits the topic under discussion.

We'll look at each of these uses more closely.

Using a Formal Definition as the Basis of a Paragraph   A valid formal definition of the term *university* might be the following:

> A *university* is an institution of higher learning that includes one or more undergraduate schools or colleges, graduate programs leading to advanced degrees, and one or more professional schools.

The following paragraph is devoted to an expanded version of this formal definition:

> A *university* is an institution of higher learning that has three components. First, a university includes one or more undergraduate schools or colleges, such as a school of education and a college of arts and science. Second, a university offers graduate programs leading to advanced degrees. The graduate school of arts and science, in particular, grants M.A. and Ph.D. degrees. Finally, a university has one or more professional schools under its jurisdiction. It may have, for example, a school of law or a school of medicine or—as is frequently the case—both. The law school grants J.D. or LL.D. degrees; the medical school grants M.D. degrees. Some universities, moreover, have schools of dentistry, veterinary medicine, architecture, and other professional areas.

This entire paragraph is a formal definition. The topic is the term *university*, and the controlling idea indicates that the term *university* belongs in the class "institutions of higher learning" and "has three components," which are its distinguishing characteristics. The remainder of the paragraph describes these components.

Sometimes in a paragraph using definition you may find it necessary to define more than one term. In defining one term, for instance, you may have to use another term that must be explained as well. It's best to define the second term as quickly and efficiently as possible, for it is not central to your plan. Thus, in a paragraph that includes a definition of a *motocross* as a "race against time by one motorcycle and driver through a course containing a number of hazards such as rough patches of ground and pylons," the writer must pause long enough to define *pylons* as "slender structures that mark the race course at various points, narrowing it and thus providing a challenge to the driver's skill." Having made it clear that pylons are obstacles between which a driver must steer, the writer can proceed with his work of defining *motocross*.

Using a Formal Definition to Clarify the Controlling Idea   A formal definition may also be used to clarify or explain a term that is vital to understanding a controlling idea. With this method, the topic sentence is followed by a definition, and the topic sentence and the defining sentence together function as a control for the paragraph. Support actually begins with the third sentence, and the rest of the paragraph aims to show that the topic under discussion fits the definition. For example, in a discussion of the suitability of calling an educational institution a *university* rather than a *college,* one might find the following paragraph:

> Pinkerton College deserves its new name of Pinkerton University. A *university* is an institution of higher learning that includes colleges, graduate programs leading to advanced degrees, and one or more professional schools. For the last twenty-five years, Pinkerton has had a college of liberal arts, a college of fine arts, a college of physical sciences and mathematics, and a college of education. Pinkerton offers graduate programs leading to the M.A. and M.S. degrees

in the various colleges. Pinkerton has also had a distinguished medical school. And for the past twelve years it has had a school of law that is gaining a solid reputation in this part of the country. Thus, Pinkerton College has actually been a university for quite a long time—all it lacked was the name.

The idea the writer hopes to convey is that Pinkerton was already a university before it was officially called one. The best way to do this is to tell what a university is—that is, to define *university*—and then to present facts showing that the school in question conforms to the definition. By this method, the writer establishes the idea expressed in the topic sentence.

Informal Definition

A formal definition places the term being defined into a class, or category, and then lists the traits that distinguish that item from other items in the same class. An informal definition, on the other hand, gives the meaning of the term in a less structured manner. In informal definition, the rules used in formal definition may be relaxed. One may assign a term to a class, but the class does not have to be strictly precise. If, for example, one were to call a *book* "an inexpensive way to travel," one would be putting the term *book* into the loose class "travel"—which would have no meaning in a formal definition of *book*.

Many terms do not lend themselves to formal definition. Because everyday terms, such as *book,* are so well known, informal definition of such terms is frequently more appropriate and meaningful than formal definition. Abstract terms, also, are often defined informally. Formal definitions of terms such as *patriotism, love,* or *hate* are infrequently called for and hard to make meaningful. One may define *patriotism* formally by calling it "loyalty" (class) "to one's native land" (differentiating characteristic), but this formal definition does not convey the spirit of patriotism, which is also important to an understanding of the term.

Although some terms require definition by the formal rather than the informal method (for example, *calorie* or *ion*), most terms may be defined by either method. In setting out to define a term, a writer must choose between these two types of definition. Making this choice involves two basic considerations: context and tone.

Context   If a paragraph using definition is to appear in a formal context, formal definition will most likely be called for. For example, in a textbook intended for use by a university class in architecture, the term *kitchen* would probably be placed in the class "room" and then be described according to architectural characteristics that distinguish it from other rooms in a house. Specific distinguishing characteristics would include the details that a student must consider in designing the kitchen of a house.

In a less formal context, the writer would find it more natural to use informal definition. In a general essay on the house one would not have to define *kitchen* formally because the term is well known to everyone. Instead, the writer would take an informal approach, bringing out some of the many connotations of the term *kitchen*. For instance, it might be defined in terms of the importance of this room to the American family: readers who are familiar with the formal meaning of the word would be made aware of other aspects of its significance.

Tone   The tone of any piece of writing conveys the author's attitude toward the material. If the writer's attitude is impersonal and precise, he or she is likely to use formal definition when developing a paragraph by means of definition. If, on the other hand, the writer's attitude is personal, or if the writer's intention is evaluative—that is, if he or she wishes to bring out the value or significance of the item under discussion—he or she will probably make use of informal definition.

In the following paragraph, for example, the writer conveys a personal attitude in an informal definition of the term *dog:*

> A dog can be an owner's best friend. My dog is always there when I need a friend. He keeps me company when I am alone. I would have spent many difficult nights alone if it had not been for my dog. My dog forgives and forgets when I am moody and take my feelings out on him. He never holds a grudge against me. He just seems to understand. He is there to listen to my gripes when no one else has the time. He is always patient with my shortcomings and always celebrates my arrival home no matter how long I have been away from the house. A dog gives love and demands little in return.

While not all dogs and dog owners have this kind of relationship, most dog owners would agree that this informal definition reveals an important aspect of the meaning of the term *dog.*

There are no hard-and-fast rules for developing a paragraph by informal definition; the writer enjoys a great deal of freedom. The writer of the paragraph above simply made a series of statements showing the ways in which her dog was her "best friend." The point for you to keep in mind is that in any paragraph developed by informal definition, the topic sentence should state the special significance of the term to be discussed, and the rest of the paragraph should explain the topic sentence.

■ SUMMARY

---

1. A formal definition of a term identifies the class to which the term belongs and the specific characteristics that differentiate it from other members of the class.

2. A formal definition may form the basis of a paragraph.

3. A formal definition may also be used to clarify the controlling idea of a paragraph that is not primarily concerned with the definition itself. When used in this way, the definition of an important term in the topic sentence is interposed between the topic sentence and the rest of the paragraph.

4. Informal definition is less structured and precise than formal definition. It aims to bring out the special connotations of the term being defined.

5. Informal definition is often used to define abstract terms that do not lend themselves to satisfactory definition through formal definition, or to define everyday terms that are already well known.

6. The choice of formal or informal definition is determined by context and by the attitude of the writer toward his or her subject.

■ EXERCISES

I. Following are seven topic sentences that lend themselves to development by means of definition. Consider them carefully, and for each sentence write out the answers to questions A, B, C, and D.

A. Should the paragraph be developed by formal or informal definition?

B. If by formal definition, what term should be defined? Should the formal definition itself form the basis of the paragraph, or should the definition provide clarification of the controlling idea?

C. If informal definition seems appropriate, what term should you define? What are the qualities you should bring out in order to give a clear impression of the object or idea being defined?

D. Could the topic sentence be developed by both formal and informal definition?

TOPIC SENTENCES:

1. Weeds are worthless plants.
2. Microwave ovens provide an efficient alternative to other forms of cooking.
3. "Homemade" food is not always made entirely at home.
4. Video cassette rental stores have become more common than libraries in most American towns.
5. One way to help prevent cancer is to eat large quantities of cruciferous vegetables.
6. The gifted child is easy to identify if one knows what signs to look for.
7. Reggae has had a noteworthy impact on contemporary American music.
8. School is a building that houses the future.

II. In each of the following paragraphs, a student has attempted to develop a paragraph by means of definition. Read each paragraph carefully and with a partner discuss possible answers to the following questions:

A. Does the writer attempt to use formal or informal definition?

B. Is the attempt successful or not? Consider the following questions in your answer:

1. What term is being defined?
2. If the definition is formal, into what class does the author place the term? What are the distinguishing characteristics that set the item apart from other members of the class? Does the paragraph itself constitute a definition, or is the definition a clarification of the controlling idea followed by sentences that support the controlling idea?

3. If development is by informal definition, how does the writer go about making the reader grasp the special significance of the object or concept being defined?

PARAGRAPHS:

a. Alcoholics and other individuals suffering from addictive behaviors tend to become emotionally involved with a personality type that sociologists and psychologists call "enablers." An "enabler" is a significant person in an addict's life who helps to maintain the addiction. For instance, in a marriage between an alcoholic and a nonalcoholic spouse, the nonalcoholic enabler might enable the other's drinking in a variety of ways, including covering up or excusing excessive drinking. Curiously, though, the enabler might appear to be working against the addictive behavior while in reality enabling it: continuous nagging to "stop drinking so much" might cause the alcoholic to perceive the nagging as an irritant that can be stopped only by drinking even more. An enabler, then, enables by focusing on the behavior of the other, the addict, instead of focusing on the self. In order to stop enabling, enablers must learn to stop attempting to control the addict and to start looking after themselves. As the saying made famous by Alcoholics Anonymous states, enablers need to seek the courage to change what they can change—not others, but themselves.

b. *Sickle-cell anemia* is a disease in which red blood cells become sickle-shaped because of the malformation of the large oxygen-carrying molecule, hemoglobin. Although the malformation involves only a tiny part of the molecule, it causes a great reduction in the ability of the entire cell to carry oxygen. In addition, the distorted cells cannot pass through the capillaries. Instead, the sickle cells form clumps that can grow and collect, sometimes blocking important larger vessels and preventing whole sections of tissue from getting necessary oxygen. This causes cell death and can be excruciatingly painful for the victim. Another problem is the fact that the blocked vessels do not allow free passage of antibodies and other substances necessary for protection from diseases and repair of damaged tissue. Perhaps the greatest problem, though, concerns treatment: there is neither a cure nor a preventive for sickle-cell anemia. The disease is inherited, occurring most often in blacks, although members of other groups may suffer from it. Because it is possible to carry the trait for the disease without being harmed by it, it is wise for all couples who are considering having children to be tested for the trait. Those people who do carry the gene for sickle-cell anemia should think carefully about the chances their children might have for a healthy life.

c. A *black hole* is not a hole at all. Rather, it is the remains of a star that in dying collapses on itself. As this happens, the star becomes dense enough to develop a very strong gravitational field, pulling in all matter surrounding it, including its former planets. As time goes on, the black hole becomes increasingly strong and dense as it "eats" more and more galactic matter. Eventually, it begins to migrate from one galaxy to another, its own gravity pulling it toward other bodies. When scientists first noticed these wandering phenomena, the black holes seemed to them to be areas containing a strong force but no matter—mysterious moving vacuums. Later, however, astronomers discovered that there was indeed a tremendous amount of matter in a black hole's center, which in volume might be no larger than the head of a pin.

d. Music can influence and express thoughts, feelings, and emotions. Have you ever been in a bad mood or feeling rather sad when a song suddenly came over the radio that made you feel even worse? Have you ever been in a good mood and feeling rather happy, when a song came over the radio that made you feel even better? Many songs contain a mysterious force that releases listeners from reality and awakens the inner spheres of their emotions. So powerful is this force that people have always used music to convey their emotions to others, knowing that if, even for just an instant, the listener feels the flow of emotion from a memory or dream, the music maker has communicated with the listener on a profound level.

e. Snow is a wolf in sheep's clothing. Snowflakes fall from the sky with silent grace, and on the ground they can form a blanket that covers the earth's imperfections, but they can also cause trouble. A single, lovely, little, white, feather-like flake of snow cannot do much damage, but several million can combine to knock down power lines, bury cars, and cave in roofs. Snow also produces dangerous driving conditions, and it can leave cities and towns isolated and immobilized for weeks.

III. Using either formal or informal definition, develop a paragraph on one of the following topics. Decide whether the paragraph can be developed better by formal or by informal definition. If you choose formal definition, first jot down the class to which the term belongs and the characteristics that make the item different from other members of the class. If you use informal definition, jot down the special qualities you wish to bring out. Then proceed.

A. anger
B. cult
C. brunch
D. comic books
E. sororities (or fraternities)
F. mascots
G. museum
H. grass
I. sexual harassment

IV. Write two paragraphs on a topic or topics of your own choice. Develop one by formal definition and the other by informal definition. You can use one topic for both paragraphs or two different topics. Be sure that the terms that you define lend themselves to the method of definition you have chosen.

V. Examine other paragraphs that you have placed in your portfolio. Do any of them employ formal or informal definition as a development strategy? If so, can they be improved? If not, could any of their topic sentences have been developed by means of formal or informal definition? While you are thumbing through your folder, ask yourself if you could write a formal definition paragraph on the word *portfolio.* Or has the term taken on a personal meaning for you? Could you write an informal definition paragraph focusing on this topic?

COMPARISON AND CONTRAST

The fifth method of paragraph development is comparison and contrast. Although the term *comparison* is often loosely used to refer to an evaluation of both likenesses and differences in two or more items, in our discussion we will reserve it to refer to a consideration of likenesses only. When you consider likenesses between two or more items, you are *comparing* them; when you concentrate on differences, you are *contrasting* them. Understood in this sense, the two methods are—as we said of cause and effect—two sides of the same coin. The techniques you will use in the two approaches are the same, and we will take a look at those techniques in this section.

Whether you compare or contrast will depend on whether the items being considered are substantially alike or unlike. It may also depend on your intention—whether you want to show similarities or differences. In some cases your instructor may specify whether to use comparison or contrast in a paragraph assignment. Most often, however, your task will be to consider two people, objects, or ideas carefully and to relate them in a paragraph. It will be up to you to examine their likenesses and differences and to decide which are important and more useful to discuss. You will then express your decision in a topic sentence that probably focuses the paragraph on either comparison or contrast.

Although in a single paragraph it is usually best to concentrate on either comparison or contrast (and not attempt to cover both), there may be occasions when an examination of your subject leaves you convinced that likenesses and differences are equally important. If you feel that this is the case, your topic sentence should make it clear that the two items you are considering are much alike in certain respects but strikingly different in others.

We have seen that definition can be either formal or informal. When comparison or contrast is used to support and develop a paragraph's controlling idea, it, too, can be either formal or informal. Formal comparison and contrast are guided by specific rules that must be strictly adhered to. In informal comparison and contrast, those rules can be relaxed.

Formal Comparison and Contrast

There are three things to keep in mind when you develop a paragraph through formal comparison and contrast:

1. Compare or contrast items in the same class.
2. Identify a class sufficiently narrow for comparison or contrast to be meaningful.
3. Make the basis or bases of your comparison or contrast clear.

Compare or Contrast Items in the Same Class   In formal comparison and contrast, the items you consider must be in the same *class*—that is, in the same related group or category. It makes no sense, for example, to compare an alligator and a banana, or, for that matter, to contrast them. It would be hard indeed to put these two items in the same class. On the other hand, it would make a great deal of sense to compare (or contrast) an alligator and a crocodile. These reptiles are related—and in fact many people confuse the two animals. A workable paragraph of comparison, then, might explain their similarities in some detail. If, on the other hand, you felt that readers would benefit more from a discussion of the differences between the two animals, contrast would be the appropriate method of development.

You might, too, profitably compare bus travel and air travel; both belong to the class "modes of travel." They may be compared and found to be alike in a number of ways. But since each has its own advantages, they can also be usefully contrasted. In a paragraph of formal comparison, you would focus on the similarities; in a paragraph of formal contrast, you would focus on the differences.

Identify a Class Sufficiently Narrow for Comparison or Contrast to be Meaningful   If the items being considered are not in a sufficiently narrow class, comparison or contrast becomes pointless. The two items discussed in the following paragraph, a Hyundai Excel and a Cadillac Eldorado, are both in the broad class "automobiles." Therefore, the student who wrote the paragraph felt that the contrast would be appropriate:

> There are many differences between a Hyundai Excel and a Cadillac Eldorado. The Hyundai is an economy car. It averages thirty-five miles to a gallon of gas. The Cadillac Eldorado is a luxury car. It averages fewer than twenty miles to a gallon. The Excel has less leg-room and is not as comfortable as the more spacious Eldorado. The list price of a new Excel is approximately $8,000, while the list price of a new Eldorado is more than $35,000. Thus the differences between the two cars are decisive.

In this paragraph, developed through formal contrast, the topic sentence points to differences between the two cars. However, while the paragraph is technically a proper contrast between items in the same class (automobiles), the point made in the topic sentence and in the paragraph itself is not very significant because the cars are so far apart in price that few people would ever seriously consider the two together. A prospective buyer of a Hyundai might more profitably compare or contrast this car with other cars in the lower price range.

Make the Basis or Bases* of Your Comparison or Contrast Clear   When you compare or contrast two items, you must have a good basis—or, what is

---

*The word *bases,* pronounced "bayseez," is the plural form of the word *basis.*

often even better, several bases—on which to judge the items. In the paragraph contrasting the Hyundai Excel and the Cadillac Eldorado, the writer considered the cars on three bases: mileage per gallon of gas, comfort, and list price. If, instead of selecting a basis (or bases) for direct comparison or contrast, you randomly give facts first about one of the items and then about the other, the result will very likely be haphazard, as in the following paragraph:

> Both today's farmers and the American farmers of a century ago work to make a living, but today's farmers have a wide variety of machinery to help them in their every task. They have heavy machinery not only to plow and harvest but also to do other heavy work around the farm. They get much of their information about farming from books. They can begin their study of farming in high school and then go on to a university to study farming and animal husbandry. But early farmers got their education from practical experience, learning mostly by working with their parents. Old-time farmers usually built their own houses, perhaps with the aid of neighbors, and they had only what today's farmers would call primitive appliances for their use. They kept warm by making a fire in a fireplace. They cooked on a wood-burning stove. And they lighted their homes with oil-burning lamps. Today's farmers have had their lives changed drastically by the introduction of electricity. And they have automatic machinery to help them in their every task about the farm. Finally, yesterday's farmers were interested only in producing enough food for their own dinner tables, and perhaps a little to take into town to sell. But today's farmers think about producing enough food to feed the world. So while early farmers, like farmers of today, produced vegetables and meat for the dinner table, early American farmers would scarcely recognize the farming profession as it is practiced by farmers in America today.

The writer of this paragraph comes up with only a sketchy view of farming in either early America or the present time and leaves us with no strict contrast between the situation of farmers of yesterday and today. We might say that there are certain bases for contrast lurking in the author's mind. For example, the author considers farm tools, household equipment, and education. However, these bases aren't used to contrast farmers of today with farmers of yesterday *directly*. We are told about the heavy machinery the farmers of today have at their disposal but nothing about the tools used by yesteryear's farmers. Similarly, we find comment about the household equipment that old-time farmers used but nothing about the contrasting modern equipment available to farmers of today. After reading the paragraph, we have only an imperfect picture of the farmers of either period under consideration and no sense of contrast of farming in the two periods.

Four bases on which the farmers of today and yesteryear might be contrasted are the following:

1. farm equipment
2. education
3. house and household equipment
4. outlook and objectives

There are other bases on which farmers' situations might be compared or contrasted. However, a consideration of four specific bases will leave the reader with a clear impression of the idea of contrast the writer wishes to convey. Following is a revised version of the student paragraph:

> Today's farmers, like the early American farmers of a century ago, work to make a living, but today's farmers have come a long way from yesteryear. Early farmers, like today's farmers, used machinery on their farms, but there is a wide difference in what the word "machinery" denotes in the two cases. Early farmers used plows pulled by animals to plow their ground. They had push planters to plant their seeds, or they planted them by hand. In contrast, today's farmers have tractors for plowing and heavy machinery to do most of the heavy work on their farms. Again, the education provided for prospective farmers today is very different from that available a century or so ago. Early farmers got their education from living and working on a farm, usually starting as a child, walking side by side with their parents and learning firsthand. Today's farmers often start the study of farming in high school and then attend an agricultural college or university where they study the science of cultivating the soil and raising animals. Early American farmers lived in houses they built themselves, and the equipment was simple. They had oil-burning lamps and a fireplace. Their kitchens were equipped with a woodstove. Water was brought in from a pump outside. Their counterparts today have central heating and, frequently, air conditioning. They turn a tap to get water instantly and flick a switch to get a blaze of light. The kitchens are electric, with modern appliances that start with the touch of a button. Finally, the outlook and even objective of early farmers were narrower than those of farmers in America today. The interests of early farmers were largely local, and they were concerned mainly with producing enough food for their families. Today, farmers must be concerned with the national and international forces that affect them. And their objective is producing enough food to help feed the world. So while early farmers, like farmers of today, produced vegetables and meat for the dinner table, early American farmers would scarcely recognize the farming profession as it is practiced by farmers in America today.

Here, the writer considers four of the most prominent features of farm life in early America and the present. For each of the four bases a brief but specific comment points up contrast. The writer succeeds in leaving the reader with a clear and specific idea of the contrast between the life of the American farmer in two periods of our history.

Two Ways to Organize and Present Your Material

Two ways are commonly used for structuring material in a formal comparison or contrast. The best way to understand these procedures is to set up a paragraph first by one arrangement and then by the other.

Suppose that you have been asked to write a paragraph comparing or contrasting two economy cars. You should then go through the following procedure:

Step 1. Select two items that might be usefully compared or contrasted from the class "economy cars"—say, the Nissan Sentra and the Toyota Corolla.

Step 2. Compare the two items, looking for likenesses.

Step 3. Contrast the two items, looking for differences.

Step 4. Decide whether it is better to focus on likenesses—to compare—or on differences—to contrast. Suppose you decide that differences are more important because through understanding the differences you can better choose which car to buy.

Step 5. Next, go back over the various bases on which the two cars might be contrasted and select the most useful. You might decide that the following three are the most worthy of attention:
1. gas mileage
2. size
3. interior design

You are now ready to set up an outline and work up a plan for a good paragraph using one of the two methods of structuring your material in a formal contrast. You can make the two items being contrasted—the Sentra and the Corolla—the main entries in your outline and consider the bases under these headings, as in the following outline:

I. topic sentence
   A. Nissan Sentra
      1. gas mileage
      2. size
      3. interior design
   B. Toyota Corolla
      1. gas mileage
      2. size
      3. interior design

Alternatively, according to the second method, you can establish the three bases of contrast as main headings and then consider how each car measures up under each heading:

I. topic sentence
   A. gas mileage
      1. Sentra
      2. Corolla
   B. size
      1. Sentra
      2. Corolla
   C. interior design
      1. Sentra
      2. Corolla

Experienced writers generally agree that the second method of organizing material is usually better. If you adopt the first method, you run the risk of writing at length on the Sentra and in the process making points that readers may forget when they reach the material on the Corolla. The contrast, therefore, may not be completely successful. On the other hand, if you follow the second method and take up each basis of contrast in turn, immediately treating first one car and then the other, the contrast may be sharper and more effective. In a brief paragraph, however, either method can work well.

Informal Comparison and Contrast

An informal comparison or contrast, like an informal definition, is not bound by strict rules. A comparison or contrast of two or more items must take place, but the rule that the items must be in the same class is not treated rigidly. In fact, the items under consideration may be placed in a class so large or so indefinite that it does not narrow or limit the discussion significantly. An airplane may be compared to an eagle, for instance, and the two may be said to belong to the broad class *objects that fly*. This class would be too large to focus and limit a formal comparison. However, a writer who desires to show the power and grace of an airplane may compare it informally to an eagle in order to create a sharp image of strong and graceful flight.

Informal comparison or contrast is sometimes used to clarify an idea that might be harder to explain by another method of paragraph development. In the following paragraph, a student writer effectively uses informal comparison to express her attitudes toward television:

> My television set reminds me of a story I once read. A man found the most beautiful egg he had ever seen. The shell was very unusual because it looked like a piece of the rainbow. It seemed to glow with secret promises of wealth and fortune. The man took the egg home with him, and he polished it until it shone like glass. He placed it near the fire in his front room. Early the next morning the egg began to hatch. Soon there was an ugly monster standing in his front room. The man still tried to love it, but it turned on him and drove him from his home. Television is like that monster. Americans welcomed it into their homes and placed it at the heart of their lives. They idolized the stars who marched across the TV screen. Only recently have Americans realized that they have innocently harbored a monster. Hour after hour the television spits out nonsense like "Just Do It!" or "Pizza! Pizza!" The monster blinks at us unceasingly. It has hypnotized our children. Youngsters try to copy every move their TV idols make, and those moves are not always in the children's best interest. You can argue all day, but you will never convince a child that the characters of *Beverly Hills, 90210* are shallow and disturbed. And so involved are our children with the fiend television that they can't do their homework until they have seen the latest episode of *Power Rangers*.

The informal method of expressing feelings used in this paragraph is much more effective than a straightforward statement of complaints about television would be. Here the writer has taken a class—the class "monsters"—and stretched it imaginatively to cover an item that, strictly speaking, does not belong to the class at all. For the moment, the television set becomes a monster, and the writer's point is made strikingly and effectively.

■ SUMMARY

1. Use comparison to consider the likenesses between two items.

2. Use contrast to consider the differences between two items.

3. In formal comparison or contrast, consider items that are in the same class, and make sure that the class is sufficiently narrow for the comparison or contrast to be meaningful.

4. In formal comparison or contrast, select definite bases on which to rest a comparison or contrast, and restrict yourself to these bases in writing your paragraph.

5. In a paragraph developed by formal comparison or contrast, you may use either the items under consideration or the bases as main headings in outlining your paragraph. Usually the latter is preferable.

6. In informal comparison or contrast, you may relax the rules for formal comparison or contrast in order to support the controlling idea in a more effective way than formal comparison or contrast would allow.

7. In informal comparison or contrast, you may place one or both items under consideration in a very broad or even an imaginary or "far-fetched" class.

■ EXERCISES

I. Analyze each of the following topic sentences carefully. Which sentences invite development by formal comparison or contrast? If formal comparison or contrast is indicated, in what class would the two terms be placed? What basis or bases would you use to rest a comparison or contrast on? If informal comparison or contrast is indicated, what broad or imaginary class might you employ?

A. There are many fascinating similarities between Greek mythology and the stories in the Old Testament.
B. Driving an automobile is more dangerous than flying in a commercial airplane.
C. American football is a derivative of rugby.
D. Life is often likened to a voyage.
E. Parents of infants have to choose between cloth diapers and disposables.
F. Health Maintenance Organizations offer more (or fewer) benefits than traditional healthcare providers.

II. Carefully read all the following paragraphs. Then, with a classmate, select three paragraphs and discuss the answers to the questions about each:

1. Is the paragraph developed by comparison or by contrast or by some other method?
2. Is the comparison or contrast formal or informal?

3. If formal comparison or contrast is used, what are the bases for the comparison or contrast? Are the bases clear? Does the writer develop them fully?
4. If informal comparison or contrast is used, what is the *class* into which the terms being compared or contrasted are placed?

In each case, explain whether or not the paragraph is effective. If the paragraph is poorly developed, jointly identify ways in which it could be improved.

A. The Ibos and the Yorubas, prominent African tribes living in the Republic of Nigeria, are similar in many respects, but one striking difference between them has impressed itself on the minds of visitors more than the similarities between the two cultures. The Ibos have been much influenced by their contacts with Europeans. They have acquired a very deep consciousness of the value of education. Many of them have also become Christians. The Yorubas, likewise, have acquired many Western ways and values. They devote themselves seriously to education, and some, like many of the Ibos, have adopted Christianity. The Ibos, except for the Christians among them, practice polygamy. Christian Ibos, of course, respect the Christian taboo on the practice. The Yorubas who have not been converted to Christianity also practice polygamy. The Christians among them do not. What separates the two tribes decisively in the minds of outsiders, however, is a wide difference in the attitude of the two peoples toward the supernatural. Belief in supernatural powers does not play an important part in the life of the Ibos. On the other hand, the Yorubas find life governed to a large extent by a real belief in the existence of spirits and supernatural powers that are very close and that must be considered in daily life. Belief in such spirits is obvious in the stories, art, and customs that visitors become aware of.

B. Kung fu, the Chinese form of self-defense fighting, differs considerably from the modern Japanese version, known as karate. "Karate is straight line action," say some kung fu instructors, "while kung fu involves circular motions." Kung fu uses punches and kicks similar to those in karate, but kung fu movements are more flowing. A karate session looks like an army drill; a kung fu practice resembles a ballet. Karate fighters generally stand in one position and step forward or backward, while kung fu fighters move sideways and back and forth continually. Clawing and scratching are important in karate. Karate is easier to learn because the fighter remains relatively stationary, moving only the arms and legs. The kung fu fighter, on the other hand, is always moving and therefore needs to develop a high degree of coordination.

C. To an inexperienced person, a hunting rifle and a target rifle may look alike, but to an experienced shooter, the differences are readily apparent. The mechanical build of each of these guns sets it apart from the other. The hunting rifle, which is often carried for long distances, is reasonably light. A target rifle, on the other hand, can weigh up to twice as much as a hunting rifle, since portability is not among the considerations that influence its design. The target rifle is delicate and must be protected from dust and moisture. Sights on a target rifle are often quite elaborate. If steel sights are used, they are usually intricate peep sights. The wide variety of scopes found on target rifles ranges up to 20 or 24 power. Those on hunting rifles range from 1.5 to 12 power.

D. Several recent movies have made progress in correcting the negative and erroneous view of Native Americans that Hollywood has historically presented. For example, Hollywood movies have traditionally portrayed Europeans coming to America as benevolent emissaries of a superior culture. However, the Canadian-Australian film, *Black Robe,* correctly challenges this view. *Black Robe,* based on the novel by Brian Moore, points out the narrow-minded and intolerant attitudes that Europeans have often displayed toward other groups of people. Moreover, it accurately depicts a Native American culture as moral, tolerant, and extremely complex. Hollywood, in movies like John Ford's *The Searchers,* has also traditionally portrayed European Americans as the victims of Native American aggression. Nevertheless, Kevin Costner's *Dances with Wolves* provides a more accurate picture by reversing the roles. Costner's film, which won an Academy Award for Best Picture, depicts European Americans as aggressive opportunists who will go to any lengths to acquire tribal lands. In this film, as was often the actual case, the rapacious greed of European Americans forces Native Americans to respond to violent attacks on their land, heritage, and culture. Finally, Hollywood movies have repeatedly implied that Native Americans would benefit by abandoning their traditional values and adopting European ones. Conversely, the movie *Thunderheart* rightly questions this assumption. In this movie, which is based on an actual incident, an FBI agent of Native American extraction travels to an Ogala Sioux reservation in order to investigate a murder. Until the visit, the agent has disavowed his own Native American background. However, his experiences at the reservation reawaken his inner being and he grows to recognize the spirituality and beauty that characterize the Native American cultures.

E. Prejudice works like a slow poison after it has seeped into a human being. Like poison, it usually enters without the victim's knowledge. Poison and prejudice can enter the mind or spirit and spread to do their dark work. The person who is affected by prejudice is, unlike the recipient of poison, rarely aware of the ailment and does nothing to counteract the sinister agent. Just as slow-acting poison cripples the body, prejudice warps the human mind and spirit and frequently distorts the victim's thoughts and actions. Unlike poison, prejudice does not kill its victim, but its effects are insidious and permanent unless the victim becomes aware of his condition and seeks an antidote.

F. For most Americans, breakfast is radically different from lunch and dinner: whereas most foods eaten at lunch can be served at dinner as well, breakfast foods are often reserved exclusively for the morning meal. Cereals, for example, are rarely served except at breakfast. The same is true for toast, which often appears on the breakfast table but rarely on the lunch or dinner table. In fact, part of the breakfast ritual in America involves browning bread to the desired shade and then buttering it. Bacon and eggs are a breakfast staple across the United States, but they are rarely served as a main dish at other meals. Jam and jelly appear most often at breakfast and only as an occasional extra at lunch and dinner. Unless one eats at an establishment that specializes in waffles and pancakes, these foods are usually consumed only for breakfast. On the other hand, most items found on lunch and dinner tables never show up at breakfast. Roasted meats and fowls, for example, are hardly ever eaten for breakfast. Salads and vegetables are likewise reserved almost exclusively for other meals. And those all-important dishes—soup and dessert—that frequently begin and end lunch and dinner just aren't to be found on American tables before noon.

III. Write a paragraph on one of the following topics. Develop the controlling idea by means of comparison or contrast. Employ either a formal or informal approach. Before you start writing, be sure to establish *definite bases* for any formal comparisons or contrasts that you make. Discuss these bases with a small group of classmates. When you have finished your first draft of your paragraph, share it with your partners. Get their feedback on how well you have accomplished your goals.

A. attending a small college or attending a large university
B. two popular music groups
C. dogs or cats
D. two television advertisements
E. previously owned car or a new car
F. college sports versus professional sports (you may choose one particular sport to discuss)
G. getting a college degree early in life or getting a degree after being "out in the world" for several years

IV. Write a paragraph on a topic of your own choosing. Develop your paragraph by means of formal or informal comparison or contrast. If you use formal comparison or contrast, be certain that the *bases* for your comparisons or contrasts are definite and clear.

V. Examine two paragraphs from your portfolio: one from earlier in the term and one you have written recently. Do you see similarities and differences between the two paragraphs? Write a paragraph of comparison or contrast in which you support your answer to the previous question.

CLASSIFICATION

In paragraphs developed by classification, a writer makes a meaningful statement about a subject by analyzing its parts. And, as with definition or with formal comparison or contrast, the writer follows a set of established principles. It is also possible, however, to relax those principles and develop a paragraph by informal classification.

Formal Classification

In developing a paragraph by comparison or contrast, the writer evaluates objects and ideas by weighing their likenesses or differences. With classification, the writer examines an object or idea by considering the parts of which it is composed. How formal classification works is illustrated in Figure 5–1, which shows the relationship of the large class *movies* to the types, or *classes,* of movies that make it up.

Figure 5–1 Movies

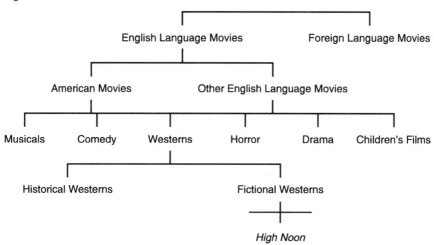

Figure 5–1 shows a *hierarchy,* or series of levels. In this hierarchy, the highest level that a writer might be concerned with is "Movies." The next highest level in the hierarchy shows the classes that make up the highest level. The third level shows the classes that belong to, or make up, the level just above. Each item in a hierarchy can be subdivided into the classes that make it up. For example, the item "Foreign Language Movies" is not classified further; however, if you were interested in supporting the thesis "Many foreign language films have wide distribution in the United States," for ease of discussion you might divide "Foreign Language Movies" into the classes that it includes. You might, for example, divide foreign language movies into the following classes: French Films, Italian Films, German Films, Scandinavian Films, and Other Foreign Language Films. You could then discuss each of these classes. You can classify until you get to a level that cannot be significantly classified further. Thus, at *High Noon,* you have reached an ultimate, or final, level. *High Noon* belongs to the category "Fictional Westerns," which belongs to the class "Westerns," which is a class of "American Movies," which is a class of "English Language Movies," which is, of course, a class of "Movies."

We would like to point out that you might select any item in this hierarchy except the lowest level (which cannot be divided further) and write a classification paragraph about it. For example, although the writer who devised the set of levels that we present here was interested in Western movies derived from fiction, you might be more interested in "Historical Westerns." If this were the case, you could consider the classes of movies that would fall under the "Historical" category. You might create the following classes: "Movies about the Euro-American Conquest of the West," "Movies about the Spanish Period" (think of the Alamo!), "Movies about the Civil War Period in the West," and so on according to time periods. A topic sentence for a paragraph might be "Some of the most important films to come from the American film industry are films about historical incidents connected with the old West." You would then discuss typical movies from each class.

We would like to make another useful point. It should be obvious that you do not have to draw up a broad hierarchy, with many levels, like the one presented in this chapter. You may have a very simple set of two levels in mind. If you are interested in Western movies, you need to be concerned only with your subject level—"Western Movies"—and with the level immediately below it containing the classes of movies, or simply examples of the individual movies, which make it up.

There are two rules to remember in developing a paragraph by formal classification or division:

1. Select a basis or bases for classification and formulate those bases precisely before you begin writing.
2. When you are classifying, your categories must be mutually exclusive; if one item fits into more than one category, your categories are faulty.

Selecting Precise Bases for Classification   In a paragraph developed by classification, *you must be sure that the bases on which you classify are suitably precise* and that you do not stray from them. Without clear bases for classification, your paragraph is likely to become muddled. Consider the following paragraph in which a student classifies the student body of Pinkerton University.

> The student body of Pinkerton University is highly varied. Although most of the students are from North America, many are also from Europe and Asia. Some are from South America, and others are from France and Germany. Pinkerton is especially noted for its musicology department, and some of the college's best students are musicology majors. Some of the musicology students are also interested in languages or fine arts. There are also students in the colleges of Liberal Arts, Business Administration, and Education. There are many English majors. Pinkerton offers a wide choice of majors for its students.

In this paragraph, the bases on which the writer classifies the subject "student body" are not at all clear. He begins by classifying the students according to *place of origin;* he has apparently not decided, though, whether place of origin should be specified in terms of continents (North America, Europe, and so on) or countries (France and Germany). The precise basis for classification should have been either *continental origin* or *national origin,* and the writer should have used one or the other consistently. The writer apparently also tries to classify "student body" according to the *academic major* selected by each student, but the students are sometimes said to be majoring in a *College* (for example, the College of Liberal Arts), and sometimes in a *subject* (for example, English). Again the precise bases for classification are unclear.

Selecting Mutually Exclusive Categories When classifying, always choose categories that are mutually exclusive and do not overlap one another. This rule is violated in the preceding paragraph. The students' places of origin are identified as North America, Europe, Asia, South America, France, and Germany. The overlap occurs because France and Germany are *parts* of the broader category "Europe." By listing them separately, the writer is in effect counting French and German students twice. There is also an overlap in the division according to *academic majors*. Students with an English major are listed separately, even though they have already been included in the larger category of students in the College of Liberal Arts. Thus the divisions in this paragraph are muddled and leave the reader with imprecise information.

The paragraph might be more effectively written as follows:

> Students at Pinkerton University have varying backgrounds and academic interests: they come from different parts of the world, and they are interested in different fields of academic specialization. Although most of the students are from North America, many are from South America, some are from Europe, and a few are from Asia. Pinkerton is especially noted for its musicology department, which draws many majors each year. It also graduates a large number of majors in English, business administration, chemistry, and education. The student who attends Pinkerton will be among students of widely differing backgrounds and with widely differing academic interests.

In this paragraph, the student body is classified on the basis of *continental point of origin* and on the basis of *major subject*. There is no overlapping in the classifications, and the paragraph is successful.

Informal Classification

A paragraph can also be developed by *informal* classification. A writer using this method still establishes precise bases on which to classify but relaxes or ignores the rule against overlap. Furthermore, the classes of items are often set up in accord with the purely personal perspective of the writer. Consider, for example, the following paragraph:

> I have had many types of teachers in my fourteen years as a student, but the instructors I remember best were the intellectuals, good guys, and teachers I had crushes on. The intellectuals weren't too strict, but they were always demanding. They demanded my time, my efforts, and my brains and would, on occasion, reward me with an "A"—if I was lucky. Good guys were usually coaches who taught courses like "Popular Culture" or "National Problems" to supplement their income. Good guys would let us sleep in class if they thought we were tired. And they wouldn't get on us if we were unprepared. Finally, there were the teachers I had crushes on. They were all, to my way of thinking, either handsome or cute. They could be intellectuals or good guys, but if I liked them, I didn't care. I did my best work for them outside of class and spent time in class daydreaming about them and their private lives. Were they married? Did they have kids? Did they wear blue jeans when they weren't teaching school? Of

course, I had other teachers. Dummies, idiots, and phonies were a few I encountered, not to mention frustrated comedians, frustrated actors, and those who were just plain frustrated. But the ones I remember best are the ones who asked a great deal of me, the ones who asked only that I come to class, and the ones I hung my fantasies on.

This paragraph classifies teachers from the *personal* viewpoint of one student. There is nothing scientific about the classification. The writer puts the teachers she remembers best into three classes that are meaningful to her personally. And her classification does not observe the rule against double listing, or overlap, because the third category (teachers she had crushes on) can also include some members of the first category (teachers who were intellectuals) and the second (teachers who were good guys). The result is an interesting and well-written paragraph developed by informal classification.

A Word of Caution: Avoiding Oversimplification

In writing a paragraph developed by classification or division, avoid simplistic assertions that there are three categories of a given item: the one extreme, the opposite extreme, and the in-between. A paragraph, for example, that classifies students into three categories—"those who study hard and never go to parties," "those who scarcely study at all and spend a great deal of time socializing," and "those who balance the time they spend studying and socializing"—is not likely to be very effective. Such a classification is too pat. It overlooks many other kinds of students. There is nothing wrong, of course, with writing a three-class paragraph—provided that the three categories you include reflect your subject accurately or, as in informal classification, deal with it originally.

■ SUMMARY
---

1. Developing a paragraph by classification involves examining something by analyzing its basic parts.

2. In formal classification, you must establish precise bases on which to rest the classification.

3. In formal classification, you must be sure that no item falls into more than one class. In other words, make certain that classes are mutually exclusive.

4. In informal classification, your point of view may be personal. Classes still must have precise bases, but the rule against overlap may be relaxed or, occasionally, ignored.

■ EXERCISES
---

1. In a small group of classmates, discuss each of the following topic sentences carefully. If you were to use them as topic sentences for paragraphs, what precise

bases for classifying would you use? Could the idea contained in the sentence be developed effectively by informal classification? If so, how would you go about doing it?

A. There are many different kinds of holidays.

B. Automobile drivers fall into several basic categories.

C. Athletes are either "amateurs" or "professionals."

D. There are several ways to classify dogs.

E. Despite their different formats and personalities, television talk shows tend to focus on the same types of topics.

F. Any checker at a supermarket can tell you that every shopper falls into one of several categories.

II. In each of the paragraphs below, a student writer has attempted development by classification. Read each paragraph carefully, and answer the following questions:

1. Is the method formal or informal?

2. If the method is formal, what are the bases for classification?

3. Is there any overlap in categorizing the items?

4. Is the paragraph successful? Why, or why not?

5. If the method employed is informal, in what way are the rules for formal classification relaxed? What does the writer gain by using informal classification?

A. Carnivorous plants, which are distinguished from other plants by virtue of their ability to entrap and digest unwary insects, can be divided into two groups according to the way in which they catch their prey: active trappers and passive trappers. The familiar Venus's flytrap belongs in the class of the active trappers. The leaf structure of the flytrap contains tactile trigger hairs that protrude from a convex hinged surface. When an unsuspecting insect touches one or more of these hairs, the leaf closes, and the insect is trapped inside. Once the leaf is closed, glands on the surface of the leaf secrete enzymes that digest the entrapped victim and thereby supply nutrients to the plant. The equally well-known pitcher plant fits into the category of the passive trappers. This plant exudes an enticing nectar that lures insects into a slippery funnel containing a reservoir of digestive fluid. The fluid then digests the trapped insect, turning it into a form of nutrition that can be utilized as food for the plant. Carnivorous plants like the Venus's flytrap and the pitcher plant possess unique and subtle skills, and they must be considered one of nature's more exotic experiments.

B. The origin of English words—their "etymology"—divides them into three distinct groups: Germanic words, Latinate words, and words borrowed from just about everywhere else. Most basic English words come from the Germanic language. For example, almost all of our everyday names of people and objects—like *mother, father, daughter, home, door,* and *bed*—originate in German. Moreover, such common verbs as *walk, talk, sit,* and *sleep* also come from the Germanic tongue. On the other hand, English has also added words from Latinate languages. For example, many English words that relate to law, literature, and religion have Latin roots. For instance, words like *jury, contract,* and *legal* stem from Latin as do *crucifix, cathedral, author,* and *manuscript.* Finally, many English words come from places where English-speaking voyagers found things that did not exist in Europe. For instance, from Native American languages they derived the labels for *tobacco* and *hickory,* as well as names for places such as *Mississippi* and *Massachusetts.* From the languages of

India, English speakers obtained words such as *jungle, bandanna,* and *calico.* While in Australia, they learned words such as *boomerang,* and in Africa, it is believed, they acquired *cocktail.*

C. There are, of course, as many individual reasons for failing to vote as there are people who don't vote, but these reasons tend to fall into several categories. Unnecessarily strict voting laws often keep many people from voting. Poll tax laws and "grandfather" clauses are among the types of legislation that discriminate against voters by making it difficult for them to vote. Many college students who attend out-of-state schools cannot vote in the state where their schools are located. Other people fail to vote because they lack interest in either of the major political parties. Many of today's voters feel less and less committed to a specific party, and as a result they don't feel an allegiance to a team and have little personal motivation to vote. Probably the largest group of stay-at-home eligible voters, however, consists of people who simply have a feeling that they, as individual citizens, have little effect on the outcome of elections. These voters feel powerless and alienated. Apathy toward voting is the outcome, and recent scandals involving high-ranking public officials have contributed greatly to this apathy. In conclusion, it is safe to say that most people who don't vote are either prevented by law from voting, are apathetic to both political parties, or just feel that their votes don't count.

D. There are three major misconceptions concerning the Crusades. First, many people think that the Crusades were successful. In reality, however, they were not. Although the Christian nobles who led the Crusades achieved their goal of taking Jerusalem from the Muslims, a little more than a century later the Muslims regained control of the city. Second, many people believe that the Christian nobles who participated in the Crusades followed the codes of chivalry. In reality, however, these nobles were anything but chivalrous. On one occasion, for instance, they sacked Constantinople, a city they were supposed to protect. Most of the nobles who went on the Crusades were opportunists. They hoped that the Crusades would make them rich, and they took every opportunity, chivalrous or otherwise, to make themselves rich. In many instances, the Crusades were merely an excuse Christian knights used to plunder and pillage. Some knights even became kings of captured territory in the Holy Land. Third, many people assume that the Crusades initiated an exchange of culture and learning between the East and the West. Actually, however, there was little exchange between Muslim and Christian cultures. Muslims were highly literate and communicated primarily through the written word. Christian nobles, most of whom believed that reading and writing were below their dignity, learned little from the Muslims, and vice versa.

E. There are several ways in which car owners can prevent burglaries and can help to ensure the return of their cars in the event that a theft does take place. First, car owners can take precautions that make theft difficult. The most obvious is locking a car, even one left for a short time in a safe parking lot. At night drivers should park in well-lighted areas only. They should be sure never to leave the keys in the car, even for a few moments. The owner who parks overnight in the driveway can prevent theft by parking with the front of the car facing the street, so that a prospective car thief will run the risk of being seen tampering with the engine. Second, when buying a new car, a driver should insist on having the new devices that have been developed to discourage theft, such as tapered door locks and an alarm system. Third, the car owner can take measures that ensure against the theft of items from the car. Here, again, locking the car helps. Packages, clothing, luggage, and sports equipment should be locked in the trunk, not left on the seat in plain view. Finally, car owners can take precautions that will help the police to identify a car if it is stolen. They can remove license and registration cards from the car when it is not in use, thus making it difficult for thieves to sell the car. All car owners should know the identification numbers on their cars, and they can even mark the car somewhere out of sight with a mark known to no one else. They can also place a small card with a name on it somewhere inside a seat. Identification numbers and hidden markings facilitate the location and return of stolen motor vehicles.

F. The fabrics and colors of costumes worn by actors in Shakespeare's time were highly symbolic. Commoners wore coarse gray wool. Working men usually wore rough canvas aprons. Servants were always seen in tawny brown clothing. Fools dressed in several colors, of which yellow was usually the most prominent. Members of the nobility dressed in satin, taffeta, damask, or velvet. The queen often appeared in costumes made from scarlet or purple material. Sometimes she even appeared in a calico dress. Because calico was imported from India and hence enormously expensive, only a queen could afford to wear a calico outfit.

III. Write a paragraph on one of the topics listed below. Develop the paragraph by use of formal classification. Be sure that you establish bases on which to rest your classification, and be sure that no item in your classification falls into more than one category. When you have finished this paragraph, select another topic and write a paragraph using informal classification as your method of development. You may use the same topic for both a formal and an informal paragraph.

A. drivers
B. popular music (or music videos)
C. thieves
D. infomercials
E. parents
F. football (or hockey, baseball, etc.) fans
G. villains
H. science fiction movies

IV. Write a paragraph on a topic of your own choosing. Develop your paragraph by means of classification. If you use formal classification, be sure that you rest your classification on precise bases, and make certain that your bases don't overlap.

V. Look through your portfolio. As you browse, list the paragraphs that you have included by title on a sheet of paper. How many ways could you classify the writings that you have completed thus far? Could you divide your paragraphs into types based on method of development? Could you create classifications of your paragraphs based on the types of topics you have chosen or your performance. Create a topic sentence and rough outline for a paragraph that develops your classifications. Then write the draft of the paragraph for inclusion in your portfolio.

USING METHODS OF DEVELOPMENT

Now that you have studied six of the methods available for developing general-to-specific expository paragraphs, you can put your knowledge of them to work for you in two ways:

1. If you have been assigned a topic but are finding it hard to decide on a controlling idea for a paragraph, a consideration of the six methods may help you.
2. If you already have a controlling idea, a consideration of the six methods should help you to select the best method to use in developing your paragraph.

Deciding on a Controlling Idea

One of the important ways in which you can use your knowledge of the six methods is as an aid in thinking of a controlling idea. In Chapter 2, where we discussed the steps that you should follow in order to write a good paragraph, we placed consideration of development *after* choice of a controlling idea. You were told (1) to choose a topic, (2) to choose a controlling idea, (3) to express this idea in a good topic sentence, and *then* (4) to proceed with development of the controlling idea.

When you write, you may choose to continue to follow this pattern. However, now that you are familiar with six methods of developing your material in a paragraph, you may be able to put this knowledge to work earlier than we had indicated. Whenever you are finding it difficult to think of anything to say about a topic you want to write on—or *must* write on—let your mind run over the six methods you know in order—from example to classification. A consideration of each in connection with your topic may actually help you come up with a controlling idea for your paragraph.

For instance, suppose that one of the topics you are considering for a paragraph is *cybernetics*. You select this topic because you know a little about it and find it interesting. However, you cannot decide precisely what to say about it, how to focus your paragraph. Consider the six methods. If you use example, the first method, could you get across a message about cybernetics? After careful analysis, you decide that you have enough knowledge of the subject to give several examples of the role that cybernetics plays in our lives today, and you consider using the following topic sentence:

Cybernetics plays a prominent role in our lives today.

But before you reach your final decision, you consider another method, definition, and you realize that you could also develop a paragraph in which you define the term *cybernetics*. Because most people do not know what the word means, you decide that a paragraph developed by definition would be more meaningful to most readers than a paragraph developed by example.

After considering the other four methods, you find that you cannot use any of them as well as you can definition, and you decide to develop a paragraph devoted to a formal definition of the term *cybernetics.* You then write a new topic sentence that reflects this decision:

> Many people may have heard of the term *cybernetics,* but probably few know what it means.

Keep in mind, of course, that when you choose a controlling idea on the basis of a review of the six methods of paragraph development, the question of which method to use in developing your paragraph is also automatically answered. You will use the method that suggested the controlling idea to you.

Choosing the Best Method for Developing a Paragraph

There will be times when selecting a controlling idea for a paragraph is no problem at all. After reviewing a potential list of topics, you may realize that you have something worthwhile to say about one of them. You know *what* you are going to say; your problem is deciding *how* to say it. In this situation, a review of the six methods of development is in order. It will be your task to decide which method will work best for you.

Suppose, for example, that you plan to write on the topic *gun control,* and you know that you want to say that gun control would benefit society. When you go over the options you have for paragraph development, you may find that any of the six methods could be used but that either comparison and contrast or cause and effect seems to be the most suitable. If you know whether gun control in another country has reduced crime there, you can compare the crime rate in that country to crime in the United States. On the other hand, you can choose to support your controlling idea by showing the effects of the relatively free circulation of guns in our country—that is, the effects, or results, of the *absence* of gun control. You decide, finally, that you can most effectively use the information and ideas you have about this controversial topic in a paragraph that deals with effects.

■ SUMMARY

1. If you are having trouble deciding on a controlling idea for a paragraph, a consideration of the six methods of development discussed in this chapter and the last chapter may help you select one.

2. After you have chosen a controlling idea, a consideration of the six methods should help you select the best method for developing your paragraph. Of course, if you have selected a controlling idea on the basis of a review of the methods of development, the method that suggested the controlling idea is the one that you would use.

■ EXERCISES

I. In a small group, examine each of the following topic sentences carefully. Review the six methods of development that you have studied, and decide which would be the best for developing each topic sentence.

A. The bald eagle, our country's symbol, is making a recovery.
B. Along with the need to succeed, there exists in almost everyone an opposite need to avoid success.
C. Music surrounds us every day of our lives.
D. Conservation is the wise use of natural resources.
E. American society degrades and neglects the elderly.
F. There are many effective ways to deal with sleeplessness without having to resort to drugs.
G. Habits are actions that a person performs regularly and unconsciously.
H. The student union houses many different groups of people.

II. Read each of the paragraphs below carefully. For each paragraph answer the following questions:

1. Which of the six methods of development do you think the writer was attempting to use?
2. Was the effort successful? If not, state what other method of development could have been used more effectively, and why.

A. Most men have, it would seem, one of two attitudes toward women. And these attitudes—chauvinism and nonsexism—are as reflective of the male psyche as a mirror is of a man's appearance. The chauvinist male believes that he is superior to women in intelligence, strength, and emotional stability. Raised in an environment that toughened him while it coddled women, he truly believes that females are inferior objects to be treated with gloved hands. The concept of equality is often so alien to the male chauvinist that he can never put down his guard long enough to give the opposite sex a chance to prove its worth. This type of sexist man, while appearing to be strong, is actually concealing fears of his own inadequacy. In contrast, the nonsexist male believes that women are equal to him in intelligence, strength, and emotional stability. However he was raised, the "new man" is looking toward a future when members of the opposite sex will work and live alongside him as equals. The nonsexist male, although possibly considered naive by some people, is secure enough in his masculinity to respect and admire femininity. Instead of fearing inadequacy, he recognizes that we are all inadequate at times, just as all people—male and female—are strong at times.
B. Students can be either good students, average students, or "F" students. Good students do well on tests. They study a great deal and are willing to sacrifice leisure time for additional study time. Average students rarely sacrifice free time to study, but they do end up doing enough to receive a "C." The "F" students repeatedly flunk tests. These students never find time to study because they rarely try to make time for schoolwork. Overall, students can be people who study with effort, who get by with a little sacrifice, or who do not care at all about grades. Thus, these students can be classified as either "good," "average," or "failing."

C. Heavy social drinkers and back-alley drunks have several characteristics in common. First of all, heavy social drinkers see every cocktail party and Saturday-night social as an excuse for becoming inebriated. They are not looked down on by their peers since they are well aware of the pressures put on the social drinkers during a hard week at work. Likewise, the back-alley drunks save their money during the week so that they can spend it on their Saturday-night binges. With "booze" in hand, they find their favorite spot to settle down in and proceed to drink themselves into a stupor. By becoming thoroughly intoxicated, they can forget everyday trials and tribulations, slipping instead into alcoholic fantasies of success and contentment. Second, heavy social drinkers take their whiskey and water with companions of similar social status. They and their friends discuss business, community issues, and current world events. In the same manner, the back-alley drunks and their cohorts exchange hard-luck stories and tales of the "good old days" while becoming intoxicated on cheap liquor. Finally, the hangover that they experience the day after a drinking spree awakens both the social drinkers and the back-alley drunks to reality. With splitting headaches, the social drinkers are forced to meet the daily obligations that their families and jobs require while they await the next excuse to become drunk. The socially outcast drunks awaken to reality either on a city street or in a back alley. They, too, exist from day to day, awaiting the next time they can drink themselves into unconsciousness. The settings may be different, but the intentions of the heavy social drinkers and the back-alley drunks are the same. Both wish to escape the reality of life for a few forgetful hours of drunken existence.

D. Laughter is a way of releasing inner tensions, and there are many classes and types of laughs. A happy laugh can be heard when students finally pass an important examination that they studied for all night. It can also be heard coming from a small child running with her dog through the meadows. An inexperienced driver may find himself laughing when he tries to turn the steering wheel but ends up turning on the signal lights. His laughter stems from nervousness. The act of laughing helps him to relax. Then there is the sad laugh. This is the kind of laugh one experiences when watching a soap opera and finding out that George is leaving Helen for Jane who is married to Bob, George's brother-in-law. Laughter is the greatest of all emotional outlets.

E. Autism is a neurological disorder that impairs physical, social, and language skills and causes its sufferers to appear excessively withdrawn and self-absorbed. Autism is a relatively rare congenital condition. The disorder is present from birth and is almost always detected before two years of age. It occurs in about one out of every 2,000 births and affects boys three times as often as girls. The symptoms of autism make normal development impossible because the condition disrupts and distorts perception of the outside world. For example, autistic children have great difficulty communicating. They rarely acquire even basic speech skills, and in many cases they never learn to speak at all. Moreover, autistic children often seem insensitive to sound and sometimes show little or no reaction to pain. However, they frequently display an unusual degree of sensitivity to visual stimuli and can become extremely anxious if even the slightest detail of their surroundings is altered.

Efforts to determine the causes of autism and to devise treatments for the disorder have achieved only moderate success. Early research surmised that trauma during the birth process caused the condition, but this theory is no longer accepted. More recent studies using magnetic resonance imaging, or MRI, have revealed abnormalities in various brain structures of autistic subjects. A few experimental treatments have shown positive results. While most autistic children remain impaired into adulthood, a few have responded to treatment and have gone on to lead relatively normal lives.

F. When trying to save the life of a drowning person, you should follow a certain series of steps. After you have gotten the victim out of the water, place him on his stomach, and give three quick upward back thrusts. This action removes water from the lungs. Next, turn the victim on his side and clear his mouth of any foreign materials. This procedure guarantees that the airway to the lungs is open. Then take the victim's head in the palm of one hand and tilt the head backwards. This step opens an air passageway. Next, take the index finger and thumb of your free hand and pinch the victim's nostrils closed. Then place your mouth securely over the victim's mouth and breathe into the victim's lungs. Finally, place the heel of one hand on the top of the other and compress the center of the victim's chest. Repeat this procedure five times. It massages the heart and circulates the oxygen that you have forced into the victim's lungs. Then look to see if the victim is breathing on his own. If you cannot detect any breathing, repeat the entire process. Even if the patient recovers, transport him to the nearest hospital for further medical attention.

G. The symptoms of Attention Deficit Disorder, or ADD, can create multiple problems for students who suffer from an undiagnosed case of this neuro-logical disorder. First of all, ADD causes the brain to redirect its attention to almost any new stimulus. Students with ADD are easily distracted and have great difficulty remaining focused on any one thing. As a result, they find it nearly impossible to listen carefully to classroom lectures, study for more than a few minutes, or even read moderately long passages. Secondly, ADD creates an excessive amount of undirected energy. The disorder continually urges sufferers to move around, talk, or engage in some type of activity. Since ADD students already find it hard to concentrate on the task at hand, this symptom only compounds their problem. Finally, ADD can make its sufferers appear to be something they are not. While ADD has no effect on intel-ligence, its symptoms make learning in a traditional classroom environment extremely difficult. Consequently, students with undiagnosed cases of ADD are frequently mislabeled as either unintelligent or unconcerned with scho-lastic achievement. Moreover, the uncontrollable impulse of ADD sufferers to burn off excess energy often results in their unintentionally disrupting other students in the classroom. In such cases, ADD students can find them-selves branded as troublemakers through no real fault of their own.

H. Supermarket retailers have an arsenal of strategies that they use to extend the time that customers are likely to remain in their stores. On hot days, for instance, supermarkets always seem to be the coolest place to be. This phe-nomenon is no coincidence. By keeping their stores noticeably cool in summer and comfortably warm in winter, supermarket retailers create an atmosphere that invites customers to remain indoors. Since most shoppers tend to be in a rush, supermarkets rarely display large clocks in obvious places. Not having a clock clearly in view encourages customers to loiter, and the longer they linger, the more they are likely to spend. In fact, studies have shown that shoppers spend an additional $20.00 for every ten minutes that they stay in a store beyond the time required for their normal shopping. Among still other devices that supermarket managers use to detain their customers is the use of carefully orchestrated background music. This music is always soft and slow, and it encourages shoppers to relax and browse. Significantly, fast music usually replaces slow music during the hours when stores are closed. At this time clerks are stocking shelves, and the faster pace of the music is used to stimulate them to greater productivity.

I. Anglers generally go about locating fish in one of three ways. Those who prefer to fish the same lakes day after day usually know from experience which are the choicest spots. Experience has taught them that bass lurk in the quietly flowing water behind a certain rock, that trout hide in the calm current near an undercut bank, or that crappie and bream inhabit the sanctuary of submerged roots below a dead tree. Because new fish are constantly moving into them, these places remain good even when they are heavily fished. Other fishermen use their eyes to locate fish. While wading through the water, sitting in a slowly moving boat, or remaining stationary on the shore, they scrutinize the water for signs of feeding fish, paying special attention to unusual ripples or waves that might indicate that their dinner lies beneath the surface in wait of a tempting worm or well-turned fly. Still other fishermen learn where the fish are because they study the structure of the lake or stream where they fish. They know that fish can usually be found off sandbars and shoals, and they know that deep holes and rocky shores are often the most productive places to fish, even in an otherwise unproductive lake.

III. Select one of the following topics. Construct a topic sentence, and then write a paragraph that supports it, using one of the six methods of development.

A. bumper stickers
B. popular customs (or folk customs)
C. computers
D. divorce
E. political correctness
F. newspaper reporters (or television announcers)
G. tattoos
H. summer school
I. aging
J. gossip
K. global warming ("greenhouse effect")
L. bonding
M. ozone
N. delayed stress syndrome

IV. Write a paragraph on a topic of your own choosing. Use one of the methods of development.

V. Share your portfolio with your instructor. Provide the instructor with an opportunity to review the writing you have done so far in the course and to suggest areas of improvement. After your discussion, draft a brief paragraph that summarizes your discussion. Include a topic sentence that characterizes the value of the discussion and support that develops the issues that were raised. Then present that paragraph to your instructor for evaluation.

6

ACHIEVING
COHERENCE

Coherence means "sticking together." When a paragraph is coherent, the reader can move smoothly from sentence to sentence without becoming confused or losing the writer's train of thought. Coherence is achieved by arranging one's material in a logical order and by providing signals that help the reader understand the relationships between the ideas in the paragraph. If points are taken up in a disordered sequence, the reader will find it difficult to follow the writer's train of thought; if there are no guideposts along the way to indicate relationships between ideas, the reader may become totally lost. Achieving coherence is vital to effective communication.

In Chapters 3, 4, and 5 we saw that the success of a paragraph depends to a great extent on how well the writer has followed the principles of paragraph unity and paragraph development. In a paragraph that is *unified,* all the supporting sentences back up the controlling idea, and the reader is not presented with any facts or ideas that do not belong in the paragraph. In a paragraph that is adequately *developed,* the writer has selected one of the methods of development as a means of examining the subject and has followed that method consistently throughout the paragraph.

However, a paragraph may be unified and well developed *but still not be coherent.* The appropriate parts may be there, but they may not fit together well enough for the paragraph's overall message to be fully understandable to the reader. Consider, for example, the following paragraph:

(1) The current population explosion could yield devastating problems in the future. (2) Famine is already a serious problem in many countries. (3) If present trends continue, famine will spread. (4) The world population is rapidly outgrowing its limited food supply. (5) Famine could someday engulf most of the planet. (6) Millions of people would die daily. (7) In such a situation, full-scale wars would erupt. (8) Countries would struggle to expand their borders. (9) They would also try to take over new areas. (10) Food crops would be closely guarded and rationed. (11) Inflation would be intense. (12) Even people in higher income brackets would not be able to buy sufficient food. (13) The hungry would grow angry. (14) The anger of the hungry would cause riots to break out. (15) Humanity's full military power would be unleashed. (16) Countries would be torn apart by internal strife and rioting. (17) Those countries would begin looking to neighboring lands for natural resources and food. (18) Civilization as we know it would cease to exist.

This paragraph is unified: all the sentences back up the controlling idea, or, more specifically, all the details contained within the sentences lend direct or indirect support to the assertion that the population explosion *could yield devastating problems in the future*. And the paragraph is adequately developed: the writer has selected a method of development, cause and effect, and has followed it throughout.

But the paragraph is not coherent. Specifically, three essential elements of coherence are missing:

1. The paragraph lacks any sense of *order,* or *organization.* The writer has used ideas that together adequately support the controlling idea and has chosen to develop the topic by showing how a *cause*—overpopulation—may lead to several *effects*—famine, inflation, and war. But the writer has not arranged the supporting information according to a logical plan.
2. The paragraph lacks *transitions*—that is, signals that serve as a link between one sentence and the next. A paragraph is made up of a number of separate sentences, of course, but we usually do not think of each sentence as a distinct unit. Rather, as we read, we look for clues that help us cross sentence boundaries by showing how the ideas in one sentence relate to those in the next.
3. The paragraph lacks any *sentence combining.* As you probably noticed, it contains a number of short sentences. If the ideas in short sentences are closely related, they may be better understood when they are combined into one longer sentence that makes the relationship clear. This technique also makes a paragraph less choppy and therefore more pleasing to read.

With all these elements of coherence missing, readers will have to rearrange the ideas and discover the appropriate relationships between them if they are to get at what the writer is saying. And readers will probably be too annoyed by the paragraph to bother.

Following is a second version of the same paragraph, revised to correct the defects we have noted:

(1) The current population explosion could yield devastating problems in the future. (2) The world's population is rapidly outgrowing its limited food supply, and famine is already a serious problem in many countries. (3) If present trends continue, famine will spread and could someday engulf most of the planet, resulting in the deaths of millions of people daily. (4) In such a situation, what food crops remained would be closely guarded and rationed. (5) In addition, inflation would be so intense that even people in higher income brackets would not be able to buy sufficient food. (6) The hungry, in time, would grow angry, and their anger would cause riots to break out. (7) Eventually, countries torn apart by internal strife and rioting would begin looking to neighboring lands for natural resources and food. (8) Full-scale wars would erupt as the strife-torn countries struggled to expand their borders and take over new areas. (9) And finally, with humanity's full military power unleashed, civilization as we know it would cease to exist.

In this paragraph, the writer has arranged the predicted events in the order in which they might be expected to occur—that is, according to *time order*. Sentence 2 is set in the present, focusing on a trend that is already occurring. Sentences 3–5, in turn, include results that will appear next in time: famine, rationing, and inflation. And then, unfolding in sentences 6, 7, 8, and 9 are the final stages of unrest, internal strife, war, and extinction. Such a chronological arrangement is logical and natural because we perceive our everyday experience, our past, and our future to be made up of a sequence of events in time.

In addition, the sentences are now connected by a number of linking devices: repetition of key words (such as *problem, food*); repetition of key ideas through synonyms or closely related words (such as *riots, strife, rioting*); transitional words and phrases (such as *and, in addition, eventually,* and *finally*); and pronouns (such as *their,* in sentence 6, which refers back to "the hungry"). These connective devices bind the sentences in the paragraph together, making them a more coherent whole.

In the revised paragraph, the writer has also joined together short, choppy sentences to form longer sentences. The result is not only that the writing is more pleasing to read but also that the relationships between the thoughts are clearer. For example, the three sentences on famine in the original paragraph (sentences 3, 5, and 6) have been united into one sentence in the revised paragraph (sentence 3). This new sentence not only eliminates the repetition and choppiness of the original three sentences but also clarifies the relationship the writer sees between existing famine and future catastrophe.

Writers who order or organize their material logically and naturally, who use traditional devices where necessary, and who combine closely related thoughts in clearly developed sentences, will usually construct coherent paragraphs. In this chapter we will examine these three essentials of good expository writing.

ORDER

As we pointed out in Chapters 1 and 2, an expository paragraph begins with a general statement—the topic sentence—and then continues with supporting sentences that provide specifics to back up the topic sentence. This is the overall outline, or plan, that you have been using to write your paragraphs. But you have not been asked to think about the order in which your supporting sentences are arranged. A paragraph is well organized if the ideas and events it considers are presented in the order that best shows the relationships between them. In the following three sections we will focus on three possible organizational patterns:

1. time order
2. space order
3. order of importance

In some instances, the specific order you choose for the support in your paragraphs will depend on your controlling idea and on the method of development you have selected to support your controlling idea. For instance, a process analysis paragraph will usually involve time order for its support. In most cases, however, the organizational patterns listed above can be employed with any method of development.

Time Order

Time order, also called *chronological order,* simply means that events considered in a paragraph are arranged in the order in which they occurred or in which the reader would expect them to occur. A four-year-old child chanting "October, February, June, January, July" violates an order his older listeners take for granted. We would call his list disorganized or confused because it does not follow the established sequence of the months of our calendar. Similarly, readers expect that a paragraph focusing on a series of events will take up the events in chronological order and feel that it is disordered if it does not seem to do so.

The following paragraph, which presents directions for preparing and eating burritos, is developed by process analysis with supporting steps arranged according to time order:

> Burritos are as easy to make as they are fun to eat. First, take a package of frozen tortillas out of the freezer, remove the tortillas, and place them on a cookie sheet. Preheat the oven to 400°, place the tortillas in the oven, and bake them until they are moist. Then brown one pound of hamburger meat mixed with onion and chili seasoning. While the hamburger is browning, empty an eight-ounce can of pinto beans into a saucepan and heat them on the stove. While the beans are warming, grate four ounces of cheddar cheese, shred one quarter of a head of lettuce, and chop two tomatoes into small pieces. When all the ingredients—the tortillas, the browned hamburger meat, the pinto beans, the

cheese, the lettuce, and the tomatoes—are ready, it is time to put the burrito together. Lay each tortilla out flat. Now put some of the warm beans onto the tortilla, and spread a small amount of hamburger on top of the beans. Sprinkle the cheese over the hamburger, and top it with the lettuce and tomatoes. To enjoy a burrito, you must learn the trick of folding the tortilla so that the mixture inside will not fall out. First fold the bottom flap up, then the right side over, and finally the left side over. Now it's time to eat and enjoy!

Imagine the confusion if the writer had told the reader to insert the hamburger before it was browned or if the writer had left out a step—say, preheating the oven. In a successfully ordered process analysis paragraph, one step leads to the next, in succession, and the information provided in one step may enable us to understand how to carry out the next step.

Paragraphs developed by process analysis, like the one on burritos, almost always involve time order. But time order can also appear in paragraphs using any other method of development. The cause-and-effect paragraph about Elvis Presley in Chapter 4 is organized by time order, as is the following paragraph, developed by the use of example:

Job applicants who are well qualified for the position they are seeking sometimes fail to be hired because of a slip they make before or during the interview. For example, some candidates do not dress properly. One applicant may appear for an interview in clothes that are much too casual to convey a sense of respect for the job to a prospective employer. Another may make a bad impression by overdressing for an interview. There are applicants who, although dressed tastefully, arrive five or ten minutes late for an interview, only to find that the interviewer has moved on to the next candidate. Then there are applicants who talk too much during an interview. In their eagerness to please, they are entirely too chatty and end up annoying the interviewer. And, finally, when the interview turns to the question of salary, there are the applicants who appear more interested in this aspect of the job than in the duties they will have to perform. Such applicants may impress the potential employer as being self-seeking rather than committed to hard work.

In providing examples of reasons that qualified job applicants are sometimes not hired, the writer *first* points to failure to dress properly, *then* to arriving late for the interview, *then* to being too talkative, and *finally* to showing too much interest in money. Because these mistakes are presented in the order in which they are likely to be made, the paragraph's organization seems logical and natural to the reader.

In the paragraph that follows, time order is used to organize a paragraph developed through cause and effect:

Injuries may harm a football player physically, but worse than the physical discomfort they create is the psychological damage they sometimes bring. Even for minor injuries the athlete must undergo such treatments as ice baths, whirlpool baths, and retaping, all of which require time and patience and often make the athlete feel annoyed with himself for not having avoided the injury. Nursing the injury along in a cast, on crutches, or in a sling, the athlete is forced to adapt to a totally different life style, one that he may find difficult to accept. Accustomed to warming up with the team and getting "psyched up" for the win, he must sit on the sidelines and be a spectator. He must watch and accept, and if, for instance, his team is losing a close game—one that he knows he could help them win—his anguish is even greater. If the athlete's injury is serious enough to require his sitting out an entire season, the depression he feels may cause the injured player to lose faith in himself and the people around him. As the season progresses and as the fans see the player hobbling around on crutches, he becomes just someone who was stupid enough to get himself hurt. Eventually, the player must even confront the changed attitudes of friends and acquaintances, whose respect and admiration often become indifference and annoyance. Sensing this change, the injured athlete, at first only resentful, may eventually become hostile, perhaps even avoiding his old athletic environment altogether.

In this paragraph, the writer concentrates on the effects of physical injury on an athlete's mental outlook. In ordering his support, he presents these effects in the sequence in which they are likely to occur, using this sequence to make his paragraph more coherent.

■ SUMMARY

1. You can make your paragraphs more coherent by ordering their support according to basic organizational patterns. Three common patterns are time order, space order, and order of importance.

2. Time order (or chronological order) means simply that the supporting elements in a paragraph—examples or causes, for instance—are arranged in the order in which they occurred or in which the reader would expect them to occur.

3. In paragraphs ordered by time, you must be sure that your supporting points consistently follow a chronological sequence and that no important point is left out.

■ EXERCISES

1. The following topic sentence is followed by a series of supporting sentences. Arrange the supporting sentences according to the time sequence in which they are likely to occur.

Topic Sentence: Learning to go up and down stairs on crutches takes time, but it is not as difficult as most people think.

1. The patient quickly brings the crutches up to the next step and braces herself.
2. While going down the stairs, the patient places the crutches on the first step beneath her.
3. She repeats this process of leg first, then crutch until reaching the top of the stairs.
4. The physical therapist slowly explains and demonstrates both procedures.
5. Going up the stairs, the patient steps on the first step with the unbroken leg.

6. The patient repeats this procedure of crutch first, then leg until reaching the bottom of the stairway.

7. The patient steps down with the unbroken leg, making sure to keep the broken leg slightly in front of the other in order to prevent stumbling on the stairs.

8. After the patient has experimented on the practice stairs, she realizes that it really isn't that difficult, even though there is a little time involved.

9. After the therapist demonstrates the processes, the patient must practice until sure they have been learned properly.

II. Think of a process that you experience on a regular basis—for example, a morning ritual or a job-related activity. Then communicate that process to a partner in the precise order in which you perform it, being certain not to leave out any steps. After you have detailed that process to your partner, ask him or her to communicate orally what he or she can remember of your process back to you. Has your partner forgotten any steps? If so, why? Did he or she order any of the steps incorrectly? Would the process have suffered greatly with those steps out of order? Share your results with the class.

III. Using time order to organize your supporting sentences, write a paragraph on one of the following topic sentences. Be sure that your supporting points consistently follow a chronological sequence and that no important point is left out.

A. From start to finish, moving can be a grueling chore.

B. Teaching someone to drive a car can tax the patience of even the best of friends.

C. A handful of important inventions have changed the course of the world.

D. Day in and day out, television is very much the same.

E. Joining a fraternity or sorority involves the observance of certain rituals.

F. Given the political challenges that the discoverers of the Stone Age Iceman have faced, it is a wonder that they have been able to conduct a full investigation of this ancient treasure.

IV. Look back through your portfolio of paragraphs that you have written thus far. Are any of them ordered by time? Upon examining those you have written that are ordered by time, determine if any require rewriting because the sequence is not clear or because steps and details have been omitted.

V. Using time order to organize your supporting sentences, write a paragraph on a topic of your own choice.

Space Order

The second way to organize the support in a paragraph is according to space order—that is, according to a spatial arrangement or pattern. If, for example, you are writing a paragraph about the benefits to physically challenged students of the location of buildings on your campus, you might choose to order the paragraph according to the spatial arrangement of the campus. You might begin with a discussion of how the most important buildings are located in the center of the campus, where the most activity is, and then go on to a discussion of how outlying buildings are conveniently arranged around the center of campus so that physically challenged students have easy access to them.

Like time order, space order can appear in a paragraph using any method of development. And because it enables your reader to *visualize* what you are describing, space order can be a particularly effective way to add coherence to your writing. In the following paragraph, developed by classification, the supporting sentences are effectively arranged according to a spatial pattern:

> Each major section of Wisconsin is noted for the food it provides the nation. Bordered on the north by Lake Superior and on the east by Lake Michigan, the northeastern section of the state supports a thriving fishing industry. Every year thousands of tons of trout, salmon, perch, bass, and smelt from the region are harvested, processed, and eventually sold to the public. Indeed, few other areas in the country produce as much fish as northeastern Wisconsin. While the southeastern portion of Wisconsin also boasts a fishing industry, it is primarily noted for the fruit grown in its numerous orchards. Because it has milder winters and warmer summers than the northern part of the state, southeastern Wisconsin has a climate ideally suited to raising peaches, apples, cherries, and other fruits. The southwestern section of Wisconsin, on the other hand, is one of the most famous grain-producing areas in the world. Its rich soil, watered by frequent rains and warmed by long summers, is perfect for the growing of wheat, barley, and especially corn, the region's most important product. More rocky than the southwestern part of the state, the northwestern section of Wisconsin earns the state the title America's Dairyland. Every day the thousands of cows that graze on the gently rolling hills and slopes of northwestern Wisconsin produce millions of gallons of milk, much of which is processed into butter, cream, or cheese. Like the other regions of Wisconsin, this area has an identity all its own, created at least in part by the food it produces.

The writer of this paragraph could simply have listed the many foods produced in Wisconsin. Instead, she divided the state into four sections and discussed each region in terms of the food produced there. As a result, readers are able to "follow" the writer as she "moves" clockwise from region to region; they learn, moreover, that the state's food production and its geography are closely linked. The paragraph is more coherent than it would have been if the writer had merely listed food products one after another, and classification of the food products according to a spatial arrangement is responsible for this added coherence.

The two types of order we have discussed so far are not mutually exclusive. A paragraph can be ordered by *both* time and space. Consider, for example, the following paragraph, developed by cause and effect, about the devastation an atomic bomb dropped on Chicago would create:

> If a fifty-megaton atomic bomb were dropped on Chicago, it would have a devastating effect on an area extending for several hundred miles around the point of blast. Almost instantly, the city itself would be an inferno of death and

destruction. People in the downtown area would be killed immediately, and the buildings there would topple and disintegrate. Suburbs twenty-five miles to the north, the west, and the south of Chicago would feel the devastating effects of the bomb within minutes. Fire would destroy most of the buildings and people in those areas. Survivors of the fire would gradually be contaminated and destroyed by radiation. Within a few hours, crops and animals as far north as Milwaukee, Wisconsin, and as far south as Springfield, Illinois, would be poisoned by the spread of radiation outward from the blast. By hiding in bomb shelters and basements, a few people might manage to survive, but both farmland and water would contain high levels of radiation, making them useless for many years. Eventually, fallout from the bomb blast would radiate into all parts of the country, and cities as distant as Seattle and Miami would feel its effects.

The writer of this paragraph analyzes the effects of the explosion of an atomic bomb, ordering those effects according to both their chronological sequence and their spatial arrangement. He begins with a discussion of the immediate effects the bomb would have on the city itself, then analyzes the destruction the bomb would gradually inflict on the surrounding suburbs, and goes on to say that the bomb would eventually affect virtually every area of the country. Thus time order and space order work together to make this paragraph coherent.

■ SUMMARY

1. In paragraphs ordered by space, the writer organizes the support in the paragraph according to spatial arrangement or pattern. Space order enables a reader to visualize what is being described.
2. Space order and time order are not mutually exclusive. The supports in a paragraph can, if the topic warrants it, be ordered by both space and time.

■ EXERCISES

1. Write a paragraph using one of the following topic sentences. Order your support according to space order. Remember to try to describe your supporting details so that your readers can visualize their spatial relationships. You may combine space and time order if you feel the topic warrants it.
   A. The state of Pennsylvania (or another state) is known for its historic landmarks.
   B. From bumper to bumper, a minivan is a better buy than a stationwagon.
   C. Many American cities depend on the Mississippi River for their livelihood.
   D. Vegetable gardens are usually more productive if they are arranged with care.
   E. Most supermarkets have a familiar layout.
   F. Students sit in different parts of the classroom for a variety of reasons.
   G. Almost every kind of climate can be found somewhere in the United States.
   H. An old house frequently has a number of hidden problems.

II. Choose one of the topic sentences from Exercise I. Then, with a small group of classmates, draw a picture that could serve as a guide to a paragraph on that topic sentence. For instance, as a response to Topic Sentence F, you and your partners might draw a picture of a typical classroom and then proceed to label areas of that classroom such as the back, the front, the seats by the door, and so on. Next, discuss your drawing in relationship to the topic sentence and any paragraph that it might suggest. In the case of Sentence F, you and your classmates might want to discuss why students sit in those areas of the classroom. Does where they sit, you might ask, say anything about their attitudes toward the course? If you discover that where a student sits does indeed indicate something about that student, you will want to take the next step and organize your paragraph using the spatial relationship of the areas in the classroom as your guide. As a group project, draft the paragraph and share it with your other classmates and instructor.

III. Looking back through your portfolio of paragraphs, identify those that you have organized by space order and evaluate how well they convey their controlling ideas through word pictures. If you cannot find any paragraphs organized by space order in your portfolio, look for topic sentences whose primary and secondary supports could have been ordered spatially but were not. Briefly outline what one of those paragraphs would have looked like had they been organized by space order.

IV. Using space order to order your support, write a paragraph on a topic of your own choosing.

Order of Importance

Still another way you can organize the supporting material in your paragraphs is to arrange your ideas according to their order of importance—that is, according to how strongly you wish to emphasize each one. With this method, you present the least important idea first, then the next most important, and so on until you end the paragraph with the most important idea. This method of ordering supporting sentences according to their relative importance is probably used more often in student and professional writing than the other methods of ordering paragraphs previously discussed.

In the following paragraph, for instance, the writer uses the cause-and-effect method of paragraph development to discuss why many students dislike unannounced in-class writing assignments, and she organizes the ideas in her paragraph from least important to most important:

> Most students dislike spur-of-the-moment, in-class writing assignments. In the first place, they may not have with them the kind of paper or pen that they like to use, and they are almost certain to find themselves without a dictionary. Second, students often find that if the choice of topic is left to them, they are unable, on such short notice, to think of anything worthwhile to write about. If, on the other hand, they are given a number of topics to choose from, they may not be able to think of enough to say about any of them. A still greater source of discomfort for many students is the classroom environment itself. Nervous

students may be whispering and coughing, asking the teacher questions, or otherwise distracting those who are trying to concentrate. The most difficult problem with unannounced, in-class writing assignments, however, is the pressure involved. In part, the pressure is a matter of time: students know that they have only forty-five or fifty minutes in which to produce a finished paragraph or essay, and every glance at the clock causes a rise on the pressure gauge. Being compelled to produce a well-written paragraph or essay on demand creates so much pressure, in fact, that some students are unable to write anything and therefore turn in a blank sheet of paper. Other students, feeling the pressure almost as much, submit a few indecisive sentences. And most students would admit that whatever writing they turn in is bound to be the worst they have produced during the semester.

In this paragraph the writer discusses causes for student dislike of in-class writing assignments in this order: lack of writing materials, difficulty in choosing a topic, classroom distractions, and the pressure to perform. By moving from a valid but mild cause, to more important factors, and finally to the most important cause, pressure, the writer achieves a coherent and well-developed paragraph.

The following paragraph, developed by means of contrast, also demonstrates how effective the use of an order-of-importance arrangement can be to the achievement of a coherent paragraph:

> Many differences existed between the two earliest political parties in the United States, the Federalist Party and the Republican Party. For one thing, the Federalists favored a loose interpretation of the Constitution. Although the Constitution does not specifically mention a bank, for instance, the Federalists argued that the power to establish one is implied. The Republicans, on the other hand, believed in a strict interpretation of the Constitution; they felt that only in extreme circumstances would it be acceptable to assume the power required for establishing a bank. A second, and perhaps more significant, difference between the two parties involved their attitudes toward the structure of government itself. The Federalists believed in a strong central government geared to serving the interests of the few. Conversely, the Republicans supported the concept of a weak central government, with its powers distributed among the many. This difference resulted from what was perhaps the most fundamental dissimilarity between the parties. The "rich, wise, and well-born" were basically Federalists. They felt that the average citizen was incapable of governing intelligently. The Republicans, for their part, *were* the average citizens. Thus the difference in background and philosophy of the members of the two parties underlay their different attitudes toward specific activities of the government and toward the very nature of government.

According to the writer, the fact that members of the Federalist Party were well-born while the members of the Republican Party were largely "average citizens" was the most fundamental difference between the two parties because it *underlay* the other differences in attitude and philosophy. Because he judges this difference to be most important, the writer has made it the culmination toward which the rest of the paragraph moves. The paragraph is effective because the reader comes away with the most important support for the controlling idea clearly in his mind. Had the writer presented the other points randomly rather than according to their relative importance, the paragraph would have lacked coherence.

When you decide to arrange the supporting evidence in a paragraph according to order of importance, you may find it helpful to follow a specific procedure. After you have selected the primary supports for your controlling idea, list them according to their importance to you, with the most important point first, the next most important point second, and so on. If you have no more than three primary supports, you might make your list mentally. If you have more than three supports, though, you should write your list down. When you begin to write your paragraph, *reverse* your list and take up the least important point first; then move on up through your list so that you conclude your paragraph with the most significant point.

In this way the writer of the paragraph on in-class papers might have jotted down the following informal list of supports, giving the most important first:

1. pressure
2. noisy classroom
3. difficulty in finding a suitable topic
4. lack of writing materials

The finished paragraph, of course, takes up these points in reverse.

■ SUMMARY

1. Ordering the supports in a paragraph according to their relative importance is another way to make your paragraphs coherent. Order of importance is probably used more often than any other principle in the arranging of supports within a paragraph.

2. When you decide to order the supports in a paragraph according to order of importance, you should make a list of primary supports with your most important support first, then the next most important, and so on to the least important. When you write the paragraph, reverse the list and order your supports from the least to the most important. Fill in secondary supports as needed.

■ EXERCISES

1. The first sentence in each group below is a topic sentence. The rest of the sentences in the group are the primary supports for a paragraph that develops the topic sentence. Rearrange the supports according to what you believe to be their order of importance, placing the most important first, the second most important second, and so on. Then reverse the order of your supports according to the way they would appear in the finished paragraph.

A. *Topic Sentence:* Instituting a fall semester break at colleges results in many advantages for the student.

1. Students have the opportunity to take a break from the constant pressure of classes and exams.
2. Students catch up on work for classes that they are behind in.
3. Students have the opportunity to spend a few days at home visiting with family and friends.

B. *Topic Sentence:* Salads are beneficial in many ways.

1. Salads are inexpensive to make.
2. Salads offer many health benefits.
3. The salad chef can exercise a great deal of creativity when making salads.
4. Salads contain fewer calories than many other types of food.

C. *Topic Sentence:* A music-performance major often finds it more advantageous to drop out of college than to remain.

1. College can't provide the experience a musician needs to be able to play with a professional orchestra or band.
2. A musician has more difficulty developing important contacts in the insular setting of the college campus.
3. Not all musicians are judged by what or how many schools they have attended.

D. *Topic Sentence:* The American jury system is in jeopardy for several reasons.

1. Court testimony and evidence is becoming far too complex for the everyday juror to understand and interpret.
2. Most people consider jury duty a needless hassle that distracts from their work and their family responsibilities.
3. Lawyers often prevent potentially competent jurors from participation by excusing them without valid reason.
4. Jurors who are involved in certain types of trials run the risk of being sought out afterwards for retribution.
5. Today's trials and subsequent deliberations can be lengthy, inconveniencing jurors for long periods of time.

II. Choose A, B, C, or D from Exercise I for examination with a classmate. Focus your discussion on how you might arrive at what is the most important primary support for the topic sentence. Does varying the audience of a paragraph affect which support is most or least important? Imagine two audiences for a paragraph that uses the topic sentence and primary supports that you have chosen. Would you organize it one way for one audience and a different way for another audience? If so, divide the task with your partner, and each of you write one of the paragraphs for evaluation by your instructor.

III. Develop a set of primary supports for one of the following topic sentences; then rank each primary support according to its importance, beginning with the most important support and working down to the support of least importance. Then reverse the order of your supports according to the way they would appear in the finished paragraph.

A. Jogging is a worthwhile form of exercise.
B. An "A" on a paper means a great deal.

    C. When choosing a college, one has to consider many points.

    D. Student governments do a good deal (or do nothing) to improve life on campus.

    E. Living at home while attending college has definite advantages.

    F. Attending a distance education class is different from attending a class taught by a site instructor.

IV. Look through your portfolio of paragraphs that you have written thus far. How are you progressing? Have you seen improvements in your writing? Write a paragraph in which you explain the major differences between your writing at the beginning of the course and your most recent writing. Organize your differences according to their relative importance to you as a writer.

TRANSITIONAL DEVICES

As we pointed out in the introduction to this chapter, coherence can be achieved in three basic ways: through attention to order, through the use of transitional devices, and through effective sentence combining. In the first section we explained how order is achieved by arranging your material according to basic patterns of thought and experience that help to tie the parts of your paragraph together. Now we'll turn to the second factor in achieving coherence: transitional devices. There are many devices at your disposal for producing smooth and effective transitions from point to point in your writing. In this section, we will consider some of the more common ones:

1. transitional words and phrases
2. pronouns
3. repetition of key words and phrases

Transitional Words and Phrases

Transitional words and phrases—such as *but, therefore, in addition, for example,* and *on the other hand*—add coherence to your paragraphs by linking the ideas in one sentence with those in the next and showing their relationships. Transitional expressions (as they are also called) act as reminders of what you have already said and as signals indicating where you are going. When used effectively, they can make the difference between an easy-to-understand paragraph and one that is difficult to follow. Without transitional words and phrases, writing tends to be choppy and awkward.

The following paragraph, for instance, does not use transitional words and phrases to bring out the relationship between the ideas the paragraph contains:

(1) Owners or drivers of automobiles in this state should know the traffic laws concerning accidents. (2) Anyone involved in an accident must remain at the scene until the police arrive. (3) The drivers should exchange names,

addresses, and registration information. (4) If the police are not present, someone should phone them as soon as possible. (5) If an officer is present, the
drivers can supply the necessary information at the scene of the accident. (6) Accidents result in a great deal of damage and/or personal injury. (7) If there is
damage to one of the cars in excess of $250 but no injury, the driver of that car
must file a written report with the Department of Motor Vehicles within thirty
days. (8) If there is also personal injury, both drivers have to file a report within
five days. (9) People forget to file reports in the required time, and the result may
be a severe fine. (10) It is important to know state laws concerning the responsibilities of drivers involved in accidents.

The sentences in this paragraph are arranged in a logical order, but the paragraph lacks signals which would help the reader see the relationship between the ideas.

Following is the same paragraph rewritten to include transitional words
and phrases (shown in italics):

(1) Owners or drivers of automobiles in this state should know the traffic
laws concerning accidents. (2) *For example,* anyone involved in an accident
must remain at the scene until the police arrive. (3) *In addition,* the drivers
should exchange names, addresses, and registration information. (4) If the
police are not present, someone should phone them as soon as possible. (5) *But*
if an officer is present, the drivers can supply the necessary information at the
scene of the accident. (6) *Frequently,* accidents result in a great deal of damage
and/or personal injury. (7) If there is damage to one of the cars in excess of $250
but no injury, the driver of that car must file a written report with the Department
of Motor Vehicles within thirty days. (8) If there is also personal injury, both
drivers have to file a report within five days. (9) *Often* people forget to file
reports in the required time, and the result may be a severe fine. (10) *Therefore,*
it is important to know state laws concerning the responsibilities of drivers involved in accidents.

Unlike the first version, this paragraph is easy to follow because transitional
words and phrases provide the reader with signals to relate the sentences to
each other.

Transitional words and phrases take many forms—so many, in fact, that
a complete list of all or most of them would be unmanageably long. For your
convenience, however, we have drawn up a list of those most frequently
used, categorized according to their most common uses:

A. *Example*
   occasionally, usually, often, frequently, especially, specifically, princi-
   pally, mainly, namely, significantly, indeed, for example, for instance,
   first of all, for one thing, most important, to illustrate, in particular, in
   general
B. *Addition*
   and, also, furthermore, first, second, third, next, other, besides, too,
   likewise, moreover, last, again, finally, in addition, in the first (second,
   third) place, what is more, as well, at last, next to

C. *Comparison*
   similarly, likewise, like, as, at the same time, in the same way, in like manner
D. *Contrast*
   but, however, yet, or, nevertheless, still, nonetheless, conversely, nor, rather, whereas, though, on the one hand, on the other hand, on the contrary, by contrast, in contrast, even though, at the same time
E. *Concession*
   doubtless, surely, certainly, naturally, granted that, although this may be true, no doubt, I concede, I admit
F. *Repetition*
   again, as has been pointed out, to repeat, in other words, as I have said above, once again
G. *Result*
   then, therefore, thus, hence, so, consequently, as a result, all in all
H. *Conclusion*
   finally, then, thus, hence, therefore, so, in conclusion, to sum up, to summarize, to conclude, in short
I. *Time*
   before, earlier, formerly, afterward, later, subsequently, presently, soon, shortly, meanwhile, simultaneously, now, then, after a while, at last, at that time, in the meantime, in the past, until now
J. *Place*
   here, there, elsewhere, above, below, behind, beyond, nearby, adjacent to, farther on, in the background, opposite to, to the right

Consult this list if you are having trouble thinking of transitional words and phrases, but use it with caution. Too many transitional words and phrases, or inappropriate ones, can be just as harmful as too few. *Be sure to select the word or phrase that links your ideas logically. And always remember to use only as many transitional words and phrases as are needed to make your paragraph coherent.*

■ SUMMARY

1. Transitional devices add coherence to a paragraph by linking the ideas in one sentence with those in the next. They remind the reader of what preceded and signal what is to follow.

2. When used effectively, transitional words and phrases can make the difference between a clearly written and easy-to-read paragraph and one that is difficult to follow because it moves abruptly from sentence to sentence.

3. When selecting transitional words and phrases for your paragraphs, be sure to select only those that fit logically and to use only as many as are needed to make your paragraph coherent.

■ EXERCISES

I. Examine the following paragraphs and the lists below each. Work with a partner to choose the transitional word or phrase from each list that best fits into the indicated space.

A. The primary cause of heart attack among men in their forties and fifties is a buildup of cholesterol in the bloodstream. Particularly among men who are overweight, don't exercise, and have high blood pressure, cholesterol tends to accumulate on the walls of the arteries that supply the heart muscle with oxygen and essential nutrients. The arteries may eventually become so congested with fatty deposits that blood flow is decreased or completely shut off. A significant decrease in the amount of blood flowing to the heart can cause severe arterial damage. (1) _____ the worst damage occurs when the blood flow is completely stopped. When this happens, the area of the heart to which the blood was being pumped is cut off from its supply of oxygen and nutrients. (2) _____, the heart muscle in the receiving area cannot function, and a heart attack ensues. (3) _____, to prevent a heart attack, one should exercise and stay trim, but most of all one should avoid excessive intake of cholesterol.

1. a. But
   b. Besides
   c. As I have said above
2. a. Occasionally
   b. Nonetheless
   c. Consequently
3. a. For instance
   b. Therefore
   c. And

B. Genetic screening in business, or testing the genes of employees to see if they are susceptible to workplace-related diseases, may present problems for the tested. (1) _____, the genetic screening tests and technology in general are in their infancy stages. (2) _____, many physicians and health professionals doubt their reliability. (3) _____, once genetic information is recorded on employes, it cannot always be kept secret. Even though employers are assured that their medical files are confidential, clerical staff have access to them. (4) _____, if they are entered into a computer data base, they are available to anyone with access. (5) _____, some argue that such screening procedures are violations of personal rights. (6) _____, many cite similarities between genetic screening and drug testing, noting that both involve a process of obtaining information from unwilling individuals that might affect them adversely. Opponents of genetic screening point out that some employees with the potential for workplace diseases would rather run the risk than lose their jobs.

1. a. Granted
   b. First
   c. However
2. a. Consequently
   b. Second
   c. For instance

3. a. Nonetheless
   b. Once again
   c. Further
4. a. In addition
   b. Therefore
   c. Specifically
5. a. Occasionally
   b. Finally
   c. Thus
6. a. Therefore
   b. Next
   c. In particular

II. From the list of transitional words and phrases (pp. 117–118), select the word or phrase that best fits in the indicated spaces. In each case, the *use* of the transitional expression is specified.

A. Our state's correctional system is plagued with problems. _____, high
    (EXAMPLE)
officials increase their personal wealth by awarding building and catering

contracts to disreputable companies in return for bribes. _____,
                                                            (ADDITION)
promotions within the system are made on the basis of politics, not merit.

_____, the system is filled with people at the top who know little
(RESULT)
about what they are doing. _____, lackadaisical security measures,
                            (ADDITION)
allowing trusted inmates to control certain operations of the institution, are part of the growing plight. But one increasing tendency in particular is doing harm to the system's image and efficiency. This is the tendency of officials who are charged with important tasks and who make faulty decisions to

cover up their mistakes. _____, one would think that amid all the strife
                          (CONCLUSION)
some effort would be made to rectify these problems, but a seemingly dogged determination to resist change overshadows the system.

B. Of all the possessions successful bass anglers must have, four are highly important: a solid rod, a reliable reel, the proper bait, and a large quantity of

patience. _____, the rod should be approximately five and one-half
           (EXAMPLE)
feet in length and should have the proper degree of rigidity. The eyelets should be lined up and smoothly sanded to ensure the proper flow of the line

when it is cast. The reel, _____, must provide a smooth cast; other-
                            (COMPARISON)
wise, its "drag" system will not function efficiently. _____, successful
                                                        (ADDITION)
bass anglers need the right bait. While some anglers prefer plastic worms and others "top water" and shallow diving lures, successful anglers know that

the right kind of bait catches the most fish. _____, they must have vast
(ADDITION)
amounts of patience. Bass anglers may cast their baits for hours on end
without so much as a strike. Anglers who have patience, though, and refuse
to give up may be rewarded with a fine day's catch.

III. From the list of transitional words and phrases (pp. 117–118), select the word
or phrase that best fits each blank in the following paragraphs. Do not use the
same transition more than once in any paragraph.

A. Once you have set foot on Ireland's soil, you will never want to leave it.
A land of many outstanding characteristics, Ireland has as its most striking

quality a beautiful countryside. It contains, _____, a magnificent,
flat-topped mountain, called Ben Bella, that hovers over the landscape.

_____ the mountain there are rock-ribbed hills where for centuries

flocks of sheep have grazed. _____ lining these hills are rock fences,
originally constructed as boundaries by farmers who cleared the rocks from

their croplands. _____, the traveler who wants natural beauty cannot
visit a lovelier country than Ireland.

B. One of the most useful techniques in the sport of body building is called
supersetting. To understand supersetting, one must understand that in
weightlifting a "set" is the completion of a specified number of repetitions of

an exercise. Supersetting, _____, is the practice of combining sets of

exercises for muscles located on opposite sides of the body. _____,
one would do a set of an exercise for the muscle on the front of the arm, the

bicep, and _____ proceed immediately to a set of exercises for the
muscle located on the back of the arm, the tricep. Supersetting is valuable
because it saves time. One can work two body parts in the time it would

normally take to work one. _____, supersetting promotes cardiovascular fitness by placing a greater demand on the heart and lungs. A

_____ advantage of supersetting is the sense of both stimulation and
relaxation experienced when a part of the body is fully exercised.

C. The future promises many dramatic changes for television viewers.

_____, they will have more options for viewing. One communications

company, _____, has already introduced a small, inexpensive rooftop

dish that can deliver 150 channels. _____, a cable-tv operator is mar-

keting a device that will deliver as many as 540 channels. _____,
viewers will be able to receive upon demand any programming that they
want. Televisions will serve as entry points to vast databanks of programs. All

viewers will have to do, _____, is browse the vast store of movies, sitcoms, and other types of shows and then select what they feel like watching

at that moment. _____, the home television set will become a two-way communications device allowing viewers to broadcast as well as to receive. The benefits of this development are many. One of the most sig-

nificant assets of two-way television, _____, is the ability of the viewer to participate in educational programming.

IV. Select a paragraph from your portfolio of paragraphs that you have written thus far. Underline the transitional words and phrases that you employed in that paragraph. Do you tend to use a variety of transitional words and phrases? Or do you rely on the same ones each time you write? Are there places where you might have used transition and did not? Do you tend to use too much transition? After answering these questions, revise your paragraph employing appropriate transitional words and phrases to make it more understandable.

Pronouns

Another device that acts as a link between sentences in a paragraph is the pronoun, a word used in place of a noun. The following pronouns are frequently used to add coherence to expository paragraphs:

	SINGULAR	PLURAL
FIRST PERSON	I	we
	me	us
	my, mine	our, ours
	myself	ourselves
SECOND PERSON	you	you
	your, yours	your, yours
	yourself	yourselves
THIRD PERSON	he, she, it	they
	him, her, it	them
	his, her, hers, its	their, theirs
	himself, herself, itself	themselves
DEMONSTRATIVES	this, that	these, those

Pronouns add coherence to a paragraph in two ways: (1) they provide for smoother reading by eliminating the awkward and distracting repetition of nouns, and (2) they serve as links between parts of a paragraph by referring to a noun in a preceding or following sentence or sentence part.

Using Pronouns Effectively The following paragraph focuses on the career of Nelson Mandela. Naturally, the writer often refers to Mandela by name, but imagine how awkward the paragraph would be if the writer repeated Nelson Mandela (or even just Mandela) time and again instead of substituting pronouns at the appropriate places. All the pronouns in the paragraph refer to Mandela.

(1) The name Nelson Mandela has come to symbolize for people around the world the struggle for justice and freedom in South Africa. (2) Mandela, born in 1918 the son of Chief Henry Mandela of the Tembu tribe, eventually gave up *his* birthright to study law. (3) After qualifying to practice law in 1942, *he* joined the African National Congress (ANC) in 1944 and soon became one of that black liberation group's leaders. (4) Mandela, as an organizer of ANC's Youth League, confined *himself* and *his* group to nonviolent acts of opposition to the oppressive Afrikaner government and its racist policy of Apartheid despite persistent arrests and incarcerations during the 1950s. (5) Then in 1960, the massacre of unarmed Africans by police forces at Sharpeville and the government's subsequent banning of the ANC served to alter Mandela's philosophical stance on violence as a form of disobedience, leading *him* to form the military arm of the ANC, the Spear of the Nation. (6) In 1962, Mandela was jailed again and sentenced to five years in prison. (7) Then in 1963, *he* was tried for sabotage, treason, and violent conspiracy in the infamous Rivonia Trial and in 1964 sentenced to life imprisonment. (8) From 1964 to 1982, Mandela was incarcerated at Robben Prison, near Cape Town. (9) During the years *he* was in Robben Prison and even after *he* was shifted to a maximum security facility, *he* retained the loyalty of *his* followers and became a major focus of attention from groups throughout the world opposed to Apartheid. (10) Facing escalating unrest at home and increased pressure from abroad, Afrikaner president F. W. de Klerk released Mandela and legalized the ANC in 1990. (11) In July of that year Mandela assumed the presidency of the ANC and shortly thereafter began negotiations with de Klerk on a new constitution and free elections. (12) Their agreement was struck in November of 1993, and South Africa embarked on its new course in April of 1994, when it elected Nelson Mandela as its first black president. (13) For *his* commitment to freedom and justice, Mandela, along with F. W. de Klerk, received the Nobel Peace Prize.

The writer's use of pronouns not only makes the paragraph as a whole read smoothly but also provides links between one sentence and another. Thus, the reader has no difficulty following the progression of ideas throughout the paragraph.

Take care not to overuse pronouns, however. Like transitional words and phrases, pronouns should be used only when they are needed to make your writing smoother. Notice, for example, that in the paragraph on Mandela the writer has not replaced every instance of the name Nelson R. Mandela with a pronoun. If overused, pronouns can be as awkward as the constant repetition of the nouns they replace.

A Word of Caution: Pronouns and Their Antecedents The noun (or nouns) that a pronoun substitutes for (or, as we also say, *refers to*) is called the *antecedent* of the pronoun. When you use a pronoun in your writing, be sure that your reader will be able to identify its antecedent immediately. If your reader has to stop and hunt for a pronoun's antecedent, he or she may lose your train of thought. There are three types of pronoun-antecedent errors that writers are likely to make: *ambiguous reference, broad reference,* and *weak reference.*

An *ambiguous reference* occurs when there are two or more possible antecedents for a pronoun:

UNCLEAR: Mandela met de Klerk for the first time in 1990 at the presidential residence in Cape Town. After the meeting, *he* said that *he* was clearly interested in moving the country toward democracy. [The antecedent for the pronoun he is ambiguous. The pronouns could refer to de Klerk or Mandela or both.]

CLEAR: Mandela met de Klerk for the first time in 1990 at the presidential residence in Cape Town. After the meeting, *Mandela* said that *de Klerk* was clearly interested in moving the country toward democracy.

A *broad reference* occurs when a pronoun refers to an entire statement rather than to a specific noun or nouns:

UNCLEAR: Both Mandela and de Klerk made critical concessions during the negotiation process. *This* paved the way toward the eventual agreement that led to a majority-rule democracy for South Africa. [The pronoun *this* is intended to substitute for the entire sentence preceding it. As a result, its antecedent is unclear.]

CLEAR: Both Mandela and de Klerk made critical concessions during the negotiation process. *Their concessions* paved the way toward the eventual agreement that led to a majority-rule democracy for South Africa.

A *weak reference* occurs when the antecedent is a noun that cannot *logically* be replaced by the pronoun.

UNCLEAR: Mandela was at one time a lawyer. *This,* of course, was not a job that was totally suited to his ambitions. [The pronoun *this* is intended to substitute for the word *lawyer.* However, the reference is unclear because a "lawyer" is a not a "job."]

CLEAR: Mandela was at one time a lawyer. *Practicing law,* of course, was not a job that was suited to his ambitions.

Finally, be sure when you use a pronoun that it agrees, or corresponds in form, with its antecedent in *person* (first, second, third), *number* (singular, plural), and, if possible, *gender* (masculine, feminine, neuter).

■ SUMMARY

I. Pronouns add coherence to a paragraph in two ways: they smooth the flow of sentences by eliminating awkward repetition of nouns, and they help to knit a paragraph together by referring to nouns in previous or following sentences or sentence parts.

2. Use pronouns only when they are needed to add coherence to your paragraph.

3. Be sure that every pronoun has a clear antecedent.

4. Be certain that every pronoun agrees with its antecedent in person, number, and, if possible, gender.

■ EXERCISES

I. Collaborate with a classmate to fill in the blanks with the appropriate pronouns in the following paragraphs. If necessary, refer to the list of pronouns (p. 122).

A. Human beings are destroying their environment. It is ironic how people pollute _____ surroundings and then go to great pains to clean up the messes that _____ have made. A cheap method of getting rid of industrial wastes is to dump _____ into rivers or lakes. The result of such intrusions into nature is the death of many forms of life in and around the waters. Only when the pollution reaches _____ reservoirs, however, do people figure that the time has come to clean up _____ environment. Then _____ create a series of expensive projects to restore the water to _____ original purity. Of course, the cheapest and most effective way to get clean water is not to pollute _____ in the first place.

B. People who smoke in nonsmoking areas are _____ who irritate me the most. _____ have absolutely no respect for _____ and other people who are sitting around _____. In restaurants, for example, _____ often invade nonsmoking sections where nonsmokers have sought refuge from the smoke. Once in the nonsmoking area, these people light up and, when not sneaking a puff, clandestinely hold _____ cigarettes under the table. The result is, of course, that the smoke still circulates, and anyone who cannot stand _____ must either wear a gas mask or leave before _____ food is served.

II. The following exercise demonstrates the importance of furnishing clear antecedents for each pronoun you use. Read the paragraphs below carefully, and determine what word each italicized pronoun refers to. If there is a problem of pronoun reference, decide whether the pronoun has an *ambiguous, broad,* or *weak* reference.

A. (1) I enjoy working with children with disabilities because they look up to me as a parent figure. (2) The children are always asking me to watch what they are doing, and they inevitably quiz me on how well I thought they did. (3) Usually I show a great deal of enthusiasm and offer constructive aid. (4) *This,* of course, results in a great deal of respect from the children. (5) It seems that children without disabilities never appreciate my efforts as much as those with disabilities do. (6) And when I am successful in helping *them* complete a task or confront a problem, I feel a great deal of satisfaction. (7) *This* is why working with children with disabilities is so rewarding to me.

B. (1) Physical punishment and verbal abuse in the classroom frequently have adverse effects on children. (2) Despite the common belief that a few smacks on the behind never hurt anyone, children who are slapped or beaten by teachers may be left with both physical and mental scars. (3) Often *they* are so mad at *them* that *they* are unaware of *their* own strength. (4) Many times *this* results in serious injuries and permanent disabilities. (5) Tongue-lashings, too, can wound a sensitive child. (6) If a teacher scolds a child by using words like stupid or slow, *that* is unfortunate. (7) Children often believe what their teachers say and grow up thinking that *they* are stupid. (8) Often it takes years to reverse the thinking, and *that* sets the child back even further.

III. Choose a paragraph that you have written from your portfolio. Identify the types of pronouns that you have used in the paragraph. Have you used an appropriate number of pronouns to aid the coherence of the paragraph? Do any of your pronouns make an ambiguous, broad, or weak reference? If so, revise for clarity.

Repetition of Key Words and Phrases

Repetition of key words and phrases is another transitional device you can use to achieve coherence in your paragraphs. We do not mean to suggest, of course, that words and phrases should be repeated so often that they begin to distract the reader. We are saying, rather, that to maintain focus on your controlling idea, you can repeat particular words and phrases that emphasize this idea. The paragraph below, for instance, keeps the focus on its controlling idea—the importance of the multivitamin in a child's diet—by either repeating certain key words or using closely related phrases:

> The *multivitamin* plays an important role in a child's diet. Laboratory tests show that most children do not obtain the recommended daily allowances of *vitamins and minerals* from the food they eat. To maintain and build healthy bodies, therefore, most children need a *dietary supplement.* One *multivitamin* each day provides the *vitamins* A, B-6, B-12, C, D, and E, as well as folic acid, thiamine, riboflavin, niacin, and even iron. For children who do not eat a well-balanced diet or who are unable to absorb essential *vitamins and minerals* from their regular meals, a single *supplementary tablet* may ensure good health.

In this paragraph, repetition of the words *multivitamin* and *vitamins* keeps the focus of the paragraph clear. To avoid too much repetition, though, the writer also uses two closely related phrases: *dietary supplement* and *supplementary tablet.* These phrases add variety to the paragraph. They also add coherence because they echo the key words around which the paragraph is structured.

Again, we do not wish to tell you to repeat words and phrases needlessly. Rather, our intention is to remind you to look back over your paragraphs to make sure that, where appropriate, you have used repetition of a key word, or have introduced a closely related phrase or a synonym for a key word, to help focus the reader's attention on your controlling idea.

■ SUMMARY

I. To maintain focus on the controlling idea throughout a paragraph, writers often repeat key words and phrases that emphasize this idea.

2. Repetition of key words and phrases—either the original words, related forms, or synonyms—adds coherence to a paragraph by drawing the reader's attention to the controlling idea of the paragraph.

▪ EXERCISES

I. Underline all key words and phrases that are repeated in the following paragraphs. Also underline variations of key terms.

  A. *Lamaze,* a word that sounds exotic, actually refers to something quite practical: a method of prepared childbirth. Lamaze classes teach the expectant mother and her "coach" methods of coping with the birth process. The mother, first of all, learns breathing and hand-motion techniques to aid her during labor. These techniques often enable the mother to undergo "natural childbirth," or childbirth without anesthesia. In addition, Lamaze classes instruct the mother in how to deal with such problems as "back labor" or even an emergency delivery. The "coach" is also trained to oversee the mother's breathing techniques, to time her contractions, and generally to offer moral support to her efforts. Lamaze classes, which are intended for women in their last months of pregnancy (and for their coaches), are usually taught by registered nurses with Lamaze certification.

  B. One of the major causes of our city's traffic problems is Main Street. To begin with, the street is not wide enough to handle the flow of traffic that plagues midtown. The midtown area has expanded vastly in the last few years, and the number of vehicles traveling through it has grown. Furthermore, there is an inadequate number of traffic lights on Main Street. For example, the very busy intersection at Second Avenue, where traffic flowing onto Main Street is always backed up, is greatly in need of a traffic light. There is also an urgent need to improve the condition of the street itself. There are numerous potholes that slow vehicles down, impeding the flow of traffic even further.

II. With a partner, identify all key words and phrases that are repeated in the following paragraphs. Also identify variations of key terms.

  A. Television furnishes an effective means of advertising. One of the reasons for its effectiveness is simply that millions of Americans view television every day. It is estimated that the average American family watches television four hours a day. Second, television is more effective than, say, radio because television can appeal to the prospective buyer through both ear and eye. Viewers who can see the product that is being sold are more likely to buy it. And, finally, television advertising in the last twenty years has become so sophisticated that television advertisers have been able to determine what kinds of audiences watch at specific times of the day. They can now air commercials that appeal specifically to the audience watching at any given time, and the result is, of course, that their pitches are more successful than when they promote their products randomly.

  B. Getting a dog creates several duties for the owner. First of all, feeding the new pet regularly is necessary to its well-being. A puppy needs to be fed twice a day, as opposed to an adult dog, who needs feeding only once a day. Second, a healthy dog requires regular exercise. Taking it for daily walks or allowing it to run for lengthy periods of time increases its chances for good health and a sound muscular structure. Exercise also helps the dog to release the tension that builds up while it is confined. Finally, the dog must be protected from disease and health problems and therefore requires occasional trips to the veterinarian's office. It should be inoculated against distemper and rabies, as well as tested for worms and skin ailments.

III. Examine a paragraph from your portfolio to determine how effectively you have repeated key words and phrases in order to promote coherence. Have you used them too often? Not often enough? What synonyms have you used for these key words and phrases to provide connections without excessive repetition? Would you write your paragraph differently if you had it to do over?

COMBINING SENTENCES

The first two sections of this chapter have focused on two important means of achieving coherence in your paragraphs: arranging your supporting sentences in a logical and consistent order and furnishing transitional devices where needed. Still another way to achieve coherence is to combine two or more short, single-idea sentences into a longer sentence that will relate the ideas clearly and more effectively. Particularly if your sentences tend to be choppy, this method can help.

Combining Sentences for More Effective Paragraphs   Consider, to begin with, the following paragraph, which consists of brief, simple sentences:

(1) El Castillo is a paradoxical marvel of the Western Hemisphere. (2) El Castillo is an ancient pyramid. (3) The Maya Indians built El Castillo between 300 and 900 C.E. (4) The pyramid is located in the ruins of the Mayan city of Chichen Itza. (5) Chichen Itza is located on the Yucatan Peninsula. (6) The portion of the Yucatan Peninsula that contains Chichen Itza is in Mexico. (7) The pyramid was used for religious ceremonies. (8) El Castillo was dedicated to Kulkulcan. (9) Kulkulcan was a powerful god of creation and transformation. (10) The pyramid has four sides. (11) On each of the sides is a staircase. (12) At the base of the staircases are serpents' heads. (13) The serpents' heads point to natural wells. (14) Human bones and jewelry have been found in these wells. (15) Human bones and jewelry are evidence of human sacrifices. (16) The sacrifices were made to Kulkulcan. (17) El Castillo was also used as an astronomical observatory. (18) Each staircase has ninety-one steps. (19) The four staircases of ninety-one steps plus the top platform equal 365 steps. (20) This number of steps reflects the number of days in a solar year. (21) The pyramid demonstrates the Mayas' advanced understanding of astronomy.

This paragraph lacks the coherence readers expect in a well-written paragraph. It contains a clear controlling idea (a paradoxical marvel of the Western Hemisphere), possesses a specific method of development (example), and follows a logical order (order of importance). But because all the sentences in the paragraph are short and choppy, the reader encounters so many stops and starts that the sentence-to-sentence continuity of thought may be lost. For instance, the relationship between the ideas contained in sentences 8 and 9 is not clear. The reader does not know whether the author intends to develop the notion in sentence 9 that *Kulkulkan was a powerful god of creation and transformation* or plans to open up a new line of thought in sentence 10.

To remedy the problem posed by the paragraph on El Castillo, the writer reconstructed the sentences so that the relationships among thoughts became clear. He combined short sentences into longer ones that emphasized what needed to be emphasized and subordinated what needed to be subordinated. The chart below demonstrates how he combined his sentences for greater coherence and clarity.

The writer then combines the final sentences to produce a smoother, clearer paragraph, as shown on pp. 130–131.

ORIGINAL SENTENCE	CHANGED TO	IN FINAL SENTENCE
1. El Castillo is a paradoxical marvel of the Western Hemisphere.	(main clause)	El Castillo, an ancient pyramid built by the Maya Indians between 300 and 900 C.E., is a paradoxical marvel of the Western Hemisphere.
2. ~~El Castillo is~~ an ancient pyramid.	(phrase)	
3. ^by^ ~~The~~ Maya Indians built ~~El Castillo~~ between 300 and 900 C.E.	(phrase)	
4. ~~The pyramid~~ ^which^ is located in the ruins of the Mayan city of Chichen Itza.	(dependent clause)	The pyramid, which is located in the ruins of the Mayan city of Chichen Itza on the Yucatan Peninsula of Mexico, was used for religious ceremonies.
5. ~~Chichen Itza is located~~ on the Yucatan Peninsula.	(phrase)	
6. ~~The portion of the Yucatan Peninsula that contains Chichen Itza is in~~ ^of^ Mexico.	(phrase)	
7. The pyramid was used for religious ceremonies.	(main clause)	
8. El Castillo was dedicated to Kulkulcan.	(main clause)	El Castillo was dedicated to Kulkulcan, who was a powerful god of creation and transformation.
9. ~~Kulkulcan~~ ^who^ was a powerful god of creation and transformation.	(dependent clause)	

10. ~~The pyramid has~~ four   (adjective)   On each of the pyramid's
    ~~sides.~~   four sides is a staircase.

11. On each of the sides is   (main clause)
    a staircase.

12. At the base of the stair- (main clause)   At the base of the stair-
    cases are serpents'   cases are serpents' heads
    heads.   that point to natural
                                                      wells, where human
13. ~~The serpents' heads~~   (dependent clause)   bones and jewelry, evi-
    that ∧ point to natural wells.   dence of human sacrifices
                                                      to Kulkulcan, have been
14. ~~H~~uman bones and jew-   (dependent clause)   found.
    where elry have been found
    ~~in these wells~~

15. ~~Human bones and jew-~~   (phrase)
    ~~elry are~~ evidence of
    human sacrifices.

16. ~~The sacrifices were~~   (phrase)
    ~~made~~ to Kulkulcan.

    But that
17. ∧El Castillo was also   (main clause)   But that El Castillo was
    used as an astronomi-   also used as an astro-
    cal observatory.   nomical observatory is
    is clear from the fact that   clear from the fact that
18. ~~E~~ach staircase has   (dependent clause)   each staircase has ninety-
    ∧ninety-one steps.   one steps.

19. The four staircases of   (main clause)   The four staircases of
    ninety-one steps plus   ninety-one steps plus the
    the top platform equal   top platform equal 365
    365 steps.   steps, reflecting the num-
                                                       ber of days in a solar
20. ~~This number of steps~~   (phrase)   year and demonstrating
         ing   the Mayas' advanced un-
    reflect∧the number of   derstanding of astronomy.
    days in a solar year.

                 and
21. ~~The pyramid~~ ∧demon-   (phase)
             ing
    strate∧the Mayas' ad-
    vanced understanding
    of astronomy.

   (1) El Castillo, an ancient pyramid built by the Maya Indians between 300
and 900 C.E., is a paradoxical marvel of the Western Hemisphere. (2) The
pyramid, which is located in the ruins of the Mayan city of Chichen Itza on the
Yucatan Peninsula of Mexico, was used for religious ceremonies. (3) El Castillo
was dedicated to Kulkulkan, who was a powerful god of creation and transformation. (4) On each of the pyramid's four sides is a staircase. (5) At the base
of the staircases are serpents' heads that point to natural wells, where human
bones and jewelry, evidence of human sacrifices to Kulkulkan, have been found.
(6) But that El Castillo was also used as an astronomical observatory is clear

from the fact that each staircase has ninety-one steps. (7) The four staircases of ninety-one steps plus the top platform equal 365 steps, reflecting the number of days in a solar year and demonstrating the Mayas' advanced understanding of astronomy.

Obviously, this paragraph is clearer than its original version. In addition, the way in which these statements are linked emphasizes the relative importance of the ideas in each as they relate to the controlling idea of the paragraph. For instance, the fact that El Castillo was used for religious ceremonies is the most important idea to emerge from the original sentences numbered 4–7. Therefore it becomes the main clause of sentence 2 in the new paragraph. The details about location contained in sentences 4–6 are not as important to the controlling idea of the paragraph and are therefore subordinated in that revised sentence.

The point of this discussion is, of course, that the original sentences, when combined, not only retain their original meaning but also take their appropriate places in the presentation of ideas in the paragraph—they are emphasized or subordinated through the way in which they are combined. As a result of similar combinations of the other sentences in the original paragraph, the final sentences in the revised paragraph are less monotonous, and the ideas are more clearly presented.

A Word of Caution: Don't make the mistake of thinking that a paragraph is coherent only when its sentences are long and complicated. A series of lengthy sentences with burdensome constructions can be just as difficult to read as too many short and choppy sentences. Lengthy sentences are meaningful only when their length and structure add clarity to the ideas that they are uniting. Nevertheless, you may find it useful to look carefully at your paragraphs and see whether you write short, choppy sentences again and again. If you do, then chances are that you can improve your paragraphs by combining some of the sentences to indicate the relationships among your ideas.

▪ SUMMARY

1. By combining brief, simple sentences in longer, more developed sentences, you can render your paragraph more coherent and less choppy.

2. Longer, more developed sentences can more clearly establish the relationships among the facts and ideas in your sentences by emphasizing important points and subordinating less important points.

3. Do not, however, think that a paragraph is coherent only when its sentences are long and complicated: sentence length should reflect the relationships among the ideas being presented.

■ EXERCISES

I. Combine the following groups of sentences into one or more sentences that better express the relationship between the ideas in the original sentences.

MODEL:

    A. The ball was hit like a bullet.
    B. It whizzed by the player's outstretched racket and bounced out of bounds.

Combination: Hit like a bullet, the ball whizzed by the outstretched racket and bounced out of bounds.

1. A. The tourists crowded into the bars.
    B. They were disappointed.
    C. And they were also thirsty.
    D. The bars offered relief from the beach.
    E. They were cool.
    F. They were dark.

2. A. In the lodge, the fire thaws the skiers.
    B. The fire is hot.
    C. The fire blazes.
    D. As a result, the thawing is quick.
    E. Next to the fire, an ex-skier props his cast.
    F. The propped-up cast is uncomfortable for the skier.
    G. The fire is crackling.

3. A. In the morning, the beginners appear for lessons.
    B. It's early.
    C. The beginners are quite excited.
    D. The beginners are also quite awkward.
    E. Racquetball is an easy game to play.
    F. Racquetball is a difficult game to master.
    G. Certain skills distinguish a pro from an amateur.
    H. These skills include the pro's ability to judge angles.
    I. Also included among the pro's skills is the ability to place shots.
    J. In addition, the pro has to be able to serve effectively.
    K. The novice player often does not anticipate the ball's angle off the wall.
    L. The novice player wastes much energy by running to catch up with the ball that he missed.

4. A. Watching television is shared by young and old.
    B. Watching television is America's favorite pastime.
    C. Many programs reflect the lifestyle of Americans today.
    D. These programs are shown on television.
    E. They also reflect Americans' interests.
    F. And they reflect the current state of American ethics.
    G. There are shows such as *Getting Fit* and *In Motion*.
    H. These television shows are targeted at people.
    I. These people are into fitness.
    J. They also like to mingle viewing and exercise.

5. A. Tornadoes are found in severe thunderstorms.
    B. Tornadoes are intense low pressure areas.

C. Tornadoes are only a few hundred feet in diameter.

D. Measuring devices are broken when tornadoes hit them.

E. The measuring devices cannot measure the speed of the winds in tornadoes.

F. The tornado first touches down on a mountain top.

G. In such a situation, the tornado may skip along the mountain peaks.

H. And the tornado will leave the valleys in between untouched.

I. A tornado leaves behind a trail of destruction.

J. The trail is also of devastation.

K. Houses are leveled.

L. Buildings are torn to shreds.

M. Some trees are uprooted.

N. Other trees are blown down.

O. People are killed and injured.

II. In each of the following paragraphs, too many sentences are of similar length and structure. Collaborate with a classmate to rewrite at least one paragraph using sentence combining to make the paragraph clearer and easier to follow.

A. Blood pressure is a force. This force is the flow of blood against the walls of the arteries. The pumping action of the heart creates this force. The pressure of the blood rises with each contraction of the heart. The pressure of the blood then falls as the heart relaxes. The blood goes throughout the body. The blood goes by way of a system. This system is a system of vessels. These vessels eventually return the blood to the heart. The movement of blood is rapid. A drop of blood usually requires less than one minute to complete a trip. This trip is from and to the heart.

B. In a span of time European newcomers to the United States uprooted more than half a million Indians. The time span was three hundred years (1600–1900). The European newcomers also conquered the Indians. The Indians were friendly to the newcomers. Of course, this friendliness was naive. The newcomers' power was not foreseen by the Indians. The threat of the newcomers was also not foreseen. However, soon something became apparent. It became apparent that too many whites were beginning to arrive. Friction developed. This friction developed over land. Gradually hatred and fear of Indians grew up among the settlers. These settlers regarded the Indians as savages. The United States won its independence in 1783. By this time most of the tribes along the Atlantic coast had been dispossessed of their land.

C. Land is one of the best investments that people can make. They can do whatever they choose with land. They can build the house of their dreams on it. They can use the land as a weekend camping resort. They can cultivate the land. They can landscape it. A piece of land can be a place where the owners can put down roots. It can be "home." They can relax on their own land. They can do almost anything there without fear of reprisal. The value of land is on the rise. Land bought today may double in value in the next ten years. Land is an investment that can satisfy everyone. It is an investment people should never pass up.

D. A method of testing for fetal abnormalities has been developed. This method is called transabdominal amniocentesis. This method involves drawing amniotic fluid from the mother. Amniotic fluid is located in the uterus. The fluid is drawn for study. Requirements for the process are antiseptic solution, sterile towels, syringe and needle, and a four-inch spinal needle. The syringe and first needle are needed for inserting the local anesthetic. The four-inch spinal needle is employed to penetrate the walls of the uterine cavity. First of all, the uterus is probed. The unobstructed area anterior to the fetal shoulder is located. The selected site for needle entry is then prepared. The site is prepared with antiseptic solution. A local anesthetic may be introduced at this point. It is not always needed. The puncture needle is inserted into the cavity. From the cavity, fluid is removed. This fluid is tested. The procedure takes only a short time. It tells whether the fetus is normal or has any congenital abnormalities.

III. Select a paragraph from those you have collected in your portfolio. Could the ideas in that paragraph be more clearly connected through sentence combining? If so, combine the sentences, emphasizing the most important ideas and subordinating those ideas of lesser importance. Remember that a long sentence is not always preferable to a short one, particularly when the sentence's relationship to the other sentences in the paragraph is already clear.

GRAMMATICAL CONSISTENCY

Ordering support in a natural and effective way, providing devices of transition, and combining choppy sentences into developed sentences with clear connections between thoughts are all important means for achieving coherence. Once these techniques have been used, the writer can go one step further to ensure that a paragraph is coherent. The writer can check for grammatical consistency or, more specifically, consistent verb tense and consistent pronoun person.

Consistent Verb Tense

Briefly stated, *tense* means time. When you select a verb tense for a single sentence, you consider when the action or state of being that is expressed in the sentence occurs—in the past, in the present, or in the future. Similarly, when you select a predominant verb tense for a paragraph, you consider at what point in time a series of events or ideas exists.

There are three major tenses in English:

TENSE	EXAMPLE
1. Present	I look
2. Past	I looked
3. Future	I will look

If you begin a paragraph in one tense, you should stick to that tense throughout the paragraph. You can make exceptions, though, when a given sentence logically requires the use of another tense. For instance, when you recount a past experience as support for a topic sentence, shifting from the present tense into past tense is natural and not disturbing to your reader. Often, however, shifts in verb tense are unnecessary, and you will find that your writing is smoother and more coherent when you remain in one tense. The paragraph below, for instance, shifts back and forth unnecessarily between present, past, and future:

PRESENT	Starting college sometimes *results* in a quick weight gain for beginning students. One explanation for this
PRESENT	rapid gain in weight *is* the pressure new students *have*
PRESENT (BOTH)	*to deal* with. College students *feel* pressure mainly be-
FUTURE	cause so much more *will be expected* of them as far
PRESENT	as studies and grades *are* concerned. Such pressure
FUTURE, PRESENT	*will make* students nervous, and, as a result, they *eat*
PRESENT	more food. Social pressure also *plays* an important role in weight gain, since going to parties to make
FUTURE	friends *will increase* their consumption of beer, soda,
PRESENT	and snack foods. Another reason for weight gain *is* the quality and selection of food in the cafeteria. Many
FUTURE	students *will eat* more starches and desserts in the
PAST (BOTH)	cafeteria than they *did* when they *were* at home. In addition to pressure and cafeteria food, lack of exercise
PRESENT	*contributes* to weight gain. Instead of developing a
FUTURE	regular exercise program, the students *will stay* in their
FUTURE	rooms and talk or *will sit* in the library and study. As
PRESENT (ALL)	a result, they *do* not *burn* off the extra calories they
PRESENT	*take* in.

Had the writer stuck to the present tense instead of weaving back and forth between the present and the future, this paragraph would have been much easier to follow.

Note how much smoother and more effective the same paragraph is when a consistent tense (present) is maintained:

Starting college sometimes results in a quick weight gain for beginning students. One explanation for this rapid gain in weight is the pressure new students have to deal with. College students feel pressure mainly because so much more is expected of them as far as studies and grades are concerned. Such pressure makes students nervous, and, as a result, they eat more food. Social pressure also plays an important role in weight gain, since going to parties to make friends increases their consumption of beer, soda, and snack foods. Another reason for weight gain is the quality and selection of food in the cafeteria. Many students eat more starches and desserts in the cafeteria than they did when they were at home. In addition to pressure and cafeteria food, lack of exercise contributes to weight gain. Instead of developing a regular exercise program, the students stay in their rooms and talk or sit in the library and study. As a result, they do not burn off the extra calories they take in.

All the verbs except two in this paragraph are in the present tense. The exceptions are *did* and *were* in the sentence, "Many students eat more starches and desserts in the cafeteria than they did when they were at home." These two verbs *should* logically be in the past tense because the activity they describe occurred *before* the events on which the paragraph focuses— that is, before the students started attending college. In the revised paragraph the verb tenses are both consistent and logical and therefore do not disrupt the flow of ideas and the paragraph's coherence.

■ SUMMARY

1. There are three major tenses in English: present, past, and future.

2. If you begin writing in one tense, stick to that tense throughout your paragraph unless a given context logically requires the use of a different tense.

3. Illogical and unnecessary shifts in verb tense within a paragraph disrupt the flow of ideas and detract from the paragraph's coherence.

■ EXERCISES

I. Make the following paragraph more coherent by eliminating unnecessary shifts in verb tense. For every verb that is in an inappropriate tense, indicate the verb form that would be appropriate.

A. Driving erratically is a characteristic of some drivers. They weave all over the road as if unaware of their actions. On a four-lane road, these drivers will usually drive in two lanes because they are unable to stay in one. On a two-lane road, on the other hand, they drive down the center of the road, not only because they are unable to stay in one lane, but also because they were afraid of hitting the curb at the side of the road. When a car approaches from the opposite direction, they move into their own lane slowly, scaring the other driver half to death. Therefore, careful drivers should be on the alert for erratic drivers who will not always stay in the proper lane.

II. With a classmate, collaborate to make the following paragraph more coherent by eliminating unnecessary shifts in verb tense. For every verb that is in an inappropriate tense, indicate the verb form that would be appropriate.

A. After living in a women's dorm for a little more than one semester, I have noticed that when women come to college they immediately become fanatics. No matter what they looked like, fat or thin, the calorie count of every food item around campus became imprinted on their brains. I am not sure why this fanaticism develops. One possible reason was that living with so many other women made one realize that her own figure might have been less than perfect. Another strong possibility is that calorie counting was an activity that everybody did. Whatever the reason, however, fanaticism about dieting is apparent in every women's dorm on campus.

III. Check back through the paragraphs that you have assembled in your portfolio. Do you, overall, tend to stick to one verb tense when you write? Can you find a paragraph in which you have shifted tense? If so, was the shift supportable? If not, correct the paragraph so that the verb tense is consistent.

Consistent Pronoun Person

When you are writing, you should also be consistent in the *person* of the pronouns you use (see p. 122). You may choose, for example, to use the *first-person* pronouns *I* and *we,* or you may prefer to use the *third-person* pronouns *he, she, it, one,* and *they.* On some occasions, you may find it appropriate to use *you,* the *second-person* pronoun. But whatever pronoun person you choose, you should use it consistently throughout your paragraph.

Whether you use first-person pronouns or third-person pronouns depends, in large measure, on the kind of feeling you wish to generate in your writing. If you wish to create a personal tone, the first-person pronouns *I* and *we* are appropriate, for they convey to the reader the feeling that you, the writer, are speaking for and about yourself. If, on the other hand, you prefer to remain more detached in your presentation of facts and ideas, you should use third-person pronouns because they create distance between you and your audience and imply that you are writing from an objective stance. Because expository paragraphs are paragraphs that *explain,* they are usually written in the third person.

The pronoun *you* is used less frequently in expository writing than the first-person and third-person pronouns. It is reserved primarily for instances where the writer is speaking to a clearly defined audience. Process analysis paragraphs that give instructions, like many of the paragraphs addressed to students in this book, are often written with a direct "you."

The main point to remember about the use of pronouns, however, is that you should remain consistent in the person of your pronouns throughout each paragraph. Mixing the persons of the pronouns in a paragraph, unless there is a clear-cut reason for doing so, usually results in awkward shifts in viewpoint that can destroy the coherence of the paragraph.

Consider, for instance, the following paragraph:

> Everywhere *one* goes and everywhere *one* looks, there are different kinds of signs. Motorists rely on road signs to know when to "stop," "yield," and "detour." Lines on the road let *them* know when it is safe to pass, and speed limit signs tell *them* how fast *they* are permitted to travel. Some signs give *us* helpful information that *we* need to carry out *our* daily activities safely and efficiently. Signs in parks and zoos, for example, tell *us* to "keep off the grass" and ask that *we* "don't feed the animals," and signs where construction is taking place warn *us* about "wet paint" and "falling debris." Signs in airports and shopping centers tell passers-by where *they* can "enter" and "exit" buildings and let *them* know where *they* are allowed to smoke and where *they* are not allowed to smoke. Signs are also an extremely effective way to advertise. Many kinds of businesses

advertise their products and services on signs. America is simply cluttered with signs—but how could *we* possibly survive without them?

This paragraph begins with sentences containing both singular and plural third-person pronouns *(one, them, they)*, abruptly shifts, toward the middle, to sentences containing first-person pronouns *(us, we, our)*, and then moves back and forth between third- and first-person pronouns. The result is that the writer jars the perspective of the reader through a series of abrupt shifts in point of view.

Had the writer been consistent in the person of the pronouns he used, as in the following revised version of the paragraph, he would have maintained a consistent point of view throughout:

> Everywhere people go and everywhere *they* look, there are different kinds of signs. Motorists rely on road signs to know when to "stop," "yield," and "detour." Lines on the road let them know when it is safe to pass, and speed limit signs tell *them* how fast they are permitted to travel. Some signs provide helpful information that makes it easier for people to carry out *their* activities safely and efficiently. Signs in parks and zoos, for example, ask that *they* "keep off the grass" and "don't feed the animals," and signs where construction is taking place warn about the hazards of "wet paint" and "falling debris." Signs in airports and shopping centers tell passers-by where they can "enter" and "exit" buildings and let them know where *they* are allowed to smoke and where they are not allowed to smoke. Signs also are an extremely effective way to advertise. Many kinds of businesses use signs to advertise their products and services. America is simply cluttered with signs, but much of the information *they* give makes life safer and simpler for everyone.

In this revised version, the writer has consistently used third-person pronouns, and his paragraph is clearer and more coherent as a result.

One major problem that students frequently encounter when they write paragraphs is the incorrect use of the pronoun *you.* As mentioned earlier in this section, the pronoun *you* should be used only when the writer is speaking directly to a clearly defined audience. Students often make the mistake of using *you* without a definite audience in mind, as in the statement, "*You* have to suffer to be beautiful." They do so because they are accustomed to using the "indefinite *you*," as it is called, in their speech, where informal and colloquial patterns of pronoun usage are permissible. In written language, however, where clarity of expression is necessary, frequent use of the indefinite *you* creates an overly informal tone and sometimes results in confusion for the reader. The more precise third-person pronouns—*he, they she,* or even the formal-sounding *one*—are usually more appropriate.

The use of the indefinite *you* becomes an especially annoying problem in paragraphs such as the following, in which the writer alternates between *you* and the third-person pronouns *they, their,* and *them:*

Living on campus is a learning experience. Not only do students grow mentally, but *you* also learn to be independent. Many young people fear moving away from home; *they* fear facing the world alone. But as a result of *their* experiences on campus, *they* become more self-assured. For instance, on campus *you* have to do everything for *yourself,* from laundry to cleaning. And students must decide how much time to devote to studies and how much time to devote to social activities. A party invitation for the night before an exam is a test of *your* acquired self-discipline; turning such invitations down demonstrates that *you* have learned a great deal from *your* experiences on campus. Finally, the greatest learning experience comes from the exposure students gain in the dormitory setting to people from different backgrounds. Tolerance, flexibility, and other traits that will aid *them* in the adult world are generally learned by students who successfully adjust to living on campus.

By shifting from the use of third-person pronouns to the use of the indefinite *you* in observations such as "on campus you have to do everything for yourself," the writer of this paragraph creates on inconsistency in tone and a confusion in point of view. The focus of the paragraph is on "young people" and "students," which are most appropriately referred to as "they." When the pronoun "you" suddenly appears, the reader wonders to whom it refers: students? the reader? people in general? While *you* is often used in conversation as a substitute for *people in general,* it should not be used in this way in expository writing. And it should never be used interchangeably with third-person pronouns in the same paragraph.

Notice how much more clearly the same paragraph reads when the writer sticks to third-person pronouns throughout the paragraph:

Living on campus is a learning experience. Not only do students grow mentally, but *they* also learn to be independent. Many young people fear moving away from home; *they* fear facing the world alone. But as a result of *their* experiences on campus, *they* become more self-assured. For instance, on campus *they* have to do everything for *themselves,* from laundry to cleaning. And students must decide how much time to devote to studies and how much time to devote to social activities. A party invitation for the night before an exam is a test of *their* acquired self-discipline; turning such invitations down demonstrates that *they* have learned a great deal from *their* experiences on campus. Finally, the greatest learning experience comes from the exposure students gain in the dormitory setting to people from different backgrounds. Tolerance, flexibility, and other traits that will aid *them* in the adult world are generally learned by students who successfully adjust to living on campus.

With the indefinite *you* removed and the person of the pronouns made consistent, the sentences and ideas in this paragraph flow more smoothly, and the paragraph gains coherence.

Remember, then, never use the pronoun *you* in your writing unless you have a definite audience in mind, and never use the indefinite *you* in paragraphs in which third-person pronouns are more appropriate.

■ SUMMARY

1. Another way to ensure that your paragraphs are coherent is to maintain consistency in the person of the pronouns that you use.

2. Whether you use first-person pronouns or third-person pronouns largely depends on the tone you wish to adopt in a paragraph. First-person pronouns are informal and personal; third-person pronouns are more distant and objective. Most expository paragraphs are written in the third person.

3. In expository writing, the pronoun *you* is used less frequently than first- and third-person pronouns and is reserved primarily for instances where the writer is speaking to a clearly defined audience.

4. Remain consistent in the person of the pronouns throughout a paragraph. Mixing the persons of the pronouns in a single paragraph, unless there is a clear-cut reason for doing so, results in awkward shifts in perspective that can destroy the coherence of the paragraph.

5. Avoid using the indefinite *you*. Although it may be appropriate in conversations, in written paragraphs the indefinite *you* creates vagueness and an overly casual tone.

■ EXERCISES

1. Read each of the following paragraphs carefully. Identify any pronouns that are improperly used and indicate the correct pronoun.

   A. Final exams are psychologically difficult for students and, with few exceptions, students hate them. They know that finals can make or break your grade, regardless of how well you have done previously in the semester. So students usually cram relentlessly; they bury themselves in notes, texts, and supplementary readings with the hope that something will sink in. Soon, though, the pressure begins taking its toll: you may become discouraged, frustrated, short-tempered, and fatigued. Regardless of whether a student has one or all of these symptoms, he is sure to have the disease: "finalitis."

   B. I enjoy using my creative abilities when I teach elementary school. I prefer making my own teaching materials, such as educational games, learning centers, drill cards, and exercises. So when funds for professionally made textbooks and workbooks are low and materials are difficult to obtain, my students never suffer. And you find that your materials are better anyway. I also enjoy creating my own bulletin-board materials. Why should you go out and buy snowflakes or Thanksgiving scenes or letters made by a machine when you can make them yourself? My students appreciate the items on the bulletin board more when they realize the effort that I have put into them. And I find that my creative efforts help students to discover the rewards of using their own creative abilities. Can you imagine the satisfaction they feel when they see something they made—a map or a picture—up on the bulletin board? No professionally made materials can instill that sense of accomplishment and pride.

II. Work with a classmate to identify any pronouns that are improperly used in the following paragraphs. Then supply the correct pronouns.

A. Cashiers are expected to handle any situation that may arise in the course of a day's work without becoming disgruntled or unpleasant. For instance, when you buy something, you expect it to be in working order, and if it is not, you become upset. Generally, when the disappointed buyer returns a broken item, he takes out his feelings on the first person he sees. And that person is usually the cashier. Sometimes the dissatisfied customer can be violent, cursing loudly and even threatening physical harm if his demands are not immediately met. You must keep your cool through it all and wait until the emotion has subsided; then you can deal with the problem in an efficient and appropriate fashion. After the merchandise has been returned and a refund has been made, the customer feels embarrassed. All of the apologies in the world, however, cannot make the job of a cashier any easier.

B. A home garden offers an inexpensive and nutritious alternative to paying exorbitant prices for supermarket produce. Green beans, for instance, cost as much as a dollar a pound in the supermarket, but you can grow a year's supply of beans on a small plot of land for only a few cents and a little effort. Apples and oranges, too, can be expensive, especially during off-season months. But if the climate is right, you can plant a fruit tree in your backyard, store the fruit in a cellar or garage, and enjoy fresh fruit all year round at a fraction of the price you would pay for it in a grocery store. In addition to beans and fruit, you can grow tomatoes, squash, peas, potatoes, beets, lettuce, and other types of produce in your garden. The savings to your pocketbook can prove phenomenal: if properly planted and tended, a ten-foot-square plot of land can produce several hundred dollars' worth of produce.

III. Select a paragraph from your portfolio. Then underline all of the pronouns in that paragraph. Upon examining the pronoun choices you have included in the paragraph, determine whether the pronoun person is consistent. If not, locate the inconsistent pronouns and replace them with choices that aid the coherence of the paragraph.

7

FROM PARAGRAPH
TO ESSAY

Thus far you have learned how to plan, unify, develop, organize, and order paragraphs. Of course, single, isolated paragraphs are not the most common form in which written work appears. But because they do serve as building blocks for longer forms of writing, learning how to structure paragraphs effectively represents an important step in mastering the longer forms.

This chapter will teach you how to apply to the short essay the principles you have learned about writing paragraphs. The paragraph is, in essence, an essay in miniature, and what you have learned about concepts like unity and development will be useful to you as you begin to write essays.

THE 1-3-1 ESSAY

One of the most commonly assigned forms of the essay consists of five paragraphs: an *introduction,* three *body paragraphs,* and a *conclusion.* Because of its five-paragraph structure, this type of essay is often called the 1-3-1 essay. The first paragraph in the 1-3-1 essay, the introduction, states the writer's *thesis* in a *thesis sentence* and indicates how the writer will go about developing this thesis. The thesis sentence is the most important sentence in an essay. Like the topic sentence of a paragraph, it expresses a controlling idea (the thesis), which the rest of the essay develops and supports. The three paragraphs that follow the introduction are the body of the essay. Together these paragraphs support and develop the thesis of the essay, in much the same way that the primary supports in a paragraph back up the controlling idea of the paragraph. The final paragraph in the 1-3-1 essay is the conclusion. In it the writer ties together the thoughts presented in the essay and brings the work to a close.

The following essay illustrates the 1-3-1 form:

THESIS (ITALICIZED)

When the famous magician Harry Houdini performed one of his fantastic escape acts, members of the audience invariably experienced a thrill. *Houdini, a successful showman, knew how to captivate his spectators.* He could excite them with the danger and suspense of his acts, amuse them with unexpected touches of humor, or stimulate their curiosity.

BODY PARAGRAPH 1

A performance of the "metal trunk act," for example, was certain to convey a sense of danger and suspense to Houdini's onlookers. The act began on a shaky, abandoned suspension bridge at least one hundred feet above a raging river. Hundreds of people gathered along the banks of the river and listened to an announcer standing at the edge of the bridge. Shouting into a megaphone, the announcer described the upcoming act in detail, always emphasizing the element of danger the stunt entailed. Following the announcer's introduction, four members of Houdini's company fitted the artist into a straitjacket, wrapped him in chains, and placed him in an airtight metal trunk. As the crew shut the trunk lid, members of the audience could be heard to murmur, "I can't believe it" and "He'll surely be killed." The crew then took the trunk to the edge of the bridge and hurled it into the swirling water. For ten suspenseful minutes the audience anxiously waited— and then suddenly Houdini rose to the surface of the water, waving his arms victoriously as two members of his company pulled him from the water into a boat.

BODY PARAGRAPH 2

While tricks like the "metal trunk act" were intended to create an element of danger, other acts appealed to the audience's sense of humor. The "swinging straitjacket act" was one of these humorous stunts. When the curtain opened, members of the audience began to laugh as they viewed the unexpected sight on the stage. Houdini was hanging upside down above a tankful of mud, suspended from a rope that extended to the ceiling and through a pulley back down to the stage. The presence of a stagehand holding the end of the rope was particularly amusing, for the spectators knew that if the stagehand released the rope Houdini would fall into the slimy mud below. An announcer soon appeared on stage to warn the audience that the stagehand would begin to lower the rope slowly—but that if Houdini could escape from the confines of the straitjacket within thirty seconds, he would be spared the dunk in the mud. As Houdini began to disengage himself from the straitjacket, the stagehand gradually lowered the rope. Inches before reaching the mud, Houdini freed himself from his bonds, smiled at his audience, and shouted, "I made it!" Then, to the surprise of everyone in the audience, the stagehand seemed to let go of the rope accidentally, and Houdini took his mud bath after all. This was a delightful finishing touch, and the crowd responded with a great deal of laughter.

BODY PARAGRAPH 3

Stunts like the "glass case act," finally, captivated onlookers by arousing their curiosity. At the beginning of the act, the curtain opened on a stage that was completely empty except for a large glass case filled almost to the brim with water. Members of the audience, not receiving any explanation, stared at the large container for two long minutes. Their curiosity now aroused, they eagerly awaited the coming attraction. Suddenly, Houdini, wearing a bathing suit, walked across the stage. He stopped in front of the glass box and turned quickly to face the spectators, who seemed to be sitting on the edges of their seats as the announcer dramatically described the event that was about to take place. As soon as the announcer finished his introduction, two stagehands bound the escape artist from head to toe with chain and rope, raised him to the top of a stepladder that had been placed beside the glass box, and dropped him headfirst into the water. Curiosity quickly changed to feelings of danger and suspense as most of the onlookers jumped to their feet and some even ran to the edge of the stage. Meanwhile Houdini, during the self-imposed time limit of a minute and a half, struggled to free himself from the chain and rope. When he had accomplished the feat, he quickly swam to the surface to inhale a breath of fresh air and to receive the enthusiastic applause of the audience.

CONCLUSION

Houdini's performances were successful not only because of his amazing stunts but also because of his ingenious use of dramatic devices that kept his audiences enthralled. In some acts he created an atmosphere of suspense and danger that kept his spectators breathless. In other acts he included elements of humor that drew laughter and applause. And in still other acts he appealed to his spectators' sense of curiosity. These dramatic devices were effective in capturing the attention of his audience, holding it while the actual stunts were performed, and keeping Houdini in the spectators' minds even after the performance was over.

In order to clarify the structure of this essay on Houdini, we have diagramed it in Figure 7–1. As the diagram illustrates, the first paragraph of the essay contains the thesis sentence, "Houdini, a successful showman, knew how to captivate his spectators." The paragraph also indicates that the author will support the thesis sentence by giving examples of the ways in which Houdini captivated his audiences, namely through (1) *danger and suspense,* (2) *humor,* and (3) *curiosity.* The three paragraphs in the body of the essay take up these points one by one. The final paragraph brings the essay to a conclusion by restating, in different words, the thesis and the divisions used to support the thesis. Together these sections of the essay illustrate the 1-3-1 form: a *one-*paragraph introduction, *three* body paragraphs, and a *one-*paragraph conclusion.

You may feel, at first, that the 1-3-1 essay is a confining form, one that stifles creativity by putting restrictions on the writer. But keep in mind that there is no hard-and-fast rule that requires you, when writing an essay, to follow the 1-3-1 formula—to use three paragraphs for the body of your essay or, for that matter, only one paragraph for the introduction or conclusion. In fact, two well-developed paragraphs can often support a thesis sentence. And, of course, you may often find that you need more than three body

Figure 7–1

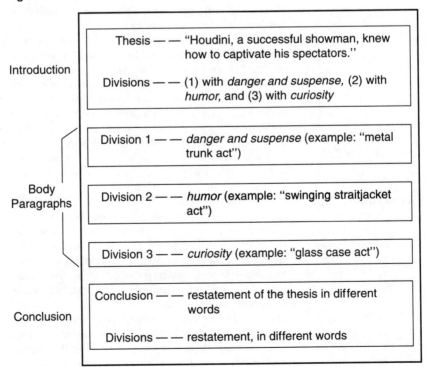

Introduction	Thesis — — "Houdini, a successful showman, knew how to captivate his spectators." Divisions — — (1) with *danger and suspense,* (2) with *humor,* and (3) with *curiosity*
Body Paragraphs	Division 1 — — *danger and suspense* (example: "metal trunk act")
	Division 2 — — *humor* (example: "swinging straitjacket act")
	Division 3 — — *curiosity* (example: "glass case act")
Conclusion	Conclusion — — restatement of the thesis in different words Divisions — — restatement, in different words

paragraphs to back up your thesis sentence. But the 1-3-1 formula, while it may seem mechanical, has the value of providing you with a skeletal structure upon which to construct an effectively developed short essay.

You may find it useful to keep in mind, too, that the primary purpose of much of the writing you do in college is simply to learn to write well—to communicate effectively—and to do so you must concentrate on acquiring a number of particular writing skills. Writing practice in one or more selected forms—the paragraph, the essay, the research paper, and so on—will provide you with the opportunity to gain these skills—skills that will serve you well no matter what type of writing you ultimately do, either for pleasure or on the job. Thus, learning the 1-3-1 essay is not an end in itself but rather a beginning, a way to start you on your way to becoming a self-confident, skillful writer.

■ SUMMARY

1. The "1-3-1" essay form consists of the following elements:
   a. An introductory paragraph stating the writer's thesis in a thesis sentence and indicating how the writer will develop this thesis.
   b. Three body paragraphs that support and develop the thesis sentence according to the divisions presented in the introductory paragraph.
   c. A concluding paragraph that ties together the thought presented in the essay and brings it to a close.
2. Because the 1-3-1 form provides the writer with a skeleton on which to construct an effectively developed short essay, mastering this form is an extremely useful way for students to learn how to write essays.

■ EXERCISE

1. Read the following essay carefully. As you will notice, it follows the 1-3-1 formula. On your own or with a small group of classmates, identify the thesis sentence and the three divisions that constitute the body of the essay. Then discuss how the final paragraph in the essay functions as a conclusion.

Suicide and Its Causes

Every year more than half a million people not only contemplate suicide but actually succeed in taking their own lives. This high suicide rate is influenced by a number of factors. Among them are psychological states, sociological conditions, and ineffective means of prevention. If we can learn to recognize these factors, we may become more successful at preventing suicide.

First, various psychological states may lead to suicide. One such state is depression, the most prevalent mental disorder in the world today. Depression itself is often caused by loneliness, loss of a loved one, or feelings of inadequacy. Individuals experiencing depression may be plagued by a sense of hopelessness and helplessness: they may feel that there is nothing they can do to make a real change for the better in their lives. Another psychological state that sometimes leads to suicide is intense guilt. People afflicted with such guilt sometimes believe that they have committed such unforgivable acts that they no longer deserve to be alive. A third mental state that often results in suicide—tension—may stem from a variety of causes. Pressure from deadlines, excessive work or family demands, or the unreasonable expectations that, for example, parents sometimes place on their children can produce such severe tension that some individuals are unable to cope with it. One source of tension especially noticeable these days is financial insecurity. In the face of the fluctuation of the stock market and devaluation of the dollar, even the rich are often overcome by anxiety and may end up taking their lives. The reason? The same that led to so many suicides during the Great Depression—fear of poverty.

Like economic insecurity, many psychological problems are rooted in sociological conditions. In fact, there are several sociological factors—including national or ethnic identity, race, sex, and age—that play a role in the majority of suicides. For instance, the suicide rate in certain societies is high because of ancient traditions that condone suicide as an honorable alternative to hardship. In the United States, recent studies have shown that suicide rates are increasing among minorities, particularly among blacks and Native Americans. There are also differences in suicide rates among men and women. Women lead men in the category of attempted suicides, but men are apparently more successful when they do try. Their success is probably due to their ability to get their hands on lethal weapons more easily. While few children commit suicide, the rate of attempts among adolescents is steadily rising. The breakdown of the family structure and the increased availability of drugs and alcohol are undoubtedly contributors to this trend. Among adults, suicide attempts at middle age are most common; at the midpoint in one's life, escape from past failures often seems attractive. Those who survive middle age, however, are less likely to attempt to take their lives. With age comes, it seems, the ability to accept the stresses and disappointments of life.

Finally, the last and perhaps most perplexing factor contributing to the high suicide rate is the ineffectiveness of present means of suicide prevention. For several reasons, suicides are difficult to prevent. First of all, in order for suicide to be prevented, the troubled individual must seek help. Many people never seek aid, and those who might be able to help never have the chance to do so. Even when distraught people contemplating suicide do call hotlines or friends, they may be so emotionally overwrought that they cannot tell the person on the phone where they are, even if they want to. And the problem does not end when one suicide attempt is prevented because there is no assurance that another attempt won't be made. In many cases, a person who has tried once to commit suicide eventually tries again. The problems that person sought to escape are still there when he or she returns to daily life, so it is not surprising when there is another attempt.

A better understanding of the main factors contributing to our high suicide rate, including psychological states, sociological factors, and ineffective means of prevention, is vitally necessary in our society. Perhaps as we become more aware of suicide as a growing problem and more knowledgeable about its contributing factors, we will be able to do more to prevent this wasteful tragedy.

WRITING THE ESSAY

There are two basic ways to go about writing a 1-3-1 expository essay. The first is to expand a general-to-specific paragraph of the kind that you have been writing into an essay. The second is the more direct procedure of simply writing an essay from scratch. In the remainder of this chapter we'll show you how to write essays using both methods.

Paragraph into Essay

As we pointed out at the start of this chapter, an expository paragraph—one that explains—is often, if it follows the patterns suggested in this text, an essay in miniature. Each of the paragraphs in the body of the essay supports the thesis sentence in the introductory paragraph in the same way that each of the primary supports in a paragraph backs up the topic sentence. To reshape an expository paragraph into an essay, you follow a relatively simple procedure involving *five* basic steps:

1. Make the topic sentence of the paragraph the thesis sentence of the essay. (The thesis sentence will appear in the introductory paragraph.)
2. Use each of the primary supports in the paragraph as the topic sentence of each of the body paragraphs in the essay.
3. Write the body paragraphs of the essay.
4. Write an introductory paragraph.
5. Write a concluding paragraph.

To understand how the procedure works, you may find it helpful to examine the diagram in Figure 7–2. As the diagram indicates, the topic sentence of the paragraph furnishes a basis for the thesis sentence in the introductory paragraph of the essay, and each of the primary supports in the original paragraph furnishes a topic sentence for a body paragraph in the essay. By completing the body paragraphs and then supplying an introductory paragraph and a concluding paragraph, the writer can construct an essay by expanding the ideas in the paragraph.

Consider, for example, the following paragraph as potential material for a 1-3-1 essay:

> After leaving the sports arena, many of today's athletes have excelled in other professions. Communications, for example, is one profession many athletes have found to be both lucrative and rewarding after their sports careers were finished. Frank Gifford, who was an All-American tailback for the University of Southern California football team and who played twelve years in the NFL, is now a major football announcer for ABC Sports. Similarly, Wayne Walker, a former All-Pro defensive linebacker for the Detroit Lions, works today as a local news reporter in Detroit, as does Johnny Morris, former receiver for the Chicago Bears, for a major Chicago network. A remarkable number of former

Figure 7–2

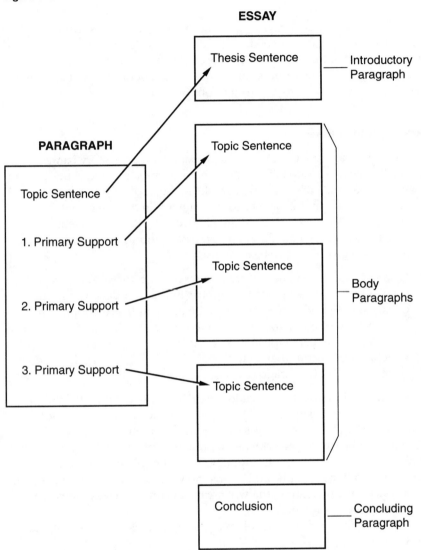

athletes have also achieved positions of prominence in politics and the related field of law. Two former athletes, Bill Bradley and Jack Kemp, have successfully run for seats in the United States Congress. Still another former athlete, Gerald R. Ford, attained this nation's highest political office when Richard Nixon resigned the presidency in 1974. More than any other field, however, business has attracted athletes seeking success after their careers in sports have ended. For instance, Don Shula, former NFL linebacker and the most successful coach in the history of professional football, is also a successful restaurateur in South Florida.

Likewise, Joe Black, after completing a successful career with the Brooklyn Dodgers, has served as vice-president of Greyhound, Inc., a major U.S. firm.

By following the steps for converting a paragraph into an essay, the writer can construct an essay from this paragraph on athletes.

Step 1: *Take the topic sentence from the paragraph and use it as the basis for the thesis sentence of the essay.* With slight modification, most topic sentences can function as thesis sentences because both topic sentences and thesis sentences introduce a topic, both make a statement about the topic, and both become the central focus of the writer's attention. They are, as we stated earlier in discussing paragraphs, a contract that the writer establishes with the reader. The difference between the topic sentence of a paragraph and the thesis of an essay is the amount of space the writer has available for making a point. In a paragraph, for example, the writer must drive home a controlling idea in a few hundred words or fewer, while in an essay the writer has several paragraphs in which to develop a thesis. Thus, in constructing an essay from the paragraph on athletes, the writer would begin by simply taking the topic sentence, "After leaving the sports arena, many of today's athletes have excelled in other professions," and using it in the introductory paragraph of the essay as the thesis sentence.

Step 2: *Take the primary supports in the paragraph and use each one as the topic sentence for each of the three body paragraphs in the essay.* If you find yourself with fewer than three primary supports and wish to remain within the 1-3-1 formula, you can construct an additional body-paragraph topic sentence that supports and develops the thesis sentence; if you have more than three primary supports, you can select the three supports that you feel will provide the most convincing back-up for the thesis sentence. In the paragraph on athletes, there are three points of primary support, each dealing with a different aspect of "other professions" former athletes have excelled in:

PRIMARY SUPPORT 1:	Communications, for example, is one profession many athletes have found to be both lucrative and rewarding after their sports careers were finished.
PRIMARY SUPPORT 2:	A remarkable number of former athletes have also achieved positions of prominence in politics and the related field of law.
PRIMARY SUPPORT 3:	More than any other field, however, business has attracted athletes seeking success after their careers in sports have ended.

In an essay on the successful careers of former athletes, these points of primary support will serve as the topic sentences for the body paragraphs.

Step 3: *Write a paragraph developing each point of primary support.* These three paragraphs will be the body paragraphs in the essay. To carry out this step, follow the procedure you learned for writing paragraphs: select primary supports with secondary supports, choose a suitable method of development, and organize your material to give the paragraph coherence.

In constructing the *primary* supports for the topic sentence of each body paragraph, you may find that you can use facts and ideas that served as *secondary* supports in the original paragraph. You may, however, have to furnish additional primary support—just as you may have to supply a topic sentence for one of the body paragraphs of the essay. In the first body paragraph of the essay you are about to read on former athletes, for instance, the writer uses two secondary supports from the original paragraph as primary supports: *Frank Gifford* and *Wayne Walker.* But the writer adds additional primary supports: *Pat Hayden, Kathy Johnson,* and *Howard K. Smith.* Moreover, the writer provides, for *secondary* support, some information that did not appear in the original paragraph. You will probably find, as the writer did, that because you can explore a topic further in the essay than you can in the paragraph, you'll want to supply more supporting material and revise some of your sentences to fit the essay format.

Finally, for the sake of overall coherence, it may often be necessary to add transitional material at the beginning of a body paragraph to smooth your reader's way between paragraphs—just as within a paragraph you use transitional devices to enable your reader to move easily from one idea to the next or from one sentence to the next. Always keep in mind, however, that the function of the body paragraphs is to support the thesis of the essay. Transitional devices that are too long or too elaborate may distract your reader from the essay's central idea and undermine the unity and coherence of the essay. A single transitional word or phrase is usually enough to prepare your reader for the topic sentence of the paragraph.

The author of the paragraph on athletes wrote the following three body paragraphs for her essay:

Body Paragraph 1:

TOPIC SENTENCE   *Communications is one profession many former athletes have found to be both lucrative and rewarding after their careers in sports were finished.* Frank Gifford, who was an All-American tailback for the University of Southern California football team and who played twelve years in the NFL, is now a major football announcer for ABC Sports. In addition, Mr. Gifford hosts other major sports events for the network, including the Olympics and the World Series. Similarly, Pat Hayden, who played six years with the Los Angeles Rams and who guided his team to the playoffs for three seasons, and Kathy Johnson, former United States Olympic gymnast, are both highly respected and successful professional sportscasters. A Rhodes Scholar while he attended the University of Southern California, Mr. Hayden now works as a major sports analyst for CBS. Specializing in women's sports events, Ms.

Johnson announces for ABC, where she frequently appears in commercials. Another sports star, Wayne Walker, former All-Pro defensive linebacker for the Detroit Lions, works today as a local news reporter in Detroit, as does Johnny Morris, former receiver for the Chicago Bears, for a major Chicago network. Finally, Howard K. Smith, a distinguished news reporter who has interviewed dignitaries around the world, was a star track and field performer during his college years at Purdue University.

Body Paragraph 2:
Transition

TOPIC SENTENCE (WITH TRANSITIONAL PHRASE)

  In addition, *a remarkable number of former athletes have achieved positions of prominence in politics and law.* Two former athletes, for instance, have served in the United States government. Once a star performer for the NBA's New York Knickerbockers, Bill Bradley is now a senator from the state of New Jersey. Likewise, Jack Kemp, former star NFL quarterback for the Buffalo Bills, ran successfully for Congress and was subsequently appointed Secretary of Housing and Urban Development. Many former athletes work for prestigious law firms and serve as either elected or appointed judges. Allan Page, who played professional football for fourteen years in the NFL, is now an associate with a Minneapolis law firm. Similarly, Fred "Duke" Slater, who played football in the Big Ten and was a professional from 1918 to 1931, was elected to the bench in Chicago in 1949 and remained a judge until his death in 1967. Moreover, one former athlete has attained this nation's highest political office. At one time a center for the football team at the University of Michigan, Gerald R. Ford became the thirty-eighth president of the United States when Richard Nixon resigned that office in 1974.

Body Paragraph 3:
Transition

TOPIC SENTENCE (WITH TRANSITIONAL WORD)

  But *more than any other field, business has attracted athletes seeking success after their careers in sports have ended.* Many former athletes, for example, have formed their own businesses. A former professional basketball star who retired from the NBA in 1978, Dave Bing founded a steel-processing plant in Detroit. Don Shula, former NFL linebacker and the most successful coach in the history of professional football, is also a successful restaurateur in South Florida. Other athletes have proven themselves successful in other types of roles in the business community. After completing a successful career with the Brooklyn Dodgers, Joe Black, for example, has served as vice president of Greyhound, Inc. Jim Lindsey, former Minnesota Vikings halfback, now heads one of the most successful real estate firms in northwest Arkansas. Furthermore, many former athletes have held important positions in the area of investment counseling. For example, Gale Sayers once an All-Pro running back in the NFL, has since achieved success as a stockbroker.

Each of these paragraphs develops its topic sentence in full. Body paragraphs 2 and 3 contain transitional words and phrases that lead the reader from the previous paragraph to the paragraph at hand. Together the paragraphs support the essay's thesis that "after leaving the sports arena, many of today's athletes have excelled in other professions."

Step 4: *Write an introductory paragraph for the essay.* Once you have completed the body paragraphs and furnished necessary transition, you are ready to write an introductory paragraph to the essay. In writing such a paragraph, keep in mind that the introduction to an essay should accomplish three things:

1. Capture the reader's interest.
2. State the thesis.
3. Introduce the divisions in the body paragraphs.

While there is no hard-and-fast rule to follow when you write an introductory paragraph, most introductions begin by attracting the reader's interest, *then* go on to state the thesis and introduce the divisions to be discussed in the body paragraphs.

The following diagram illustrates the structure which introductory paragraphs usually follow:

```
InterestInterestInterestInterest
InterestInterestInterestInterestInterest
InterestInterestInterestInterestInterest
InterestInterestInterestInterestInterest
Interest ThesisThesisThesisThesisThesis
ThesisThesisThesisThesisThesisThesis
ThesisThesis DivisionsDivisionsDivisions
DivisionsDivisionsDivisionsDivisions
```

How does a writer succeed in capturing the attention of a reader? Or put another way, how does a writer convince a reader that the essay to come will be informative, interesting, entertaining, or otherwise worth reading? There are a number of well-established devices a writer can use to stimulate reader interest. For the essay on Houdini, for instance, there are many possible "lead-ins," each involving a different interest-catching technique. The introduction of the essay, as it appears at the beginning of this chapter, employs *a simple, well-focused generalization:*

> When the famous magician Harry Houdini performed one of his fantastic escape acts, members of the audience invariably experienced a thrill. *Houdini, a successful showman, knew how to captivate his spectators.* He could excite them with the danger and suspense of his acts, amuse them with unexpected touches of humor, or stimulate their curiosity.

Other methods that could be used to introduce the Houdini essay are these:

1. PERSONAL TESTIMONY

Reading the biography of the great escape artist Harry Houdini has been an enlightening experience for me. Although the book has made me admire the Great Houdini and his amazing feats even more than I did before, it has shown me that only half of Houdini's performance was magic. The other half was showmanship. *Houdini, a successful showman, knew how to captivate his spectators.* He could excite them with the danger and suspense of his acts, amuse them with unexpected touches of humor, or stimulate their curiosity.

2. ANECDOTE

Harry Houdini, the great escape artist, never ran out of ways to attract the interest of the general public. Even the events surrounding his death demonstrate his flair for the dramatic. According to an often quoted story, Houdini, just before he died, told his wife that he would communicate with her from "the other side." From his death to just before her death in 1943, when she gave up trying to reach him, this promise kept his widow from fading to obscurity. It was this ability to stimulate the interest of the public that also served him well in life, particularly during his performances. *Houdini, a successful showman, knew how to captivate his spectators.* He could excite them with the danger and suspense of his acts, amuse them with unexpected touches of humor, or stimulate their curiosity.

3. FACTUAL DATA

Harry Houdini, the great escape artist, was born in 1874. There has been some controversy over where he was born. Some biographers argue Budapest, Hungary; others, however, support his claim of having been born in Appleton, Wisconsin. This controversy notwithstanding, Houdini's real name was Erich Weiss, and at an early age Erich demonstrated an uncanny grasp of the art of trapeze flying. As he grew older, he became fascinated with magic and with the fantastic tricks of such performers as the French magician Robert-Houdin, from whose name he later derived Houdini. It was from such magicians that he also gained his showmanship. *Houdini, a successful showman, knew how to captivate his spectators.* He could excite them with the danger and suspense of his acts, amuse them with unexpected touches of humor, or stimulate their curiosity.

4. QUOTATION

In his article on "conjuring" in the 1926 *Encyclopaedia Britannica,* the great master of escape Harry Houdini asserted that he owed his success to his "great physical strength and the fact that he [was] slightly bowlegged." But when one reads about the remarkable career of this amazing performer, one finds the man's showmanship more impressive than his athletic attributes. *Houdini, a successful showman, knew how to captivate his spectators.* He could excite them with the danger and suspense of his acts, amuse them with unexpected touches of humor, or stimulate their curiosity.

5. A COMBINATION OF DEVICES

Born in 1874, the great escape artist Harry Houdini lived in an age that, as a result of new advances in science, was fascinated with the unusual and inexplicable. The Great Houdini took advantage of his audiences' taste, performing seemingly impossible tasks and reaping their wonder and appreciation. If his audiences only had known that most of what they saw during a performance was easily accomplishable for a "slightly bowlegged" man of "great physical strength," they might not have been quite so impressed. *Houdini, however, was a successful showman who knew how to captivate his spectators.* He could excite them with the danger and suspense of his acts, amuse them with unexpected touches of humor, or stimulate their curiosity.

To introduce the essay on the careers of former athletes, any of the devices we've considered might serve as a means of gaining the reader's interest. In the following paragraph, for example, the writer attracts the reader's attention through a combination of generalization, quotation, and personal testimony:

INTEREST According to an ancient Roman proverb, a sound mind usually accompanies a sound body. Nonetheless, when we think of the word "athlete" today, all too often the term "dumb jock" also comes to mind. Dozens of contemporary athletes, however, have proven this label a myth. *After leaving the sports arena, many of today's athletes have excelled in other professions.* Communi-

THESIS DIVISIONS cations, politics, and business, for example, are just a few of the many highly competitive professions in which former college and professional athletes have succeeded after completing their sports careers.

Step 5: *Write a concluding paragraph for the essay.* Once you have completed the introduction, you should carefully reread the four paragraphs you have written and prepare to write a concluding paragraph that will accomplish the following:

1. Restate the thesis and divisions of the essay (in different words).
2. Bring the essay to an appropriate end, without digressing into any new issues.

In its most basic form, the concluding paragraph may consist of a brief summary of what has been said in the essay. At first you may find this approach the easiest to use. Such a concluding paragraph should simply restate the thesis and the divisions of the essay, using different wording from that used in the introductory paragraph. The essay on Houdini, for example, closes with this paragraph:

> Houdini's performances were successful not only because of his amazing stunts but also because of his ingenious use of dramatic devices that kept his audiences enthralled. In some acts he created an atmosphere of suspense and danger that kept his spectators breathless. In other acts he included elements of humor that drew laughter and applause. And in still other acts he appealed to his spectators' sense of curiosity. These dramatic devices were effective in capturing the attention of his audiences, holding it while the actual stunts were performed, and keeping Houdini in the spectators' minds even after the performance was over.

As you become more comfortable writing essays, you can vary the form of your concluding paragraphs. A concluding paragraph should always summarize your main ideas by restating the essay's thesis and divisions in different words. But in addition, you can use other techniques to bring your essay to a smooth and significant close. You can, for example:

1. Refer to a particular *fact, idea,* or *quotation* that you presented in the introduction as a means of tying the beginning and the end of your essay together:

   > Houdini was therefore not being totally candid when he asserted that he owed his success to his strength and bowleggedness. Certainly, he also owed a great deal of his wide acclaim to the fact that he was a splendid showman. As a performer, Houdini achieved great feats by exciting his audiences with the elements of danger and suspense, amusing them with humorous antics, and arousing their curiosity.

2. Make a *prediction* after you have restated the thesis and divisions:

   > . . . Had Houdini been just another escape artist, his name might soon have been forgotten. But because he added the qualities of a skillful showman to those of a daring performer, Houdini will probably always be remembered.

3. Make a *recommendation* after you have restated the thesis and divisions:

   > . . .When it comes to showmanship, a budding performer would do well to model his or her techniques after those of the Great Houdini.

In concluding your essay, you should also keep in mind that just as some devices for introducing a thesis sentence are more effective than others for a given topic and controlling idea, so too are some devices for concluding an essay more appropriate to a topic than others and hence more effective. In addition to bringing your essay to a close, you want to make your ending meaningful and appropriate. Try asking yourself questions—"What do we learn by knowing this information?" or "How should this information change our way of thinking about this subject?" or "If this information is true, what are its implications and what can be done about it?" Often these questions lead you to discover the best device for concluding your essay.

In an essay on spouse abuse—a disturbing topic—a recommendation on how to deal with this problem and perhaps prevent future incidents would probably be more meaningful and effective than simply echoing a quotation on domestic violence that you used to gain reader attention in the introductory paragraph. Rather than leaving the reader with a sense of hopelessness, you would close with suggestions of ways the reader could perhaps use the information in your essay to help recognize and deal with the national problem.

In short, the device that you use to close your essay, like the device or devices that you used to begin it, should always be appropriate to the topic and, if possible, should draw meaningful conclusions from the essay without bringing up any essentially new or unrelated issues.

As a conclusion to the essay on athletes, the following paragraph is effective because it restates the thesis and divisions presented in the introductory paragraph (p. 149) and also refers to the quotation and generalizations made at the beginning of that paragraph:

RESTATEMENT OF THESIS **RESTATEMENT OF DIVISIONS** **REFERENCE TO POINTS IN INTRODUCTION**	Clearly, then, the highly successful careers of many former athletes have demonstrated that athletics often attracts "brains" as well as "brawn." As broadcasters and news announcers for major television networks, as politicians, lawyers, and judges, and as leaders of the business community, former athletes have achieved positions of authority and respect. Ironically, we who are willing to pay our athletes thousands and even millions of dollars for entertaining and inspiring us are all too often at the same time willing to stereotype them as unintelligent or "dumb." The ancient Romans, however, held no such false stereotypes. For them a sound body was the sign of a sound mind.

As a result, the essay is brought to a logical and significant conclusion, and the reader is left with the feeling that the writer has accomplished what he set out to do.

Once you have completed the five steps, you have succeeded in constructing a 1-3-1 essay from a paragraph, and you are now ready to combine the parts. The complete essay would read as follows:

According to an ancient Roman proverb, a sound mind usually accompanies a sound body. Nonetheless, when we think of the word "athlete" today, all too often the term "dumb jock" sometimes comes to mind. Dozens of contemporary athletes, however, have proven this label a myth. After leaving the sports arena, many of today's athletes have excelled in other professions. Communications, politics, and business are just a few of the many highly competitive professions in which former college and professional athletes have succeeded after completing their sports careers.

Communications is one profession many former athletes have found to be both lucrative and rewarding after their careers in sports were finished. Frank

Gifford, who was an All-American tailback for the University of Southern California football team and who played twelve years in the NFL, is now a major football announcer for ABC Sports. In addition, Mr. Gifford hosts other major sports events for the network, including the Olympics and the World Series. Similarly, Pat Hayden, who played six years with the Los Angeles Rams and who guided his team to the playoffs for three seasons, and Kathy Johnson, former United States Olympic gymnast, are both highly respected and successful professional sportscasters. A Rhodes Scholar while he attended the University of Southern California, Mr. Hayden now works as a major sports analyst for CBS. Specializing in women's sports events, Ms. Johnson announces for ABC, where she frequently appears in commercials. Another sports star, Wayne Walker, former All-Pro defensive linebacker for the Detroit Lions, works today as a local news reporter in Detroit, as does Johnny Morris, former receiver for the Chicago Bears, for a major Chicago network. Finally, Howard K. Smith, a distinguished news reporter who has interviewed dignitaries around the world, was a star track and field performer during his college years at Purdue University.

In addition, a remarkable number of former athletes have achieved positions of prominence in politics and law. Two former athletes, for instance, have served in the United States government. Once a star performer for the NBA's New York Knickerbockers, Bill Bradley is now a senator from the state of New Jersey. Likewise, Jack Kemp, former star NFL quarterback for the Buffalo Bills, ran successfully for Congress and was subsequently appointed Secretary of Housing and Urban Development. Many former athletes work for prestigious law firms and serve as either elected or appointed judges. Allan Page, who played professional football for fourteen years in the NFL, is now an associate with a Minneapolis law firm. Similarly, Fred "Duke" Slater, who played football in the Big Ten and was a professional from 1918 to 1931, was elected to the bench in Chicago in 1949 and remained a judge until his death in 1967. Moreover, one former athlete has attained this nation's highest political office. At one time a center for the football team at the University of Michigan, Gerald R. Ford became the thirty-eighth president of the United States when Richard Nixon resigned that office in 1974.

But more than any other field, business has attracted athletes seeking success after their careers in sports have ended. Many former athletes, for example, have formed their own businesses. A former professional basketball star who retired from the NBA in 1978, Dave Bing founded a steel-processing plant in Detroit. Moreover, Don Shula, former NFL linebacker and the most successful coach in the history of professional football, is also a successful restaurateur in south Florida. Other athletes as well have proven themselves successful in other types of leadership roles in the business community. After completing a successful career with the Brooklyn Dodgers, Joe Black, for example, has served as vice-president of Greyhound, Inc. Jim Lindsey, former Minnesota Vikings halfback, now heads one of the most successful real estate firms in northwest Arkansas. Furthermore, many former athletes have held important positions in the area of investment counseling. For example, Gale Sayers, once an All-Pro running back in the NFL, has since achieved success as a stockbroker.

Clearly, then, the highly successful careers of many former athletes have demonstrated that athletics often attracts "brains" as well as "brawn." As broadcasters and news announcers for major television networks, as politicians, lawyers, and judges, and as leaders of the business community, former athletes have achieved positions of authority and respect. Ironically, we who are willing to pay our athletes thousands and even millions of dollars for entertaining and inspiring us, are all too often at the same time willing to stereotype them as unintelligent or "dumb." The ancient Romans, however, held no such false stereotypes. For them a sound body was the sign of a sound mind.

■ SUMMARY

1. There are two basic ways to go about writing 1-3-1 expository essays. The first is to expand a general-to-specific paragraph into an essay. The second is the more direct procedure of simply writing an essay from scratch.

2. To turn a paragraph into an essay, follow these five basic steps:
   a. Make the topic sentence of the paragraph the basis for the thesis sentence of the essay.
   b. Make the primary supports in the paragraph the topic sentences for the body paragraphs of the essay.
   c. Write the body paragraphs of the essay.
   d. Write an introductory paragraph for the essay.
   e. Write a concluding paragraph for the essay.

3. When turning a paragraph into an essay, you will find that the secondary supports in the original paragraph can often be used as primary supports in the body paragraphs of the essay.

4. The introductory paragraph of an essay should accomplish three objectives. It should (1) capture the reader's interest, (2) state the thesis of the essay, and (3) introduce the divisions in the body paragraphs of the essay.

5. There are several devices that you can use in an introductory paragraph to capture the interest of your reader. You may use (1) a personal testimony, (2) an anecdote, (3) a simple but well-focused generalization, (4) factual data, (5) a quotation, and (6) a combination of these devices.

6. The concluding paragraph of a 1-3-1 essay should accomplish two main objectives: It should (1) restate the thesis and the divisions of the essay using words different from those in the introductory paragraph and (2) bring the essay to an end smoothly, without digressing into any new issues.

7. There are several devices you can use to write effective concluding paragraphs for your essays. You can (1) refer to a fact, idea, or quotation that you presented in the introduction as a means of tying the beginning and conclusion of the essay together, (2) make a prediction after you have repeated the thesis and divisions, and (3) make a recommendation after you have repeated the thesis and divisions.

■ EXERCISES

1. Furnish an introductory paragraph and a concluding paragraph for the following three body paragraphs. To help you get started, we have provided the thesis

sentence. Once you have created your introduction and conclusion, share them with a classmate. Then have your partner critique your paragraphs using criteria from the previous section of the chapter. In the same way, provide feedback on your partner's introduction and conclusion.

THESIS SENTENCE: Winter temperatures need not be uncomfortable if one learns to dress properly.

BODY PARAGRAPH 1   Layering, or putting on two light garments instead of one heavy one, is the first way to dress properly for winter temperatures. It is not the *thickness* of a garment that keeps one warm but rather the garment's ability to trap air in its fibers; the air remains enclosed and is eventually warmed to the body's temperature. And layering garments on top of each other traps air between garments as well as within the garments themselves. Of course, some fibers trap more air than others, and garments made with such fibers naturally provide the best source of layering. Goose down, for example, is an excellent insulator because the feathers fluff up to two or three times their size, filling the spaces between them with warm air. Other effective insulators are duck down, polyester, wool, and cotton, in that order. Polyester and wool have the added advantage of providing insulation even when they are wet.

BODY PARAGRAPH 2   Wearing a hat and a vest is another way to protect against the cold. Most of the warm air in the body escapes through the top of the head and from the trunk (chest and abdomen). These areas of the body are vitally involved in maintaining warmth because the organs that they contain are the source of body heat. The extremities—legs, arms, toes, and fingers—do not produce heat themselves; they are warmed by the heat that circulates through the body. A protective hat and a vest prevent heat from escaping from the head and the trunk and thus enable the bloodstream to distribute more heat to the extremities.

BODY PARAGRAPH 3   If clothing is properly layered and one is wearing a hat and a vest, the best way to keep the extremities from feeling the cold is to keep them moving and to insulate them with gloves and socks. By moving the fingers and toes, one forces blood to circulate through them, and, as was noted, circulation keeps them warm. Wearing gloves and mittens should prevent the warmth of the blood from escaping through the hands. And mittens, because they allow the fingers to warm each other by contact, are more effective than gloves. Wool socks are an excellent way to keep the toes warm because wool resists water, and feet tend to get wet if snow and slush are on the ground. For added insulation, moreover, mittens and socks can themselves be layered in the same way that coats and other garments are.

II. Expand one of the following paragraphs A, B, or C into an essay. Be sure that the paragraph you choose is on a topic that you know enough about to discuss effectively in an essay. First examine the model paragraph and essay.

MODEL (PARAGRAPH)

Life insurance comes in three basic forms. The most common type of life insurance is called *ordinary* life insurance. An ordinary life policy states that premiums are payable for a designated number of years and that the person insured is protected for the face amount of the policy. Ordinary life insurance also guarantees its cash value and provides great flexibility to the owner. *Term* life is the second type of life insurance. Under a term insurance policy, premiums are payable for a specified period of time, and the insured person is covered for the amount stated in the contract. Because term insurance builds no equity or residual value, it is usually the least expensive form of insurance. The third kind of life insurance is *endowment* insurance. An endowment policy also requires that premiums be paid during the maturity period, while the insured person is protected for the face value of the contract. In addition to being covered for the face amount of the policy during its term, the insured receives, at the point when the policy matures, the face value plus interest.

MODEL (ESSAY)

Mention life insurance to most people, and they confess they are confused about the subject. People need not be confused, however, because there are actually only three basic types of life insurance—ordinary life, term life, and endowment life—and each has features designed to meet particular requirements.

The most frequently purchased type of life insurance is called *ordinary life insurance*. Ordinary life insurance has two features in common with term and endowment policies: a specified number of years during which the premiums are payable and a specified amount of coverage to be paid when the policyholder dies. It is probably the flexibility of ordinary life insurance, combined with low-cost premiums, that makes it the most popular type. Under an ordinary life insurance policy, premiums are usually payable until the policyholder reaches the age of ninety; thus, the cost of the insurance is spread out over a long period of time. Moreover, premiums can be discontinued by the policyholder prior to age ninety. If they are stopped, the accumulated cash value can be used to buy a fully paid-up life insurance policy. And while an ordinary life insurance policy provides benefits at the time of the policyholder's death, it also accumulates cash value while the policyholder lives (cash value is available under endowment life as well, but at greater cost). The cash value can be borrowed from the policy, or it can be left in the policy to accumulate until the policyholder retires; at that time, it can supplement other retirement income. The features of ordinary life insurance make it flexible enough to suit the needs of many people; some individuals, however, have special needs that require other types.

Term life is the second type of life insurance. Like ordinary life, it has a specified amount of death coverage and a specified number of years during which premiums are payable. Although term life is not as flexible as ordinary life, it also is popular, for two reasons. First, it is the least expensive form of insurance. Since no cash value accumulates during the life of the policy, the cost to the policyholder is just for life insurance. Second, many people purchase term insurance to protect themselves in case of major debt. In particular, people who buy homes secured by a mortgage or business executives who borrow large sums of money may buy term insurance because the period of the insurance can be coordinated to provide coverage if the policyholder dies before the mortgage or the loan is repaid. Although term insurance is attractive because of its relatively low cost and its debt protection, there are occasions when the third type, *endowment insurance*, is the most desirable to buy.

Like the two other kinds of insurance, *endowment life* provides a specified number of years during which premiums are to be paid and a specified amount of death coverage. And, like ordinary life insurance, endowment insurance accumulates cash value. What distinguishes endowment insurance from the other two types is, first, that it works like a savings account. Because it represents a harbor for savings, endowment life is frequently purchased on young children in order to provide cash to pay for their college education. Second, the cost for endowment policies is generally higher than for ordinary or term policies because endowment premiums are payable over a shorter period of time and their cash value is greater. It is easy to understand why an endowment policy is a plan that appeals especially to people who can commit themselves to saving money.

Many people never fully understand life insurance. The fact that there are only three basic types of such insurance should make the subject less confusing—particularly because each of the types has distinguishing characteristics. Ordinary life combines death protection and cash value with a low premium. Term life provides death protection and no cash value, but it is the least expensive. Endowment provides death protection, savings facilities, and higher cash value, but it is the most expensive of the three.

A. Living in a dormitory, with many other students as my too-close neighbors, has been enough to try my nerves. First of all, I have had no real privacy or solitude since I moved into the dorm. People are constantly bursting into my room to ask a question or just to chat. I cannot turn them away because I do not want to be rude or unfriendly. Second, at least once a day—and sometimes more often—I have to stand in a long line to wait for something I need. The washers and dryers are always taken, and the showers seem to be in greatest demand whenever I am in the biggest hurry. By far the most irritating aspect of dorm life, however, is the noise. I find it almost impossible to concentrate when music is blaring so loudly that the walls shake. And it is certainly difficult to get enough sleep with all the yelling and screaming I can hear through the building's paper-thin walls. Perhaps a happy medium could be reached, and the dormitory could become a more comfortable place to live—and study—if my neighbors acted with a little more consideration and I exercised a little more patience.

B. Regardless of the time of day or of the station, most television game shows follow a predictable format. First of all, every game show has a host. At the beginning of the show, the host jogs to center stage, asks for a round of applause, and smiles at the audience. The host is usually dressed in the latest fashion: male hosts wear well-cut suits, and female hosts wear stylish dresses. When explaining the rules of the game, the host frequently speaks in a rapid manner, using the catchy language of a radio disc jockey. Most game shows feature a guest star or two. Such a "star" is frequently an out-of-work actor or actress whose big series was canceled two or three years ago and whom no one has heard of since. Like the host, the stars are dressed stylishly, and—also like the host—they have the ability to smile nonstop for an entire program. Finally, there is the contestant. Favorite contestants are people who wear the most outrageous outfits or who easily become hysterical at the sight of a major prize. Whichever category the contestants fall into, they have considerable trouble deciding which prizes to keep and which to give away. Because game shows resemble one another so closely, viewers can't help but wonder where producers find the endless stream of predictable hosts, guest stars, and contestants who people the game-show airwaves.

C. Although high-school sports may not be important to everyone, most students who participate in them are favorably affected by the experience. One major advantage that students receive is the self-confidence they develop from performing before a crowd. This self-confidence contributes to the building of a positive self-image, which adults need in order to function effectively in society. Another benefit to be derived from participation in high-school sports is the friendship that students form with the other players. Because they must cooperate with one another as a team, students learn to deal with and accept the idiosyncracies of others. As a result, they develop a tolerance that should help them relate to people in later life. High-school sports also teach students the importance of discipline and determination. Participating in high-school sports may not prepare students for all the hurdles they may face in life, but it certainly gives them a healthy head start.

III. Select a paragraph that you have written from your portfolio to expand into a 1-3-1 essay.

Writing an Essay from Scratch

If you understand the format of the 1-3-1 essay and can effectively expand a paragraph into such an essay, you should have little trouble learning, in this section, how to write a 1-3-1 essay from scratch—that is, without first developing a paragraph. As in the technique of moving from paragraph to essay, there are certain steps to follow in writing an essay from scratch. These steps are as follows:

1. Select a topic.
2. Write a thesis sentence.
3. Organize the essay.
4. Write the topic sentences for the body paragraphs of the essay.
5. Write the body paragraphs of the essay and supply an introduction and a conclusion.

The remainder of this chapter shows you how to write an essay by following these five steps.

Step 1: *Select a topic.* In deciding upon a topic for a 1-3-1 essay, you should follow much the same approach you employed when you selected a topic for a paragraph. If the selection of topic is up to you, the topic you choose should be one you know enough about—from personal experience, classwork, reading, the media, and so on—to write about with confidence for several hundred words. If, on the other hand, your instructor assigns a topic, you must think carefully about the topic you have been given. Usually, assignments are given in terms of general subject areas (for example, *people, pets, college, travel, books,* and so forth), and your instructor will expect you to narrow the subject area down to a more specific topic that you can handle well.

In narrowing a broad subject area, think of aspects of it with which you are familiar and about which you can write with authority. For instance, in limiting the subject area *people,* you can probably come up with several aspects that would make a good essay: *parents, roommates, customers, sex symbols, adolescents, infants, diplomats, entertainers,* or *high-school coaches.*

If you feel that these topics are still too general, choose one and narrow it down even further. The topic *sex symbols,* for example, might be narrowed to *types of sex symbols, the differences between European and American sex symbols,* or an individual sex symbol such as *Fabio, Marilyn Monroe, Luke Perry, Tom Cruise, Demi Moore,* or *Madonna.* Under *entertainers,* to take another example, you might list *country singers, rock groups,* or your *favorite vocal soloist.* A narrowing down of the topic *customers,* to take a third example, might produce a number of more specific topics: *customers in fast-food restaurants, hotel customers,* or *the type of customer you least care to deal with on your job.*

Step 2: *Write a thesis sentence for your essay.* Once you have selected a topic, write a thesis sentence about the topic. As we stated earlier in this chapter, the thesis sentence, like the topic sentence of a paragraph, indicates a topic and expresses a controlling idea, which the rest of the essay will develop and support. The controlling idea should be broad enough to develop within the framework of a 1-3-1 essay. It should not be so broad or so general, however, that a discussion of it will become vague and meaningless. Nor should the controlling idea be so specific that you find yourself unable to develop it when you begin to write the body paragraphs of your essay.

Thus, if you were writing an essay on the topic of *customers who frequent fast-food restaurants,* you would find that the sentence

> Of the different types of customers who frequent fast-food restaurants, some are more welcome than others.

would make a better thesis sentence than the sentence

> The different types of customers who frequent fast-food restaurants are interesting.

or the sentence

> Of the different types of customers who frequent fast-food restaurants, most enjoy eating hamburgers and French fries.

The first sentence makes an effective thesis sentence because the controlling idea, that some of the customers who visit fast-food restaurants are *more welcome than others,* is a statement that is easier to develop than the more general idea that customers who frequent fast-food restaurants are *interesting* or the flat statement of fact that the customers who come to fast-food restaurants *enjoy eating hamburgers and French fries.* In writing a thesis sentence, then, you should look for a controlling idea that can be effectively and easily developed within the space limitations of an essay.

Step 3: *Organize the essay.* Once you have selected a topic and written a thesis sentence expressing a controlling idea, you are ready to begin planning the development of the essay—that is, to select a method of development and to write an outline for the body paragraphs of the essay. As we pointed out earlier in this chapter, a paragraph can be looked upon as an essay in miniature. Just as every paragraph has a method of development for its supporting sentences, so every essay has a method of development for its body paragraphs. In expanding a paragraph into an essay, you did not have to worry about selecting a method of development because you were able to use the method employed in the paragraph itself. In writing an essay from scratch, however, you have to choose a method of development. You have at your disposal the same six methods that were available to you when you wrote individual paragraphs: example, cause and effect, process analysis, definition, comparison and contrast, and classification.

As in the case of paragraphs, you should pick the method of development that *best* develops your controlling idea. The chances are that when you picked your topic and wrote a thesis sentence about it, you had an idea of which method of development was most appropriate. If, for example, you had decided upon the thesis sentence "Of the different types of customers who frequent fast-food restaurants, some are more welcome than others," more than likely the various types of customers you have observed in fast-food restaurants inspired your topic and your thesis sentence. When you thought about the fast-food customers you had watched, in other words, you placed them in categories according to certain characteristics—that is, you classified them. As a result, you now find that the best method for developing your thesis sentence is the one you had in mind from the start— *informal classification.* However, to be certain that your original choice of method is in fact the best, you should run through the list of methods of development, from example through process analysis, and check to see whether any other method might offer a more effective way to develop your thesis sentence. Probably you will decide to stick with your first choice, but at the very least a last-minute look at the other methods will make you more confident in the choice you have made.

After you have selected a method of development, you are ready to begin the second stage in the process of organizing your essay: preparing an outline for the body paragraphs. Since writing an essay involves coordinating ideas that appear in several paragraphs, writers generally find that they need an outline to enable them to map out the overall structure of the essay. An outline serves, too, as a means of checking that structure for unity and coherence. To be effective, an outline does not need to be elaborate. It should simply remind you of the major divisions of the controlling idea that the body paragraphs will take up. It is usually sufficient, in fact, to insert a word or a phrase in the outline to represent each topic sentence and each primary-support sentence you plan to include in the body paragraphs. In short, you need not be elaborate to write an effective outline. The outline is purely for your benefit when you fill in the body paragraphs of the essay. It is a way of allowing you to see the overall pattern of your thinking and to check for problems in unity and coherence.

To prepare an outline for the body paragraphs of a 1-3-1 essay, simply write down the thesis sentence and list the three major divisions in the order in which you will discuss them. If, for instance, you were writing an essay on the thesis sentence, "Of the different types of customers who frequent fast-food restaurants, some are more welcome than others," your outline might look like the following:

Thesis Sentence: Of the different types of customers who frequent fast-food restaurants, some are more welcome than others.

1. Impatient customers
2. Picky customers
3. Pleasant customers

Since the method of development you have chosen for the essay is informal classification, each of the body paragraphs in your essay should deal with a particular type of customer who eats at fast-food restaurants. The three items you've listed in the outline, therefore, represent the three classes of customer your essay will consider.

To complete your outline, you should fill in the facts and ideas you plan to use as the primary supports for the topic sentences in the body paragraphs of your essay. Again, you don't have to be elaborate. A word or a phrase is usually adequate reminder of each primary point you plan to discuss. The following outline, for example, would be appropriate for an essay on the types of customers who frequent fast-food establishments.

Thesis Sentence: Of the different types of customers who frequent fast-food restaurants, some are more welcome than others.

1. Impatient customers
   a. demand instant service
   b. angrily summon manager
   c. storm out, upsetting other customers
2. Picky customers
   a. ask for specially prepared food
   b. often return the order
   c. expect restaurant to be run according to their whims

3. Pleasant customers
   a. ask only that the food be hot and fresh
   b. understand delays
   c. are complimentary and courteous

As a final check for unity and coherence, you might find it useful to review your outline carefully before you go on to the next step. In reviewing your outline, make sure that each of the major divisions in the essay follows the method of development you have chosen for the essay and that the divisions relate directly to the thesis sentence.

Step 4: *Furnish topic sentences for the body paragraphs of the essay.* With your outline constructed, you are ready to begin the process of drafting the essay. Before you begin writing the body of the essay, however, you need to furnish a topic sentence for each of the body paragraphs. If you have constructed your outline carefully, this step should pose little difficulty. The topic sentence of each of the body paragraphs should support the thesis sentence of the essay in the same way that the sentences of primary support develop the topic sentence in a paragraph. In other words, they should relate directly to the thesis sentence, and the evidence they present should show that the controlling idea in the thesis sentence is valid.

Thus, if you were writing an essay on fast-food customers, you would examine the three major entries in the outline and come up with topic sentences like the following:

1. Impatient customers are the most difficult type of customers for employees of fast-food restaurants to tolerate.
2. Employees in fast-food restaurants also dread waiting on customers who are picky about what they eat and where they eat it.
3. Fortunately, however, many of the customers who frequent fast-food restaurants are easy to please and a pleasure to serve.

Each of these sentences supports the thesis sentence of the essay, and in the final draft of the essay, these sentences would become topic sentences for the body paragraphs.

Step 5: *Write the body paragraphs of the essay, and furnish a paragraph of introduction and a paragraph of conclusion.* To begin the final step, write the body paragraphs of the essay. As we noted at the beginning of this chapter, the body paragraphs of an essay often begin with a transitional word or phrase that serves as a bridge between the paragraph in which it appears and the one that follows. In furnishing the body paragraphs for the essay you are writing now, refer to your outline for the ideas and evidence you chose for your sentences of primary support. Write out the primary supports, and fill in secondary supports as needed.

When you have completed the body paragraphs of the essay, go back to the beginning of the essay and prepare an introductory paragraph; then go to the end of the essay and write a concluding paragraph. In writing introductory and concluding paragraphs, follow the same procedures you used when you wrote the introductory and concluding paragraphs for essays expanded from paragraphs. Keep in mind that an introductory paragraph should

1. state the thesis of the essay,
2. introduce the divisions in the body paragraphs of the essay, and
3. gain the reader's interest

and that a concluding paragraph should

1. restate the thesis and divisions of the essay and
2. bring the essay to an appropriate and effective close without digressing into any new issues.

Before writing introductory and concluding paragraphs, then, you should review the devices at your disposal for gaining the reader's interest and for bringing your essay to a satisfying close.

Thus, a final version of the essay on fast-food customers could read as follows:

> Fast-food restaurants are becoming more and more popular in the United States. The rapid pace of contemporary society and the need of those "on the go" for quick meals bring the American public through the doors of fast-food restaurants in ever-increasing numbers. No longer is the fast-food restaurant primarily a hangout for teenagers. On the contrary, during recent years people of all ages have come to rely on fast-food outlets as a means of satisfying their appetite for the all-American meal of hamburger, French fries, and soft drink. Playing host to such a mass of hungry drop-ins is bound to put a strain on the employees who work in fast-food restaurants. Of the different types of customers who frequent fast-food restaurants, some are more welcome than others. In particular, three types of customers become very familiar to those who must serve them: the impatient ones, the picky ones, and—perhaps the salvation of the employees—the easy-to-please ones.
>
> Impatient customers are the most difficult type of customers for employees of fast-food restaurants to tolerate. Such customers resent having to wait at all and, while standing in line, may rattle the staff behind the counter by making angry demands for instant service. If the employees cannot meet these insistent demands, these customers may summon the manager—who also may not be able to handle them. Impatient customers who become irritated enough may walk out of the restaurant, leaving a bag or a platter of food on the table or on the counter. They may go as far as to threaten never again to return to the restaurant—often to the relief of the employees and the other customers, who have been watching in dismay.
>
> Employees in fast-food restaurants also dread waiting on customers who are picky about what they eat and where they eat it. Because hamburgers cooked the normal way are either *too* rare or *too* well done to suit picky customers' refined tastes, they may, for instance, put in an order for a burger "medium rare, slightly browned on one side" with "half the usual amount of ketchup, no mustard, no onions, two slices of tomato instead of one, and a dash of Worcestershire sauce to be added when the hamburger is precisely half-

cooked." Even after they are given special considerations of all sorts, though, picky customers are likely to return an order just for the sake of being able to inspect it a second time—and, perhaps, for the pleasure of being able to annoy the staff. Fussy customers seem to expect, in fact, that the restaurant be run according to their whims: utensils washed and dried with extra care, tables and floors swept or wiped two or three times during their stay—there is no end to the demands picky customers may make. Surely, the fewer such patrons the staff has to deal with, the better.

Fortunately, however, many of the customers who frequent fast-food restaurants are easy to please and a pleasure to serve. Pleasant customers demand little from the restaurant and its employees except that the food be hot and fresh. They accept delays and are satisfied with the food as it is ordinarily prepared. And pleasant customers may actually go out of their way to make an employee's job a little easier. They may compliment the staff on the neat appearance of the restaurant or on the polite and friendly service. Such customers compensate for the impatient and the picky and make working in a fast-food outlet more pleasant.

The recent increase in the popularity of fast-food restaurants has brought a variety of customers through the doors of local drive-in hamburger spots. Restaurant employees, feeling the pressure of working fast and nonstop, of preparing special orders, and of trying to keep everyone satisfied, have come to identify three types. Two—the impatient and the fussy—make a difficult job much more so. The third type—pleasant customers—makes a difficult job a little easier.

■ SUMMARY

1. If you understand the structure of a 1-3-1 essay and can effectively expand a paragraph into a 1-3-1 essay, you should have little trouble writing this type of essay from scratch.

2. To write a 1-3-1 essay from scratch, follow these five basic steps:
   a. Select a topic.
   b. Write a thesis sentence.
   c. Select a method of development and organize the essay.
   d. Write topic sentences for the body paragraphs of the essay.
   e. Write the body paragraphs of the essay, and furnish a paragraph of introduction and a paragraph of conclusion.

3. In selecting a topic for an essay, use the same criteria that you used when selecting a topic for a paragraph. In order to write effectively about a topic, you need to be familiar with it, either from personal experience or from reading, watching television, and so on.

4. If you are assigned a topic, be sure to narrow it down sufficiently to make it manageable within the space of an essay.

5. When writing a thesis sentence for an essay, be sure the thesis statement (or sentence) expresses a controlling idea that is neither too broad nor too specific to be developed effectively.

6. To organize an essay, select a method of development and write a basic outline for the essay.

7. Often you will decide upon the method of development you want to use when you select your topic and write your thesis sentence. To make sure that you have chosen the best method available for developing your thesis sentence, check through the other methods before you finally settle on one.

8. In writing an outline, begin by listing the major divisions that the body paragraphs in your essay will discuss; then fill in the primary supports that each body paragraph of the essay will contain. The entries in your outline need not be elaborate. Generally, a word or a phrase for each topic sentence and each primary support sentence will be sufficient.

9. For each body paragraph, furnish a topic sentence that directly relates to the thesis sentence and that is developed by the primary supports of the paragraph.

10. When writing introductory and concluding paragraphs, follow the same procedure that you used for writing introductions and conclusions to essays based on individual paragraphs. Keep in mind that an introductory paragraph should (1) state the thesis of the essay, (2) introduce the divisions in the body paragraphs of the essay, and (3) gain the interest of the reader. A concluding paragraph should (1) restate the thesis and divisions of the essay and (2) bring the essay to an appropriate and effective close without digressing into new issues.

■ EXERCISES

I. With a small group of classmates, narrow each of the following general subject areas (A–H) down to six different topics suitable for 1-3-1 essays. Follow the model given for *student life*.

MODEL: Student life
   1. Final examinations
   2. Living off campus
   3. Coed dormitories
   4. Intramural sports
   5. Campus activities
   6. Fraternity/sorority parties

A. Music   E. Films
B. Health   F. Automobiles
C. Fashions   G. Education
D. Drugs   H. Computers

II. Read the following sentences and identify which ones would make good thesis sentences, which ones are too narrowly focused for discussion within the framework of a 1-3-1 essay, and which ones are too broadly focused.

A. At different stages in our lives we regard Santa Claus differently.
B. One reindeer, in particular, was Santa's favorite.
C. Santa Claus is based on a number of myths and legends about both real and fictitious people.
D. The computer center is really great.

  E. The computer center was constructed for one principal purpose.

  F. The computer center on campus should have been built in a more convenient location.

  G. The life of a professional bowler can be extremely monotonous.

  H. A recent poll showed that most men wear size eleven bowling shoes.

  I. Hard-soled shoes are not permitted on bowling lanes.

  J. The new tennis court is finally finished.

  K. The new tennis court is unique.

  L. The new tennis court is surrounded by a twelve-foot fence.

  M. "Love," in tennis, means "no score."

  N. The word "love" has many definitions.

  O. There are many different types of discrimination.

  P. Discrimination is the source of many recurrent social problems.

  Q. Despite significant gains made during the turbulent sixties, discrimination is still alive and still horrible.

  R. Soap operas are fun.

  S. Soap operas are successful for a variety of reasons.

  T. Most soap operas are on television between the hours of 1:00 and 4:00 P.M.

III. Write *one* thesis sentence for each of the following topics. Feel free to narrow the topics in whatever way you think best.

MODEL

  Topic: Student evaluations of the faculty

  Thesis: There are several reasons why student evaluations of the faculty are important.

  A. *Topic:* Privatizing schools

  B. *Topic:* Blizzards (or hurricanes, earthquakes, or tornadoes)

  C. *Topic:* Teenage pregnancy

  D. *Topic:* Intramural sports

  E. *Topic:* An embarrassing accident

  F. *Topic:* Genderspeak

  G. *Topic:* Health clubs

  H. *Topic:* A life-changing experience

IV. Write an outline for an essay based on one of the following thesis sentences.

MODEL

  Thesis sentence: Tourists visit vacation resorts for various reasons.

   1. Socializing
    a. meet different types of people from different backgrounds
    b. enjoy outings with other families
    c. meet members of the opposite sex
   2. Activities
    a. sports
    b. amusement parks
    c. nightspots
   3. Escape
    a. get away from family
    b. break away from daily routines
    c. get away from cities

A. *Thesis sentence:* Having to take basic courses in order to graduate from college can often be very frustrating.
B. *Thesis sentence:* Babysitting is a good job for a teenager to consider.
C. *Thesis sentence:* Living in the country is better than living in the city.

V. Write topic sentences for each of the body paragraphs you outlined in Exercise IV. Base your sentences on the notes in your outlines.

VI. Write a 1-3-1 essay based on your outline for the thesis sentence in Exercise IV. When you begin writing, be sure to use the topic sentences that you wrote in Exercise V for the body paragraphs of the essay.

VII. Write a 1-3-1 essay on *one* of the following thesis sentences.

A. Modern society is sold on the idea that the "new and improved" product is automatically the best.
B. Renewable energy sources are the salvation of our future.
C. There are many different ways of coping with the monotony of everyday jobs.
D. Crime victims should (not) be reimbursed by their victimizers.
E. The seasons of the year no longer control human activities in the way that they once did.
F. Juvenile criminals should (not) be treated as adults.
G. Money doesn't buy as much as it used to.
H. Infidelity is a natural phenomenon.
I. Modern standards of heroism are so vaguely defined that the hero in one movie (or television program) could easily be the villain in another.
J. You can tell a great deal about instructors from the way they arrange and maintain their offices.
K. Despite the many services and products it offers, the supermarket will never match the convenience and charm of the old-fashioned country store.
L. Where students choose to sit in a classroom may reveal several facets of their personalities.
M. You can tell New Englanders (Southerners, Westerners, Texans, and so on) by the way they talk.
N. There is evidence to suggest that the theories of Dr. Benjamin Spock have done more to determine the future of American society than the work of our diplomats and political leaders.
O. Building homes for people is the best form of philanthropy.

VIII. Write a 1-3-1 essay on *one* of the following topics. Feel free to narrow the topics in whatever way you think best.

A. role models
B. extraterrestrials
C. monotony
D. talk shows
E. U.S. presidents
F. courtesy
G. billboards
H. teenage sex
I. phobias
J. quarks
K. traffic problems

        L. health hazards
        M. civil defense
        N. condominiums
        O. the armed forces
        P. professional sports
        Q. cellular phones

IX. Write an essay on a topic of your own choosing. When you write the essay, be sure to follow the five steps we have given for writing a 1-3-1 essay from scratch. After you have finished your essay written from scratch and after your instructor has had an opportunity to evaluate it, measure it against the essay you wrote that derived from a single paragraph. Consider which approach to essay writing you prefer: developing a paragraph into an essay or writing the essay from scratch. Support your conclusion in a short essay, which can ultimately be shared with classmates and instructor. Remember to include all of your work in your portfolio for eventual submission to your instructor for overall evaluation.

8

ANSWERING DISCUSSION QUESTIONS ON QUIZZES AND EXAMINATIONS

Earlier in this book you followed the steps to develop a good expository paragraph. Then you followed the steps to develop an expository paragraph into a good 1-3-1 essay. Now you will discover one of the most practical applications of your knowledge of the paragraph and the essay: as forms that you can use to structure written responses to quiz and examination questions known as discussion questions.

HOW TO RECOGNIZE A DISCUSSION QUESTION

One way to decide whether a question needs a paragraph or essay response is by process of elimination. You already know that a "true-false" or "multiple-choice" question simply requires that you check a correct answer from among answers provided for you. A second kind of question you can rule out is the "ID" (identification) question to be answered in several sentences or occasionally in a single sentence. Usually the directions will say, "Identify briefly" or "Comment briefly" and list various terms or topics. In such cases the instructor checks to see whether you know the most significant information about the items listed. He or she does not expect or want a lengthy discussion. A third type of question you should rule out may require a fairly long answer: the question that asks you to "list" certain items or facts. Your instructions may say, "List the Middle Atlantic States," or "List the nations that fought on the side of the Allies in World War I," or "List the causes of the French and Indian War." Such questions do not require discussion; answering thêm does not involve writing an expository paragraph or an essay.

Questions that *do* require essay or paragraph answers usually have a recognizable key word or phrase embedded in the directions. For example, you may see the phrase *Discussion Questions* or simply *Discussion* as a heading for several questions on an examination. Or the individual question may say *discuss* a topic. The key word *explain* also signals an essay-type question, for usually if you are asked to explain something, you cannot do it in a sentence or two. Or discussion questions contain the key phrase *do you think.* The directions may open with *Why do you think . . .* or *What do you think . . .* about some subject, idea, or statement. You are being asked for your opinion, and you cannot justify your answer without writing an essay or paragraph by way of support. Further, such words as *why, which, what,* or *how* often introduce a variety of questions that require essay or paragraph answers.

However, you may not always recognize discussion questions so easily. Remember: any question that requires you not only (1) to *supply facts* but also (2) to *relate these facts in a significant way* requires an essay or paragraph answer.

■ EXERCISE

Which of the following questions would seem to require a paragraph or essay answer?

A. Why did the Portuguese lead world exploration and trade during the fifteenth and early sixteenth centuries?
B. True or false? "The Halls of Montezuma" and "The Shores of Tripoli" in the "Marine Hymn" refer to Mexico and the Libyan city of Tripoli, respectively.
C. Explain the difference between a pidgin and a creole language.
D. Briefly identify the "Northwest Passage."
E. Energy units in food are called which of the following?

  1. vitamins
  2. calories
  3. amino units

F. Discuss the chief types of waterfowl popular with American hunters.
G. How is a bill introduced and processed in the United States House of Representatives?
H. What is the difference between "discipline" and "punishment" as means of dealing with behavioral problems among children?

RESPONDING TO A DISCUSSION QUESTION

Far more challenging than recognizing the need for a paragraph or essay response is the actual process of writing one. Students who may have little trouble writing papers outside of class sometimes have tremendous difficulty answering written examination questions. The reason for this problem is easy to understand. The pressure to organize and write a paragraph or essay in a short space of time can lead to a sense of panic, which in turn can bring about writer's block, a phenomenon that leaves writers staring at blank pages racking their brains for an idea. Just as you can avoid writer's block outside of class by approaching your writing systematically and following certain steps and guidelines that generally lead to effective writing, so too can you avoid writer's block during written examinations by following a set of helpful steps and procedures.

In writing paragraph and essay answers to examination questions, you may find it comforting to know that most instructors do not expect the same degree of sophistication and polish from an in-class answer as they would from an out-of-class assignment. They do, nonetheless, require that you present a topic or thesis sentence with a clear controlling idea. They further expect you to explain your controlling idea in a clear and orderly way, with as much supporting information as possible. By writing in well-structured paragraphs and essays, you make it easy for your instructor to grasp how well you know the material. Assuming that you have studied for your examination and have at your command the information you need to answer an examination question with a paragraph or essay, you should have little difficulty writing the kind of response that your instructor will understand and respect.

Once you have determined that a question requires a paragraph or essay answer, you should proceed, in answering it, to follow four basic steps:

1. Make sure that you understand what the question asks you to do.
2. Mentally collect and then jot down any facts that may be useful in your answer.
3. Decide whether to write an answer in one paragraph or to write an essay of several paragraphs.
4. Organize and write your answer, using the techniques for structuring paragraphs and essays discussed in Chapters 1 through 7 of this text.

We will take up these four steps in order.

Understanding the Question

Regardless of the amount of prefatory or background matter in the question itself, the assignment usually requires that you do two things:

1. Furnish information, that is, *facts*.
2. Arrange and relate the facts in a *specific* way.

A great many facts simply listed on paper seldom constitute an effective answer to a discussion question. In evaluating your answer, your instructor is concerned with seeing how well you can relate these facts in a particular, organized way. Before beginning to answer a discussion question, reread the question carefully to determine exactly what the question is requiring you to do. A "why" question, for example, usually signals the need for a paragraph or essay giving reasons or causes for an event or state of affairs. Remember the six methods of development discussed in Chapters 4 and 5. Frequently, you will find that the question requires that you do one of the following:

1. Give *examples* to support a point.
   Sample Question: Discuss the following statement: Christopher Columbus was probably not the first European to "discover" and visit the Americas.

2. Give the *causes* and/or *effects* of a happening or a state of affairs.
   Sample Question: Discuss the factors that resulted in China's Boxer Rebellion.

3. Detail a *process.*
   Sample Question: How does a single-celled organism divide?

4. *Define* a term or a series of terms.
   Sample Question: What did Freud mean by the terms *id, ego,* and *superego?*

5. *Compare* or *contrast* two persons, things, happenings, or ideas.
   Sample Question: Discuss the advantages (disadvantages) of owning stocks instead of bonds (or the opposite) during the last twenty-five years.

6. *Classify* people, things, or ideas under consideration.
   Sample Question: Illustrate three different types of learning styles.

Following is a question from a quiz given students in an "Introduction to Language" course. It is followed by an answer furnished by a student in the class.

Question: Demonstrate your grasp of the term "folk etymology" by giving specific examples of the working of the process in English.

Answer: "Folk etymology" is a change in the form of a strange-sounding word made by the people in order that it look and sound more familiar. Such change occurs when an unusual word is misunderstood and interpreted in line with something native speakers are more comfortable with, even if there is no connection between the new word and the thing that it represents. One of the best known examples is reflected in the term *coleslaw.* This term is derived from a Dutch word *koolsla,* which means "cabbage salad." Unfamiliar to English speakers, the Dutch word was quickly transformed into an English word even though *Kool* originally meant cabbage. A word commonly used to designate a popular cut of steak is "sirloin." People who think about it may assume that it came into existence when someone christened the famous cut "Sir Loin." However, the first part of the word comes from the French preposition *sur,* meaning "above," which, with the English word *loin,* referred to the position of the cut in the animal. Speakers of English, unfamiliar with French, translated the unfamiliar *sur* by the familiar English *sir,* and so we have sirloin steak today. Many examples of the working of folk etymology are to be seen in words that early American settlers thought that they heard in unfamiliar Indian words. They heard the American Indian word *otchek,* representing a small native animal, and transformed the word into *woodchuck,* which sounded more familiar. Similarly, they heard the Algonquian word *musquash* and thought that they were hearing *muskrat,* which is a name for the little animal that is still with us. One last example of folk etymology may be seen in the transformation that American settlers in the Southwest made in the Spanish word *cucaracha,* which referred to a wood louse. The settlers transformed it into the more familiar-sounding *cockroach, cock* naming a rooster and *roach* naming a fish, neither in any way connected with the insect in question. Hundreds of words in the English language today came into existence when early Americans, sometimes in a fit of humor, made transformations in strange-sounding words they heard in the New World.

In the above answer, the student writer does exactly what the question requires. The writer demonstrates knowledge of the term "folk etymology" by writing a long paragraph developed by examples. The examples involve changes made in words from four different sources: Dutch, French, American Indian, and Spanish. The examples are suitable and varied. The student felt, rightly, that a multi-paragraph answer was not needed to satisfy the requirements of the particular question, especially as it was one of three questions to answer during a fifty-minute class.

Below is another question, this one found on a history exam, which is followed by a much longer, multi-paragraph answer:

Question: Discuss the principal reasons for the fall of the Roman Empire.

Answer: The Roman Empire is probably as celebrated today as it was at the height of its power nearly two thousand years ago. Because of its importance, people have always been interested in the fact that, like many other empires, it did not last. In the historian Edward Gibbon's terms, it fell. The reasons for its decline are many and varied, and authorities do not agree on all of them. But certainly there are a number of causes that have frequently been cited by many students of Roman history.

Among the main reasons proposed as causes for the fall of the empire are its size, its dependency on slave labor, and its inefficient economy. Gibbon thought that the Empire was just too big to endure. The extensive land mass that it encompassed and the varied population, together with differences in local governments and cultures, all made it unwieldy, and it sagged of its own size. Roman civilization was based on slave labor. Victories of Roman legions provided large numbers of captives for the Roman slave market who worked the soil and carried out simple manufacturing processes, but these workers lacked the interest in the prosperity of the Empire that native free workers would have had, and their work was poorly done. Further, the economy was inefficient. Rome never organized a systematic manufacturing of goods. Goods were produced locally on a hit-or-miss basis, with little attention to selling for profit in foreign markets. Rome imported many necessities and even more nonessential items to support the luxurious lifestyle of many Romans. Because exports rarely exceeded imports, the trade balance was not in Rome's favor, and the imbalance made for a monetary drain.

Then, too, the fragmented nature of the Empire's population and pressures from groups outside the Empire contributed to its eventual demise. By location and character, the population of the Roman Empire was splintered: the Celts of

Britain and the Semitic peoples of Asia Minor had widely different cultures and needs. Inevitably, regional patriotism was stronger than love of Rome. In addition, the Roman population was decimated by Bubonic Plague, which ravaged many parts of the Empire. Some of Rome's most serious problems arose because of pressure from outside tribes, specifically the Germanic tribes in the North. Under Theodoric the Great, the Goths actually ruled Rome for a time. German threats and successes north, west, and east of Italy demanded the engagement of Roman legions, which were often spread thinly along an expanded frontier. Supply lines and communications to the troops were poor. Wealth was drained away to pay for military defense against thousands of tribal outsiders eager to get a piece of Rome's wealth.

Certainly, however, one of the most important factors in Rome's decline was the inefficiency of its central political apparatus. Rome had no certain machinery to provide for succession of power. An imperial government this year might not be in power next year. Popular generals were elevated to power by the support of legions under their command. Julius Caesar is just one prominent example. When central government and government loyalties weaken, control over regional governments becomes slack, and an empire becomes less unified and secure.

Historians do not, of course, agree about all of the causes for the failure of the Roman Empire. However, an economy flawed by dependence on slave labor and too little attention to the export market, a very diverse population whose primary loyalties were not focused on Rome, outside enemies—especially the Germanic tribes—and an unstable central government all surely contributed to a final weakening of the giant empire that stretched from Gibraltar and Britain to India. Gibbon was, in the last analysis, probably correct. The Roman Empire was just too big.

The answer above is much more complex than the answer provided for the language question. Remember that the question asked for the *reasons* for the fall of the Roman Empire. It also asked the student to *discuss* these reasons. The word *discuss* indicates the need for a developed written response. The word *reasons* shows that the instructor wants to know the causes—*why* the classic state failed to endure. Moreover, the question was one of two to be answered in a ninety-minute examination. Thus the student rightly assumed that an essay of causal analysis was needed, not just a paragraph.

■ SUMMARY

1. Following a series of helpful steps can aid you in answering a discussion question.

2. Before you begin to organize an answer, you must determine exactly what the question asks you to do.

3. The question will require you to supply pertinent facts.

4. The question will also require you to organize these facts in a specific way.

5. The way you organize the facts for an essay question will correspond to one of the six methods of development covered in this book.

▪ EXERCISE

Read each of the following questions and decide which method of development should be involved in an answer.

    A. Analyze the demographic divisions of the population of Switzerland.
    B. Explain the prevailing theory regarding the origins of stars in the universe.
    C. Discuss the causes of the Whiskey Rebellion in the early years of the American republic.
    D. Consider the Gothic elements in the short stories of Edgar Allan Poe in relation to Gothic elements in the short fiction of Nathaniel Hawthorne.
    E. What is the "Whorfian Hypothesis" relating thought processes to language?
    F. Illustrate F. Scott Fitzgerald's use of color symbolism in *The Great Gatsby*.

Collecting Facts

As soon as you satisfy yourself that you understand exactly what your instructor expects of you—that is, whether you will have to gather facts to establish causes, arrange facts to reveal a process, or assemble examples to illustrate a statement—you will have to shift quickly into another gear and set about getting together the information you will need to write an answer. On scratch paper, jot down any facts you feel might be useful. Do not try to decide now what you can use; jot down everything that seems to offer possibilities. Because you know what the question asks of you, you have already set certain restrictions. For instance, if you know that you are going to discuss the reasons why something happened, you will not list facts that compare one event with another.

Suppose you must respond to the last question from the last exercise:

Illustrate F. Scott Fitzgerald's use of color symbolism in *The Great Gatsby*.

You first establish that the question requires you to give examples of *(illustrate)* Fitzgerald's use of color in his most famous novel. Jot down anything that comes to your mind having to do with color in the novel. You might start as follows:

Daisy's white dress

Jordan Baker's white dress

Daisy's daughter's white dress

Daisy's rose brick house

rosy atmosphere in the living room

Daisy's white sports car

Gatsby's yellow car

the green of money

the gold and silver of money

Gatsby's closet full of pastel shirts

the green light on the dock

If you are thoroughly familiar with *The Great Gatsby,* your list will probably go on much longer. Notice that although every item pertains to color, there is no effort to organize the items according to color. Your list will provide raw material from which you will select support for your answer as you begin to write it.

The first items on your list will come spontaneously. But before you use your list, think about the commentary in your textbook (if you have one that discusses Fitzgerald's novel). Do you recall anything that you can jot down? Next think about any outside reading that you have done on the novel. Jot down whatever facts you recall about color symbolism. Finally, think of class lectures and discussions. Review your class notes to call to mind any interesting comments on color patterns made by your instructor or classmates. When your list is as long as you can make it, you are ready to begin considering the structure of your response.

■ SUMMARY

1. Understand exactly what the question asks of you so you can begin collecting facts.
2. Jot down any facts you can recall that appear relevant to the topic and approach suggested by the question.
3. Jot down facts that occur to you spontaneously.
4. Jot down facts brought to mind by a mental review of secondary sources you have read.
5. Jot down facts you can recall from lectures by your instructor or from class discussions.

■ EXERCISES

I. Clip three or four articles from magazines or newspapers, selecting articles devoted to a single problem or issue. Formulate a question suggested by your reading of the articles. Now, jot down a list of items that might be useful to you if you were asked to write a paragraph or essay answer to your question. Add the articles and your list to your portfolio for later use.

II. Recall a question that your instructor may have asked the class recently. According to the steps outlined in this chapter, compose a list of facts that you might use to answer this question if it were put to you later in the semester on an examination. In writing the list, be sure to review in your mind your instructor's comments on the topic, comments by other students, and any attention given the topic by your text.

III. Gather together in a small group. Share the articles from magazines or newspapers that you may have collected for Exercise I. Discuss one of these articles together at length; then formulate a discussion question that an instructor might ask about the article on an examination. As a group, compose a list of information that you might consider important should you be asked to write a paragraph or essay in response to the question you formulated. Share with one another your reasons for including significant bits of information in your notes.

Choosing between a One-Paragraph and a Multi-Paragraph Response

Before you begin writing your answer in its final form, you will have to decide how much you are going to write—approximately how long and how complex your answer will be. Are you going to pack your answer into one good, long paragraph? Or should you organize it as an essay with introductory and concluding paragraphs and a number of supporting paragraphs? A number of factors will enter into your decision.

Time   After the instructor has distributed the test and finished making comments about the exam, and after you have given the question-sheet a quick reading, look at the clock. How much time do you have left? If the class is a fifty-minute period, you will probably have no more than forty minutes left in which to think and write. On the other hand, if you are taking a final examination, you may have nearly two hours remaining. Let us suppose that you are taking a quiz in a fifty-minute class period. You see that you have to answer ten true-false questions, followed by two discussion questions. Allotting just a minute each for the true-false questions, you will have thirty minutes left for the discussion part, or approximately fifteen minutes for answering each of the discussion questions. Obviously, you will not have enough time to write two five-paragraph essays. In this case, the time schedule suggests that a lengthy paragraph response to each question will be sufficient and appropriate. Then, once you have decided on a division of your time, stick with it. If you can't answer one of the true-false questions in a minute, go on to the next question, returning to the questions you are uncertain about if you have time at the end of the period. This way you will have enough time to answer each section of the exam in some detail.

Nature of the Question   As you consider whether to write one paragraph or more for each answer, you should think about the nature of the question. Often a question itself provides some indication of how long a given response needs to be. How complex is the question? If it requires that you give examples and if you know that you can give those examples briefly and concisely, one well-developed paragraph may suffice. If, on the other hand, you are going to explain causes or effects and you know that each cause or effect is fairly complicated, you will realize that, time permitting, you should write a short essay, devoting one whole body paragraph to each cause or effect. Use common sense when evaluating whether a question warrants a response in paragraph or essay form. Unless a series of questions clearly specifies otherwise, devote a relatively equal amount of attention to each question. When you are asked to discuss three or four topics in a section, you should avoid writing an extremely long essay on one question and then only short paragraphs for the remainder in that section.

How Much You Know   Obviously, how much you write will depend on how much you know. If you realize that you know more about one question than you do about another, you will probably answer more fully the question you feel secure about. If you find yourself eager to respond to a particular question, you may have thought more about the area it covers than about the area another question covers and you may be inclined to treat it more fully. Although most instructors number the questions on their exams, they rarely require that you answer the questions in the order they are presented. Start with those topics you feel most comfortable with, and you will begin your exam with a sense of confidence. This confidence sometimes makes it easier to answer more difficult questions later in the exam, and it makes a good, strong impression on the instructor as he or she begins to evaluate the answers.

■ SUMMARY

1. Before you begin to write your answer to a discussion question, decide how long and how detailed it will be.

2. Allot your time according to the number and nature of the questions on the quiz or examination.

3. Finally, take into consideration how much you know about the question, and try to begin by answering those questions about which you feel the most confident.

Organizing and Writing the Essay

The final step in answering an essay exam question is to plan and write your answer. If you understand what the question requires of you, you have probably decided which method of development you will use. Likewise, if you have studied the test structure carefully and analyzed the amount of time available to answer each question, you probably also know whether each answer will be a single paragraph or an essay. For example, if a question asks you to examine the cultures of a nation at two different periods of its history, you will know that you are going to use comparison or contrast, depending on the question, to develop your answer. Now examine the list of facts you have jotted down based on your immediate response to the question, your text, and your outside reading and notes. If the question does not specify comparison or contrast, decide whether the two cultures are strikingly alike (in which case you will use comparison) or whether they are decidedly different (in which case you will use contrast), or both. Then consider the question in relation to the whole test. If the question is one of several on a short examination, one-paragraph responses are probably in order. If, however, the question is one of two or three to be answered during a period of several hours, you know that a multi-paragraph or essay response is probably advisable.

Having determined the overall method to use in writing your answer and having decided whether your response will be a paragraph or an essay, choose a controlling idea. If you are writing a one-paragraph answer, state your controlling idea in a topic sentence. If you are writing a multi-paragraph essay, state the controlling idea in the thesis sentence. For example, suppose that your question asks you to "discuss the differences between the early seventeenth-century colonies in Virginia and those in Massachusetts." The question implies that you will use contrast in your answer. If you are going to write a one-paragraph response, your topic sentence might be, "Although both the colony founded at Jamestown in 1607 and those established in Massachusetts a little later were established by English settlers, the northern and southern colonies were very different." If you plan a multi-paragraph response, you might start more expansively and then state your thesis, as follows:

> Both the colony founded at Jamestown in 1607 and the colonies established farther north in Massachusetts were organized under English sponsorship. Both ventures had the approval of the English crown. And both involved English settlers. However, the differences between the northern and southern colonies were striking.

Do not spend a great deal of time and space writing a lengthy introduction to your thesis. In an examination situation, the thesis is what is of primary importance. Your instructor understands that you are limited by time and space and is primarily concerned with your thesis and the information you use to support it. A sentence or two introducing the thesis is more than adequate. In the example above, the last sentence is the thesis, and the two sentences preceding it serve as introductory information. The same principle holds true for the concluding paragraph of a multi-paragraph essay answer. In concluding your answer, a restatement of your thesis followed by one or two sentences explaining how you supported your thesis will generally more than suffice as an effective concluding paragraph.

Your next step is to decide how to arrange your supporting material. Consult your list of facts and ideas. Can you group these in a meaningful way? If several items are related, you might put a "1" by each. If other items seem to relate to another point, you can put a "2" by each of these, and so on. If you can write a summarizing sentence for each group, you are well on your way to composing a well-structured response to the question. In the case of a paragraph response, these summarizing sentences will furnish major supports for the controlling idea in your topic sentence. In the case of an essay, they will support the thesis and furnish topic sentences for the body paragraphs of your essay.

If you should find yourself with what seems to be insufficient evidence, try to recall other factors you should reflect in your answer. Your list represents possibilities in the way of evidence, but when you force yourself to think further about what you are going to discuss, you will probably think of more supporting factors. Similarly, don't be afraid to eliminate some of your data if you feel it does not offer strong support for your topic or thesis sentence. Once you have your major supporting points before you, arrange these major points in an effective order. For example, you may want to keep your strongest point for the last if you are using order of importance to achieve coherence. Write your major points as sentences under your controlling idea (topic sentence or thesis statement). Then review your list and jot down phrases or words under each supporting sentence so you can use these notes to develop additional support for each major point.

As you actually write your answer, keep one admonition in mind: in constructing a one-paragraph answer, try to shape an answer that satisfies the requirements of a good paragraph. Make sure that you have several sentences of primary support and several sentences of secondary support, and make sure that all of your support is effective and specific. In providing an essay answer, remember the following requirements for a good essay and try to make your answer conform as well as possible to those requirements: make sure that your thesis sentence is an effective one, that each of your body paragraphs begins with a topic sentence that supports the thesis sentence, and that all of your body paragraphs are developed with adequate and effective primary and secondary supports. Regardless of whether you are writing a paragraph or an essay, try to provide as much support as time will allow. The more information that you can provide, the more successful your answer is likely to be.

Following is a question from a two-hour examination in which students were to choose one of two discussion questions to answer. The remainder of the examination consisted of short-answer questions requiring a sentence or two to answer. The discussion question counted for more than half of the points attainable on the examination. Thus, the student correctly determined that a multi-paragraph essay response was required. The student's answer to the question is provided below.

Question: Considering the conditions in Salem, Massachusetts, in 1692, try to account for the series of "witch" trials. Be sure to consider various theories that have been advanced to explain the phenomenon of the trials.

Answer: During the summer of 1692, a series of events took place in Danvers, Massachusetts (then called Salem Village), that eventually led to the destruction of more than twenty innocent men and women and the incarceration of many others. Remembered today as the Salem Witchcraft Trials, these events have both fascinated and puzzled generations of historians. Many different types of theories have been presented as possible explanations for what actually occurred in Salem and what in reality led to the trials. For the most part, these theories fall into three categories: economic, physiological, and supernatural.

One group of theories explains the witchcraft trials according to economic tensions and problems that the citizens of Massachusetts, particularly the citizens of Salem, were experiencing during the latter part of the 1680s and early part of the 1690s. According to this line of thinking, serious economic uncertainties made the people of Salem nervous and insecure. Because of problems between the colonial government and the government of England, New World currency had become devalued. The farmers and merchants of Salem had difficulty supporting themselves and their families. Land prices skyrocketed, and as a result neighbors came to look longingly at the possibility of acquiring adjoining farms. Under the terms of Massachusetts law, individuals convicted of witchcraft forfeited their estates to the crown, and these estates were sold at public auction. Hence, accusing neighbors of practicing witchcraft became a convenient way to expand one's farm and acquire additional land at a reasonable price. Most of the people executed for witchcraft were in fact wealthy landholders with jealous neighbors.

A second group of theories about the Salem witchcraft trials explains them in terms of physiological factors. One theory points to the fact that the winter preceding the trials was excessively long and cold and the summer extraordinarily hot and humid. According to this theory, extremes in weather made the citizens of Salem uncomfortable and paranoid, so they turned their attention to witchcraft. Another theory based on physiological data concludes that the young women who began the hysteria suffered from a form of lead poisoning that produced symptoms of paranoia and hallucination. Advocates of this theory have pointed out that the Puritans commonly lined their cooking pots with lead. Yet another theory in this category proposes that the people of Salem were suffering the effects of a fungus that grew on rye and, when consumed by humans, produced paranoia and hysteria in its victims. The Puritans who farmed the Salem area depended on rye as a staple of diet, and the type of fungus that could have infected the Puritans tends to thrive during hot and humid summers of the kind Massachusetts experienced at the time of the trials.

Lastly, another group of theorists simply claims that witchcraft was actually being practiced in Danvers. Pointing to the court records, these theorists maintain that the events that occurred in Danvers have no explanation other than a supernatural one. Credible witnesses, they maintain, substantiate accounts of levitations, unnatural contortions, and other such seemingly supernatural occurrences. They also point to the fact that some of the accused readily admitted to practicing witchcraft, which they refused to recant, even in the face of death. Moreover, covens of witches and warlocks commonly existed in Europe throughout the sixteenth and seventeenth centuries, and the existence of such covens in New England was, these theorists insist, a distinct possibility.

Most likely the Massachusetts witchcraft trials will never be fully understood or explained. Much of the existing evidence is fragmentary or contradictory, and no amount of historical investigation seems to get to the bottom of it. In the meantime, historians, sociologists, and psychologists continue to explain what happened at the trials in terms of factors that are primarily economic, physiological, or supernatural in nature.

The student who wrote the above answer realized that it would be the only lengthy essay answer on the examination. She first thought in terms of causal analysis, but realized, after jotting down several causes that came to mind, that the causes fell into several neat classes, and so she organized the response around classification.

The following shorter answer is one the student might have written had she been faced with either a shorter exam period or more discussion questions to answer:

> Several types of explanations have been offered by scholars to account for the trials connected with the witchcraft mania in Salem, Massachusetts, in the summer of 1692. One group of theories suggests the trials resulted from economic tensions experienced by the settlers in the previous decade. New World currency had become devalued because of problems with the mother country, England. The price of land had skyrocketed. Because Massachusetts law provided for the auctioning off of property owned by those convicted of witchcraft, many citizens began to look longingly at their neighbors' property and to view their neighbors as witches or warlocks. A second group of theories explains the trials in terms of physiological factors. Excessively long and cold winters followed by extremely hot, humid summers made the settlers paranoid, and they turned their attention to witchcraft. Another theory based on physiological data concludes that the hysteria and paranoia resulted from lead poisoning, lead being used to line Puritan pots and kettles. A third physiological theory blames the same mass behavior on a fungus that grew on the rye that was a staple of the Puritan diet. Finally, a group of theorists simply claim that witchcraft was practiced in old Salem. Pointing to court records and the accounts of credible witnesses, they maintain that the events in Salem were indeed supernatural. Some of the accused readily admitted to practicing witchcraft and refused to recant. Much of the evidence for each theory remains fragmentary and even contradictory; different historians explain the trials in different ways. However, the explanations are primarily economic, physiological, or supernatural in nature.

The answer above provides the same main points put forward in the longer answer that precedes it. Some of the primary and secondary supports in the body paragraphs of the multi-paragraph version have been omitted, but the major evidence provided by the long version remains. The topic sentences for the body paragraphs of the essay answer serve as primary supports for the paragraph answer, and various sentences of primary and secondary support in the body paragraphs of the essay answer are retained as secondary supports in the paragraph answer.

■ SUMMARY

1. After determining the method of development you will use for your answer and deciding whether your response will be a paragraph or an essay, you should establish a controlling idea for your answer.

2. If you are writing a multi-paragraph essay answer, state your controlling idea in the thesis sentence of your essay.

3. A sentence or two of lead-in information preceding the thesis will suffice for an introduction.

4. If you are writing a one-paragraph answer, state your controlling idea in the topic sentence of the paragraph.

5. Arrange your supporting material by reviewing your list of facts and ideas and then grouping those facts and ideas around similar points.

6. In writing a paragraph answer, keep in mind the requirements of a good paragraph (that is, effective topic sentence and adequate primary and secondary supports).

7. In writing a multi-paragraph essay answer, keep in mind the requirements of a good essay (that is, effective thesis sentence, body paragraphs with topic sentences, and adequate primary and secondary supports).

8. After you have finished your paragraph or essay, if time allows, review it to ensure that it answers the question thoroughly and effectively.

▪ EXERCISES

I. Read each of the following questions carefully. Decide (1) what each asks you to do and (2) what method would be the most useful in developing an answer.

A. Explain what is meant by the term *subatomic particle*.

B. Explain how the theories of Carl Jung have influenced the way psychotherapy is practiced today.

C. Discuss the life cycle of the butterfly.

D. What basic differences in philosophy distinguish the Democrats from the Republicans?

E. Discuss the following statement: The forcible removal during the nineteenth century by the United States government of the Cherokee peoples of the Southeast to lands west of the Mississippi River aptly deserves its title as the "Trail of Tears."

F. What effect has the invention of the nuclear bomb had on the world's attitude toward warfare?

II. Share with a small group of classmates a magazine or newspaper article dealing with a subject of current importance. Together, formulate three questions that an instructor might ask in a test involving that article. For each question, indicate (1) what the question asks for and (2) what method you would find most useful in answering it.

III. On your own, write an essay answer to one of the questions in Exercise I or to a question given you by your instructor. Include your essay in your portfolio.

IV. Find an essay examination that you took in another class and answer one of the questions using what you have learned about answering essay questions.

REVISING PARAGRAPHS AND ESSAYS

Experienced writers recognize the importance of revising their work. They revise while they are writing their rough drafts and when they are rewriting their rough drafts. The qualities of writing they strive for are those discussed in earlier chapters of this book: focus, unity, development, and coherence. You, too, can benefit from revising your work. Keep in mind the principles of good writing as you write, apply them again as you revise, and you will find that your writing becomes even more effective.

Besides major concerns such as focus, unity, development, and coherence, revision involves editing—style and usage. In the initial stages of writing, many good writers concern themselves primarily with matters of structure and development and do not worry extensively about proper style, grammar, punctuation, mechanics, spelling, and diction. That way, their thoughts develop freely, without distraction. Then, as these experienced writers begin a final draft, they edit their writing for wordiness, faulty subject-verb agreement, placement of commas, excessive capitalization, confusion of words such as "it's" and "its" or "there" and "their," and incorrect word choices.

There are, therefore, two major steps in revising paragraphs and essays into final form:

1. The first step occurs both during the actual drafting stage and afterwards when you are rewriting, and it involves revising for focus, unity, development, and coherence.
2. The second step is best saved for the final drafting stage, and it includes editing for style and usage.

STEP ONE: MAJOR CONSIDERATIONS

Planning, as we have stressed throughout this book, is essential to good writing. But planning occurs before you write. The act of writing itself often produces new ideas and directions that you may want to incorporate into your work. To make sure that your new ideas, as well as your original ones, follow the principles of effective writing, you might benefit from this strategy for recollecting the principles of effective writing: the checklist.

The following checklist presents major considerations you will want to keep in mind and important questions you will want to ask yourself during and after the drafting of your paragraphs and essays.

A Checklist for Major Revisions

I. Paragraphs
  A. Focus
    1. Does the paragraph have a clearly stated topic sentence?
    2. Is the controlling idea properly focused—neither too general nor too specific for effective development?
  B. Unity and Organization
    1. Does the paragraph contain enough primary support to develop its controlling idea effectively?
    2. Does each point of primary support have enough secondary support to develop it effectively?
    3. Does each primary support relate directly to the controlling idea of the paragraph?
    4. Does each secondary support relate directly to a primary support?
  C. Method of Development
    1. Which method of development are you employing?
    2. Is it the method of development best suited to your topic sentence?
    3. Do you stick to that one method of development throughout the paragraph?
    4. Check the section in this book on the method of development you are using, and make sure that you are developing the paragraph according to the directions given there.
  D. Coherence
    1. What patterns of organization do the primary and secondary supports in your paragraph follow: time order, space order, or order of importance?
    2. Check the section of this book on the pattern of organization you are using, and make sure you are following the instructions there.
    3. Are the ideas and the sentences in your paragraphs smoothly connected?
    4. Are you including sufficient transitional words and phrases between ideas and sentences?
    5. Are the transitional words and phrases you are employing appropriate and effective?

6. Are you avoiding the awkward repetition of nouns by replacing some of them with pronouns?
7. Are the tense of the verbs and person of the pronouns consistent throughout the paragraph?

II. Essays
   A. Introductory Paragraphs
      1. What device are you using to gain the attention of the reader? Do you think that this device will be successful in stimulating reader interest?
      2. Does the introductory paragraph of your essay state the thesis of the essay?
      3. Is the thesis one that can be developed effectively in a short essay?
      4. Does the introductory paragraph of your essay state the divisions to be developed in the body paragraphs of the essay? If not, is the organization strongly implied?
   B. Body Paragraphs
      1. Does each body paragraph begin with a topic sentence?
      2. Does the topic sentence of each body paragraph support the thesis of the essay?
      3. Is there adequate transition between body paragraphs?
      4. Does each body paragraph follow the principles of focus, unity and organization, development, and coherence detailed in the paragraph checklist above?
   C. Conclusions
      1. What device are you using to bring your essay to a close?
      2. Do you restate your essay's thesis and divisions in different words?
      3. Does the device you use bring the essay to a smooth close without introducing any new facts or ideas? Does the conclusion provide your reader with a sense of completion?

Sample Revision

The following paragraph represents an early draft of a student's paragraph on child abuse. The student has gathered necessary information, has thought about the topic, and has planned the contents of the paragraph, to some extent:

DRAFT #1

Child abuse is a cycle of inadequate parenting, passed from generation to generation. Families in which child abuse occurs frequently show little integration in the community. Frequent child abuse is usually resultant from social problems such as marital discord and financial difficulty. Parents who abuse children can be rigid and compulsive, lacking warmth, reasonableness, and flexibility in their thinking and beliefs. Compulsive house cleaners are among those who abuse children. Many of these parents lack the education and training to raise children effectively; they do not, for instance, know how to help them with their homework. . . .

Sensing that she is getting away from the topic and suddenly unsure of what her controlling idea is, the writer decides to stop and reconsider her goals.

Applying the checklist above, she asks herself, first of all, about her focus. Does her topic sentence limit the topic and suggest the direction she wishes to go? The topic sentence "Child abuse is a cycle of inadequate parenting, passed from generation to generation" vaguely suggests a direction for the paragraph. But the development that follows does not focus on the way abusive parents create children who, in turn, become abusive to their children. Further, the writer decides she does not really want to take that approach to the topic, so a new topic sentence is in order. Her new topic sentence, which represents a narrowing of focus, follows:

> Parents who abuse their children have been found to exhibit one of four sets of personality characteristics.

With this new controlling idea, the writer strives for more unified support by making sure that each of the primary supports develops the focus of different personality characteristics. Most of the first draft will be discarded. The information on compulsive parents, however, can be used, because it describes one of the personality types. Recognizing that what she is doing is providing classifications of abusive parents, the writer makes sure that her classes have a sound basis and that the individual classifications are mutually exclusive. The result is the following paragraph:

DRAFT #2

> Parents who abuse their children have generally been found to exhibit one of four sets of personality characteristics. Abusive parents often exhibit hostility and aggressiveness toward other people besides their children. Always angry about something or at someone, these people are plagued by internal conflicts that blow ordinary problems out of proportion. Abusive parents can be rigid and compulsive, lacking warmth, reasonableness, and flexibility in their thinking and beliefs. Often displaying this set of personality characteristics are the compulsive house cleaners who fly off the handle when a child makes a mess or interrupts routine. Parents with strong feelings of passivity and dependence can be child abusers. Sad, moody, and immature, they are ill-equipped for parenthood and its pressures. Fathers who cannot support their families and who are plagued with feelings of guilt and ineptness may transfer these feelings to their children, seeing them as the source of their difficulties.

This second draft is decidedly an improvement over the first, displaying focus, unity, and consistent development. The writer now realizes that the relationship between the ideas should be made clear, and that those ideas should be more cohesive. So she furnishes transitions and some connective devices to create a third draft that will need to be revised only for style and usage before being handed in:

DRAFT #3

> Parents who abuse their children have generally been found to exhibit one of four sets of personality characteristics. First of all, abusive parents often exhibit hostility and aggressiveness toward other people besides their children.

Always angry about something or at someone, these people are plagued by internal conflicts that blow ordinary problems out of proportion. Second, abusive parents can be rigid and compulsive, lacking warmth, reasonableness, and flexibility in their thinking and beliefs. Often displaying this set of personality characteristics are the compulsive house cleaners who fly off the handle when a child makes a mess or interrupts routine. Further, parents with strong feelings of passivity and dependence can also be child abusers. Sad, moody, and immature, they are ill-equipped for parenthood and its pressures. Finally, fathers who cannot support their families and who are plagued with feelings of guilt and ineptness may see their children as the source of their difficulties and take out their frustrations on the helpless victims.

The multidraft process represents the way writers overcome some of the shortsightedness that inevitably occurs in the planning stages of even the best writers. As you write, you will see your ideas take form, and as they take form, you will shape and reshape them into a structure that is focused, unified, developed, and coherent. In other words, writing is an unfolding process encompassing not only prudent planning but also constant revision.

STEP TWO: STYLE AND USAGE

After you have revised your paragraph or essay according to the major considerations checklist and have arrived at a draft that is focused, unified, developed, and coherent, the last step is the final editing for style and usage. The following checklist will aid you in your editing. If any of the areas in the checklist are unfamiliar to you, consult your instructor; a college English handbook; "A Concise Guide to Editing Sentences," which follows this chapter; and other sections of this book.

A Style and Usage Checklist

I. Style
  A. Conciseness
    1. Are there places in your paragraph or essay where your ideas could be presented more simply and economically?
    2. Have you overused the passive voice?
  B. Clarity
    1. Do your words clearly and precisely communicate your ideas to the reader?
    2. Are your sentences clearly constructed with appropriate length and subordination?
  C. Variety
    1. Do you vary your word choices often enough so that the ideas are not expressed redundantly?
    2. Are your sentences sufficiently varied, with different types of beginnings and structures, so that the reader's interest is sustained?

II. Usage [See the indicated pages for further discussion of each usage problem.]
  A. Grammar
    1. Is every sentence in your paragraph or essay a complete sentence? (p. 206)
    2. Have you correctly spelled the forms of your verbs? (pp. 207–210)
    3. Do the subjects of your clauses and sentences agree in number with their verbs? (pp. 210–212)
    4. Are the pronouns in your essays and paragraphs in the proper case? (pp. 212–218)
    5. Do your pronouns agree with their antecedents in number and gender? (pp. 218–219)
    6. Do your pronouns clearly refer to their antecedents? (pp. 123–124)
    7. Have you avoided confusions that can occur between adjectives and adverbs? (for example, *good* vs. *well*) (pp. 220–221)
    8. Have you eliminated any misplaced modifiers? (p. 221)
    9. Have you eliminated any dangling modifiers? (p. 222)
    10. Do any of your sentences have problems of parallelism? (pp. 222–223)
  B. Punctuation
    1. Does every sentence end with a terminal punctuation mark?
    2. Do you punctuate compound sentences correctly, avoiding comma-splices and run-ons? (pp. 223–224)
    3. Are commas and semicolons used correctly? (pp. 224–226)
    4. If your work contains apostrophes, colons, dashes, quotation marks, and hyphens, are they used correctly and effectively? (pp. 227–230)
  C. Mechanics
    1. Do you capitalize names and titles according to standard usage? (pp. 230–231)
    2. Do you avoid abbreviations whenever possible? If you have used them, are they employed correctly? (pp. 231–236)
    3. Are numbers presented in your work according to consistent practice? (pp. 236–237)
    4. Have italics (underlining) been used appropriately? (pp. 237–238)
    5. Have you avoided using parentheses and brackets whenever possible? And when you have had to use them, have you followed accepted standards for their use? (p. 238–239)
  D. Spelling
    1. Have you consulted a dictionary or the "Concise Guide" for the spelling of unfamiliar and troublesome words? (pp. 239–242)
    2. Have you checked spelling of words that you tend to misspell? (pp. 240–242)
    3. Have you taken time to make sure you have chosen the appropriate spelling of homophones or commonly confused words such as *affect* and *effect; to, too,* and *two?* (pp. 242–249)
  E. Gender-Biased Language (p. 249–250)

Sample Revision

The student who wrote the following paragraph feels satisfied with the content and is now ready to edit for style and usage. The first paragraph represents the paragraph in need of final editing, the second paragraph has been marked by the student for revision, and the third paragraph is the final draft that incorporates the changes. Note that, as in your own writing, not every item on the checklist poses a problem for the writer:

1. BEFORE REVISING FOR STYLE AND USAGE

Roberto Clemente, the famous Pittsburg Pirates outfielder, was deserving of his nickname, The Great One.   In his eighteen-year career in the Major Leagues, he was the winner of four batting championships.   He was also the eleventh man in the history of baseball to get three thousand hits.   He was equally remarkable at his position in right field.   He would make unbeleivable catches of pop-flies in shallow center field, just behind second base, and he would stole home runs from batters by jumping above the right field fence and retrieving potential home runs from the stands.   With his powerful arm, he would also intimidate hitters and runners, throwing them out at the bases or at home.   What perhaps made Robert Clemente truly "The Great One"; however, was his humanitarianism.   In fact, his death indirectly resulting from his concern for other human beings.   Heading an effort, in 1972, to bring relief to earthquake victims in Nicaragua, it was necessary for Clemente to fly a beleaguered Managua to ensure that food, clothing, and medical aid were reaching the victims.   En route, the plane crashed, killing the passengers, shocking and saddening Clemente's countless fans.

2. MARKED BY STUDENT FOR REVISION

Roberto Clemente, the famous Pittsburg~~h~~ Pirates outfielder, ~~was deserving of~~ *deserved* his nickname, "The Great One." In his eighteen-year career in the ~~M~~ajor ~~L~~eagues, he ~~was the winner of~~ *won* four batting championships.   He was also the eleventh man in the history of baseball to get three thousand hits.   ⌊He was equally remarkable⌋ at his position in right field.   He would make unbel~~ei~~vable catches of pop-flies in shallow center field, just behind second base, and he would ~~stole~~ *steal* home runs from batters by jumping above the right field fence and retrieving potential ~~home runs~~ *four-sackers* from the stands.   With his powerful arm, he would also ~~intimidate hitters and~~ *deny* runners *extra bases,* throwing them out at the bases or at home.   What perhaps made Roberto Clemente truly "The Great One~~;~~ however, was his humanitarianism.   In fact, his death indirectly result~~ing~~ *ed* from his concern for other human beings.   Heading an effort, in 1972, to bring relief to earthquake victims in Nicaragua, ~~it was necessary for~~ Clemente ~~to fly~~ *flew* to a beleaguered Managua to ensure that food, clothing, and medical aid were reaching the victims.   En route, the plane crashed, killing the passengers, shocking and saddening Clemente's countless fans.

3. FINAL VERSION

Roberto Clemente, the famous Pittsburgh Pirates outfielder, deserved his nickname, "The Great One." In his eighteen-year career in the major leagues, he won four batting championships. He was also the eleventh man in the history of baseball to get three thousand hits. At his position in right field, he was equally remarkable. He would make unbelievable catches of pop-flies in shallow center field, just behind second base, and he would steal home runs from batters by jumping above the right field fence and retrieving potential four-sackers from the stands. With his powerful arm, he would also deny runners extra bases, throwing them out at the bases or at home. What perhaps made Roberto Clemente truly "The Great One," however, was his humanitarianism. In fact, his death indirectly resulted from his concern for other human beings. Heading an effort, in 1972, to bring relief to earthquake victims in Nicaragua, Clemente flew to a beleaguered Managua to ensure that food, clothing, and medical aid were reaching the victims. En route, the plane crashed, killing the passengers, shocking and saddening Clemente's countless fans.

■ SUMMARY

1. Experienced writers recognize the importance of revising and editing their work.

2. As they write their paragraphs and essays, they keep in mind the major considerations of focus, unity, development, and coherence.

3. When they have finished structuring their paragraphs and essays and have reviewed their work for major matters of revision, they edit for style and usage.

4. To revise your paragraphs and essays effectively, follow the revision checklists supplied in this chapter (pp. 192–193 and 195–196).

■ EXERCISES

1. Using the checklist for major revisions on pages 192–193, with a classmate jointly revise the following paragraphs:

A. There are six ways to reduce one's chances of having a heart attack. One of the most important of these is to reduce the amount of saturated fat and cholesterol in one's diet. For example, cooking should be done with poly-unsaturated shortening. Also, the amount of eggs and whole-milk dairy products can be strictly limited. Another way to avoid trouble is to keep trim. Life expectancy is longer for men and women who maintain a reasonable weight. Dieting may be necessary to be sure that they do not put on extra pounds. Another important safeguard against heart attack is regular exercise. People who have sedentary jobs and who do not make an effort to get regular exercise are much more susceptible to heart attacks than are people whose jobs involve physical activity or who engage in sports or jog to stay fit. Smoking leads to heart attacks. The government should ban tobacco as being very harmful to health. If tobacco is not banned, people will continue to smoke because the average man or woman lacks enough self-discipline to keep from smoking. People can reduce the risk of heart attack by following these simple rules for maintaining a strong heart and a healthy cardiovascular system.

B. Throughout history left-handed people have been the subject of prejudice, discrimination, and even fear. Superstitious and religious traditions frequently single out left-handedness as a sign of evil. For example, in Christian religions, the devil sits on the left hand of God and is himself left-handed. Moreover, tradition requires some Christians to use their right hands to cross themselves and swear on the bible. Muslims considered the left hand unclean and refuse to eat with it. By the same token, to reach Nirvana, Buddhists must follow the "right-hand path." Even words associated with left-handedness have negative connotations in many languages. In Anglo-Saxon, for instance, the word *"lyft,"* which means broken or weak, is the source for the modern English word "left." On the other hand, the English word "sinister" means "left" in Latin. Some Gypsies refer to evil people as "bongo," the Romany word for left-handed. Most importantly, left-handed people must endure more than just traditional and linguistic discrimination. Recent studies have shown that left-handed people have an average life-expectancy as much as nine years shorter than that of right-handers. Not only do they frequently die in accidents while performing tasks and using equipment designed for right-handed people, but they may even be more susceptible to certain diseases.

II. Using the checklist for major revisions on pages 192–193 and the style and usage checklist on pages 195–196, on your own revise and edit the following paragraphs:

A. Since President Ronald Regan announced that he was suffering from Alzheimer's disease, the American public and the world have been educated about the nature of this tragic illness. Alzheimer's is a degenerative and irreversible disorder of the brain that becomes more common among people as they reach advanced ages. No one is sure just what causes Alheimer's but it effects the nerves in various parts of the brain and so people who have it generally feel pretty badly. Genetics and environment are thought to be possible factors that might be triggerring this illness. No one seems to be immunized from Alzheimer's, which strikes members of every race, both genders, and all socio-economic classes. Alzheimer's has many symptoms; the most common being impaired speech, loss of memery, physical disorientation, and generally being confused, among other things. The average Alzheimer patient does not live very long but they can live for many years before finally losing their consciousness and falling into a comma. It is the fourth leading cause of death among the elderly, as many as fifty per cent of all people more than the age of eighty-five may suffer from this disease. Lots of money is spent by many people in taking care of Alheimer patients.

B. Like many of our modern day marriage traditions, the use of wedding and engagements rings stem from ancient customs. Because of its circular shape, rings have long been considered a cymbol of eternity. Consequently, the use or exchange of rings has been used for centuries in order to cymbollize a permanent bond between to people. For example, rings were often exchanged in ancient times to seal contracts. Kings and statesmen usually wore signet rings so they could apply it's circular seal to there official documents. Nights and warriors typically swore on their own or their king's ring to declare loyalty to their leader, and in European tradition the highest honor a king could bestow on a night was the gift of a ring. Marriage has historically been seen as a contractual obligation; and marriage partners have exchanged wedding rings to seal there pact since Roman times. The Romans believed, that if the ring should break, the martial union would be unfortunate and frought with bad luck and troubles. In order to reflect the strength of the marriage bond; the Romans prefered relatively simplistic rings, made from some formidable mettle. The remant of this idea remains in our relatively unadorned modern wedding bands. When the clergyman blesses such rings he is provoking the spiritual power of this eternal cymbol. The diamonds of modern engagements rings also reflect ancient cymbollic power. In the late middle ages, the italians began exchanging diamond engagement rings; because, it was believed that diamonds were forged in the flames of love.

C. Striving to hard to win may be the greatest mistake a person can make. When a person sets their goal and then concentrates on nothing but that goal, they lose the little things in life. For example, a boy playing in a school football team. He finds the pressure to win, to reach that goal, the most important thing in his life. It is important not only to him but the coach and teammates, and his friends and his family. The pressure can result in a boy concentrating on nothing else but to win at playing football. He forgets the fun of the game, and the good times he could have doing other activities. Grown people acts this way in business where to reach an economic goal is so strong that they will even step on friends in order to obtain a higher status in life. When one sets a goal, they should be willing to except a setback or even a failure in their social life.

III. Using the checklists on pages 192–193 and 195–196, revise two or more paragraphs from your portfolio.

IV. Using the checklists on pages 192–193 and 195–196, revise and edit the following essay:

A. The traditional American funeral has been called a social function at which the deceased is the guest of honor. Approximately 22,500 funeral establishments in the United States compete to bury two million bodies a year. Next to buying a house or a car, purchasing a funeral is the largest single investment a person is likely to make in their lifetime. The average funeral is likely to cost more than two thousand dollars, and the funeral industry itself is a thriving multimillion-dollar business. Perhaps people should think twice before they decide to bury their dead in the way the funeral industry tells us the dead should be buried. Knowing the facts about such funeral items and services as caskets, embalming, and graveyard plots can put you at a decided advantage should you ever have to confront a funeral director and purchase these things for someone you love.

The casket is the single most expensive item on the funeral bill. The object of good casket salesmanship is encouraging you to spring for the higher price models. A substantial percentage of your final payment may wind up in the salesman's pocket. In an attempt to cater to and encourage the American mania for luxury items, manufacturers have produced caskets of a wide variety of materials. They offer them in glass, steel, wood, cement, marble, rubber, and even plastic. Whatever one decides to buy in the way of a casket, you should remember one thing: you will not be around to see what you look like in it. And your friends will only have an hour or so to admire your choice before it disappears in the ground encased in two thousand pounds of concrete and covered with half a ton of dirt. Something of a cross between a bed and a bomb shelter, your casket is your home for eternity. But who, including you, will remember what it looked like or how much it cost?

Embalming is also a costly item on the funeral bill, but is not as necessary a service as you may think. You are not required by law to be embalmed unless you have succumbed to a contagious disease. Too grisly to describe in detail, embalming is a process most people might be well to do without. Technically it is simply the replacing of bodily fluids with a liquid preservative but when it comes to actual methods, suffice it to say that you are lucky that you are dead when they do it to you.

Another item on the funeral bill is the cemetery plot. Depending on their location, you can buy a cemetery plot from anywhere from a hundred to several hundred dollars. You also need, in some states, some type of vault to hold the casket when it is placed in the ground. Cemetery plots can be purchased from the funeral director or from the cemetery people themselves. The cost of a cemetery plot usually depends on the social status of the cemetery where it is located. Exclusive cemeteries which cater to the wealthy resemble spacious parks, and the plots are quite expensive. Older, less exclusive cemeteries sell you plots for much lower prices.

A final note with regard to another costly aspect of funerals: the social aspect. Many homes involved in a funeral are taxed to overflowing with guests who must be fed and, sometimes, housed at motels, often at the expense of the family involved. A funeral should not be a festive occasion. And it should not become more of a financial burden because of large food bills incurred in the feeding of countless guests.

In short, funerals should not be as expensive as they are. Until people decide what they want for the bodies of their dead; American funerals will continue to be a mysterious and expensive rite. As the star of a popular television comedy once said, "There should be a new field of funeral people who are much less funereal. . . . The way they do it now is just much too serious. It should be sillier or something . . . maybe they should play games."

V. Using the checklist on pages 192–193, revise an essay that you wrote for one of the exercises in Chapter 7.

REVISING A GRADED PAPER

Revision does not usually end when your paragraph or essay is submitted for grading by your instructor. Your instructor, in fact, may return your paper to you with suggestions for improvement, and you may be asked to revise it again in the light of these comments. If you reworked your paper carefully during the earlier stages of the revision process, the changes your instructor recommends may be fairly minor. You may be asked, for example, to add, delete, or change punctuation marks or to correct a misspelled word. Or if your paper needs more transitional devices, you may be asked to insert them where your instructor feels they are necessary.

However, if you did not write your paper carefully, you may find that even at this late stage your paper requires more radical work than the addition of a comma or the correction of a misspelled word. Your instructor may feel, for instance, that a paragraph needs additional primary or secondary support or that the facts or ideas you have chosen as support can be emphasized or clarified by a reorganization of your material. Whatever suggestions, major or minor, your instructor gives you for revision, you should consider them carefully, for they constitute an evaluation of your writing from the vantage point of an observant and highly trained reader. Not only do the suggestions you receive point the way to an improvement of the work you have handed in, but they are also likely to tell you which aspects of the writing process you should devote more attention to in the future.

Editors and instructors use a more or less standardized list of symbols and abbreviations for indicating the necessity for certain types of revision. The symbols and abbreviations most instructors and readers use are shown in Figure 9–1. In addition to using some of the symbols and abbreviations

Figure 9–1

ℓ	delete	*awk*	awkward wording
⋏	add omitted word(s)	*wdy*	wordy
sp	check spelling	*cap*	change to capital letter
¶	begin new paragraph	*ℓc*	change to lower-case letter
vag	vague	*incoh*	incoherent
∩	transpose order	*ital*	italicize
∧	insert period	*;/*	insert semicolon
:/	insert colon	∧	insert comma
∨	insert apostrophe	"	insert quotation marks
no ¶	no new paragraph	*[frag]*	fragment
cs	comma splice	*ro*	run-on sentence
⟲?	insert question mark	⟲!	insert exclamation point
wdc	check choice of word(s)	*agr*	check agreement
vbt	check verb tense	*dev*	develop further
ex	give example	*mis mod*	misplaced modifier
dang	dangling modifier	⌒	close up
?	meaning is unclear	*amb*	ambiguous
cliché	trite word or expression	*trans*	add transition
S	faulty sentence structure	*not ‖*	check parallelism

listed in Figure 9–1, your instructor may make a more detailed comment in the margin of your paper or at the beginning or end of the paper.

In revising a paper, you should interpret the remarks of your instructor and then make the appropriate changes. Consider the following paragraph:

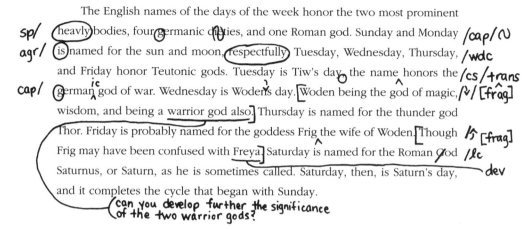

This paragraph has been marked for correction and is ready to be revised. The revision of the paragraph follows:

The English names of the days of the week honor the two most prominent heavenly bodies, four Germanic deities, and one Roman god. Sunday and Monday are named for the sun and moon, respectively. Tuesday, Wednesday, Thursday, and Friday honor Teutonic gods. Tuesday is Tiw's day; the name of this day honors the Germanic god of war. Wednesday is Woden's day. Woden was the Germanic god of magic and wisdom. Like Tiw, he was also a warrior, and the fact that two days of the week are named after gods of war is an indication of the importance of war in early Germanic culture. Thursday is named for the thunder god Thor. Friday is probably named for the goddess Frig, the wife of Woden, although it may have been named for Freya, the Scandinavian goddess of fertility. Saturday is named for the Roman god Saturnus, or Saturn, as he is sometimes called. Saturday, then, is Saturn's day, and it completes the cycle that began with Sunday.

In this paragraph, the writer has used the suggestions that she received from her instructor on her original draft as the basis for her revisions. The result is a clearer, more coherent paragraph that has benefitted greatly from the revision it has received.

■ SUMMARY

I. You may have to revise your paragraph or essay again, once you have received it back from your instructor, who has marked it with suggestions as to how it can be improved.

2. The chart on page 202 lists the kinds of marks and symbols editors and some instructors use when evaluating a piece of writing.

3. When you receive a graded paper back from your instructor, refer to the chart to determine the revisions that your instructor feels you should make.

■ EXERCISES

I. Revise one of the graded paragraphs you wrote for Chapters 4 or 5 according to the suggestions made by your instructor.

II. Revise one of the graded essays you wrote for Chapter 7 according to the suggestions made by your instructor.

A CONCISE GUIDE TO EDITING SENTENCES

This guide will help you in writing when you have problems with grammar and mechanics and are unsure how to solve them. The guide is divided into five sections: Grammar, Punctuation, Mechanics, Spelling, and Gender-Biased Language. You can use this guide with the "Style and Usage Checklist" (see Chapter 9, pp. 195–196) as you edit technical aspects of your writing during the revision process, or you may use it independently as a short handbook for the problems of sentence style and usage that all writers face as they prepare final drafts of their prose.

I. GRAMMAR

1. Writing Complete Sentences and Avoiding Fragments

A sentence is "complete" when it contains a subject and a predicate.

The drug problem has reached alarming proportions.
└──(SUBJECT)──┘ └──────(PREDICATE)──────┘

The subject of the sentence is generally the *noun* or *pronoun* that is focused upon, along with any accompanying words. The predicate contains the verb and its accompanying words. Every sentence must contain at least a subject and a verb.

When writers use a group of words that (1) do not contain a subject and a verb or (2) do not make complete sense in themselves, they are constructing *fragments* (incomplete sentences).

(A) INCORRECT:	The hurricane destroying coastal cities. (FRAGMENT)
CORRECT:	The hurricane is destroying coastal cities.
(B) INCORRECT:	Salads are an excellent source of fiber. (SENTENCE)
	Which aids digestion. (FRAGMENT)
CORRECT:	Salads are an excellent source of fiber, which aids digestion.
(C) INCORRECT:	Bored by the performance. We left early. (FRAGMENT) (SENTENCE)
CORRECT:	Bored by the performance, we left early.
(D) INCORRECT:	Dr. Radziewicz made great discoveries in her research (SENTENCE) with viruses. Because she was a hard worker. (FRAGMENT)
CORRECT:	Dr. Radziewicz made great discoveries in her research with viruses because she was a hard worker.

2. Verb Forms

How a verb is spelled often depends on its tense. Tense, briefly stated, means "time." Therefore, *when* an action or state-of-being occurs often greatly affects its form and spelling. Verbs can be roughly divided into two categories according to the ways that they are spelled in their various tenses: regular verbs and irregular verbs.

a. Regular verbs

Verbs that form their past, present, and future tenses in similar ways are called *regular verbs.* In the example below, the verb *to succeed* demonstrates regular verb endings in the present and past tenses:

I succeed, I succeeded.

The principal characteristic of the regular verb is that *-ed,* or just *-d* in some cases, ends the simple past tense forms. A unique and sometimes troublesome aspect of the regular verb formation is the occasional required doubling of the consonant before the *-ed* in the past tense forms. Some regular verbs do require this doubling *(rebelled, abetted, flipped, staffed);* some, like the verb *to program* can go either way *(programed* or *programmed, leveled* or *levelled, kidnaped* or *kidnapped, canceled* or *cancelled);* and some do not require the doubling *(limited, groveled, hungered).* Use a college-level dictionary to make a determination of whether to double the consonant.

Also, the *-s* that is added in the present tense to regular verbs when they are preceded by *he, she, it,* or singular nouns is sometimes a source of confusion, particularly when the *-s* becomes *-es,* as in the cases of such verbs as *to pitch* (She pitches), *to munch* (The gang munches), *to tax* (The government taxes), and *to dress* (He dresses).

Verbs such as *to try* and *to marry* can likewise pose problems in the third-person singular, present tense because the *-y* in each instance must be dropped and an *-i* substituted before the addition of *-es* (Our team tries; he marries).

Finally, the *future* tense is formed with the aid of the auxiliary verb *will.* These days, the auxiliary *shall* can be used interchangeably with *will* (I shall program, you shall program). Traditionally, however, *shall,* when used to indicate future action, was assigned to the first person only. While this distinction is gone, the slight variation in meaning between *will* and *shall* persists, *shall* retaining that connotation of determination that something will occur.

In addition to *will* and *shall,* there are other auxiliaries that aid in the formation of tense. *To be* and *to have* are the most important helpers because they aid in the creation of the *progressive* and *perfect* tenses. The progressive tense involves ongoing action or state-of-being (I am running. The players are being booed.). The perfect tense, on the other hand, depicts action or state-of-being accomplished prior to a fixed point in time (You have been, Our group has won). The forms of the perfect and progressive tenses are as follows:

PROGRESSIVE TENSE

(present)	I am succeeding
(past)	I was succeeding
(future)	I will be succeeding

PERFECT TENSE

(present)	I have succeeded
(past)	I had succeeded
(future)	I will have succeeded

The progressive is formed through a combination of the auxiliary verb *to be* in its various tenses and the *-ing,* or participial, form of the verb. The perfect tense is formed by the auxiliary *to have* in its various tenses plus the simple past tense form of the main verb.

Other tenses include the *perfect progressive,* which combines the two tenses presented in the previous paragraph (I have been succeeding, I had been succeeding, I will have been succeeding, and so on), and the *conditional*—a tense of sorts that relies on modal auxiliaries such as *would, should,* and *could* to establish a sense of possibility, but not certainty (I could have succeeded as a prize fighter, but I didn't). *Will, shall, can, may, might, must, ought to,* and *need to* also function as modals.

A final auxiliary that changes the tone of verbs, not necessarily their tense, is the verb *to do.* Added to a verb, *do* emphasizes its action (She does succeed). The auxiliary *to do* also functions as an important part of questions (Didn't he succeed?).

b. *Irregular verbs*

So far, the discussion of verb tense has focused on how regular verbs form their various tenses. Regular verbs, though, do not pose the biggest problems; *irregular verbs* do. Troublesome irregular verbs that form their principal parts in unusual ways are included in the following list.

PRESENT TENSE	PRESENT TENSE (3RD PERSON)	PAST TENSE	PRESENT PARTICIPLE	PAST PARTICIPLE
begin	begins	began	beginning	begun
bite	bites	bit	biting	bitten
blow	blows	blew	blowing	blown
break	breaks	broke	breaking	broken
bring	brings	brought	bringing	brought
burst	bursts	burst	bursting	burst
choose	chooses	chose	choosing	chosen

PRESENT TENSE	PRESENT TENSE (3RD PERSON)	PAST TENSE	PRESENT PARTICIPLE	PAST PARTICIPLE
come	comes	came	coming	come
dive	dives	dived (dove)	diving	dived
draw	draws	drew	drawing	drawn
drink	drinks	drank	drinking	drunk
drive	drives	drove	driving	driven
eat	eats	ate	eating	eaten
fall	falls	fell	falling	fallen
fly	flies	flew	flying	flown
freeze	freezes	froze	freezing	frozen
get	gets	got	getting	gotten
give	gives	gave	giving	given
go	goes	went	going	gone
hang (to suspend)	hangs	hung	hanging	hung
know	knows	knew	knowing	known
lay	lays	laid	laying	laid
lead	leads	led	leading	led
lie	lies	lay	lying	lain
lose	loses	lost	losing	lost
ride	rides	rode	riding	ridden
ring	rings	rang	ringing	rung
run	runs	ran	running	run
see	sees	saw	seeing	seen
set	sets	set	setting	set
shake	shakes	shook	shaking	shaken
shrink	shrinks	shrank (shrunk)	shrinking	shrunk
sing	sings	sang (sung)	singing	sung
slay	slays	slew	slaying	slain
slide	slides	slid	sliding	slid
speak	speaks	spoke	speaking	spoken
steal	steals	stole	stealing	stolen
sting	stings	stung	stinging	stung
swim	swims	swam	swimming	swum
swing	swings	swung	swinging	swung
take	takes	took	taking	taken

PRESENT TENSE	PRESENT TENSE (3RD PERSON)	PAST TENSE	PRESENT PARTICIPLE	PAST PARTICIPLE
tear	tears	tore	tearing	torn
throw	throws	threw	throwing	thrown
wear	wears	wore	wearing	worn
write	writes	wrote	writing	written

3. Subject and Verb Agreement

Subjects must agree with their predicates in *number:* singular subjects require singular verbs; plural subjects require plural verbs.

SINGULAR: Absence makes the grade grow harder.
                      (s)   (v)

PLURAL: The media were present.
                      (s)   (v)

Subjects must also agree with verbs in *person.*

1ST PERSON: I am the greatest!
                      (s) (v)

3RD PERSON: Multinational firms have world opinion to consider.
                          (s)   (v)

Sometimes you may be unsure of what the subject of a particular sentence is or whether that subject is singular or plural. The following focuses on how to treat subjects in those situations.

a.   Two or more subjects joined by the conjunction and

Sentences often have more than one subject (called a *compound* subject). Compound subjects require plural verbs.

Luck and hard work are ingredients for success.
 (s) (CONJ.)   (s)   (v)

Sometimes confusion occurs when two nouns joined by *and* appear to be functioning as a compound subject but are actually working together to form one unit. This combination requires a singular verb.

Her name and address is the following.
    └───(s)──────┘ (v)

Peanut butter and jelly is my favorite sandwich.
    └────────(s)────────┘ (v)

b.   Phrases and clauses that intervene between subject and verb

Regardless of the number of words that may come between the subject and its verb, the verb always agrees with its subject in number.

One of the benefits of a camping vacation is cost.
(s)   (v)

An individual who wears jeans to formal gatherings is not necessarily considered
       (s)   (v)
inappropriately dressed.

c. Verbs that precede subjects

Subjects usually precede their verbs. When they do not, the number of the verb is sometimes difficult to determine. To ensure correct agreement one must move into the sentence and identify the subject, then return to the verb to determine its number.

There are an estimated four million aliens in this country.
      (v)   (s)

We do not know if there is life in other systems.
                        (v) (s)

Among the problems that autistic children face are language difficulties.
                                              (v)   (s)

Attached are a memo and a draft of the speech.
     (v)   (s)   (s)

d. Indefinite pronouns used as subjects

Indefinite pronouns (with the exception of *both, few, many, most, several,* and *some*) are usually singular and thus require singular verbs.

Each of these countries has done its share.
(s)   └─(v)─┘

The most frequently used indefinite pronouns that are singular and require singular subjects are the following:

each	somebody	anybody	everybody	nobody
either	someone	anyone	everyone	no one
neither	something	anything	everything	nothing

The indefinite pronoun *none* can be either singular or plural.

None of the alternatives is feasible.
(s)   (v)

None were more excited by the news than the families of the hostages.
(s)   (v)

e. Subjects linked by the conjunctions or, nor, either . . . or, neither . . . nor, not . . . but, not only . . . but also

When two or more subjects of a sentence are connected by the above conjunctions, the verb agrees in number with the subject closest to it.

If you or a friend is planning to enter the military, ROTC may be the place
(s) (CONJ.)   (s)   (v)

to start.

Neither the president nor her sorority sisters know of the changes in campus
(CONJ.)   (s)   (CONJ.)   (s)   (v)

policy.

f.   Collective nouns used as subjects

Collective nouns (i.e., *staff, more, percent, couple, group, total, number, variety, personnel, crew, plenty,* and *range*) can require either singular or plural verbs, depending on how they are used.

An increasing number of industries are being deregulated.
        (s)   └────(v)────┘

The board of electors remains firm about its decision.
        (s)   (v)

The determining factor in these cases is whether the collective noun refers to a single unit or to parts functioning individually.

g.   Special nouns ending in s used as subjects

Some nouns (e.g., *measles, mathematics, physics*) end in *s* but are singular in number.

The news is not good.
    (s) (v)

Mumps poses a threat to adolescent men.
   (s)   (v)

Note: Some nouns (e.g., *scissors, acoustics, riches, athletics*) end in *s* and may appear singular but in practice are considered plural. Still other nouns ending in *s* can take a singular or plural verb:

The dues are unfair.
    (s) (v)

The union dues is $25.00.
            (s) (v)

4. Pronoun Case

Pronouns come in various types, and one major type, *personal pronouns,* has three cases: *nominative, possessive,* and *objective.* In other words, pronouns have different spellings when they are used as subjects, or subject substitutes; possessors; and objects in sentences. The three cases of personal pronouns are listed below:

NOMINATIVE	POSSESSIVE	OBJECTIVE
I	my, mine	me
you	your, yours	you
he	his	him
she	her, hers	her
it	its	it
we	our, ours	us
you	your, yours	you
they	their, theirs	them

The pronouns *who* and *whoever,* traditionally, also vary according to the case required:

who	whose	whom
whoever	whosever	whomever

Problems occur for writers, sometimes, when determining what case is needed in particular sentences.

a.   Nominative case

The nominative case is needed when a pronoun is used as the subject of a verb.

He is responsible for his own actions.
(PN)

Ms. Moore and I journeyed through the cave.
    (PN)

Since they visited the site, press members have changed their interpretation of
   (PN)
the accident.

The nominative case is needed when pronouns are used as subject complements.

The person talking on the telephone is she. (formal)
      (PN)

It was I who ordered the pizza. (formal)
  (PN)

The people you met at the concert are they. (formal)
     (PN)

The secretary said, "It's he." (formal)
    (PN)

Note: The objective case at the end of a sentence is acceptable in informal usage (It was her, me, and so on).

Pronouns used as appositives of subjects and subject complements require the nominative case.

The three contestants—Jeff, Rhonda, and she—congratulated one another after
        (PN)
the contest was over.

We taxpayers don't like excessive government spending.
(PN)

At least two coaches, probably you and he, will be needed to manage the team.
                (PN)

They are the same people—George, Bill, and he—whom we saw painting the
                (PN)
building yesterday.

b. Special problems in the use of the nominative case

The nominative case is needed, sometimes, when a pronoun is used in
comparisons introduced by the words *than* or *as*.

John was earlier than I.
        (PN)
(Implied: John was earlier than I am early.)

The president is as excited as they.
                (PN)
(Implied: The president is as excited as they are excited.)

More people than I saw it.
        (PN)
(Implied: More people than I saw it.)

The exam was not difficult for someone such as I.
                (PN)
(Implied: The exam was not difficult for someone such as I am.)

When a pronoun follows the infinitive *to be* and that infinitive does not
have a subject, the pronoun is in nominative case.

The pilot used to be she. (formal)
        (PN)

The driver of the automobile was assumed to be he. (formal)
                (PN)

The people in the forefront of the industry were supposed to be they. (formal)
                (PN)

c. Possessive case

Possessive pronouns serve as adjectives, modifying nouns.

While presenting her report in class, Marie dropped her notecards.
        (PN)   (PN)

Their position on gun control is questionable.
(PN)

Possessive pronouns can function as adjective complements.

The fault was hers.
        (PN)

Possessive adjectives are used in compound-modifying phrases.

He is a friend of Joe's and mine.
           (PN)

Your wife's and your gift was sincerely appreciated.
(PN)   (PN)
(Variant: You and your wife's gift . . .)

d.   *Special problems in the use of the possessive case*

Possessive pronouns precede and modify gerunds in formal communication.

My speaking to the manager probably wasn't a good idea.
(PN) (GER)

We would appreciate your attending the meeting.
        (PN)   (GER)

The possessive pronouns *its, whose, theirs, hers,* and *your* should not be confused with the contractions *it's, who's, there's, here's,* and *you're.*

There's no profession like nursing.
(Not: Theirs no business . . .)

The newspaper lost its case.
(Not: . . . lost it's case.)

e.   *Objective case*

Objects of prepositions require objective case pronouns.

The senator received information from her.
                (PREP) (PN)

Except for us, no one knows where the money is hidden.
    (PREP)(PN)

The company wrote the letter to Sarah and him.
            (PREP)   (PN)

Objects of transitive verbs (that is, verbs that pass the action to objects) need objective case pronouns.

The repairman accidentally hit him with a wrench.
           (V) (PN)

Who invited them to the reception?
(V)   (PN)

In addition to Wally and Arthur, we will consult Margaret, Doug, and her on this
                      (V)   (PN)
matter.

Appositives of objects of prepositions and transitive verbs call for objective case pronouns.

The instructor said that the report would be of interest to the two of us, Johnson and me.
L(PN)

All of us workers plan to go on strike if something isn't done to improve working
(PN)
conditions.

The governor wrote his loyal supporters, Josh and me, a letter of appreciation.
(PN)

The FBI questioned the criminals, Carrington and them, to determine how they
(PN)
gained access to Defense Systems computers.

f. Special problems in the use of the objective case

When a pronoun follows the infinitive *to be* and that infinitive is preceded by a subject of the infinitive, the pronoun is in objective case.

My nearsighted dalmatian took my friend to be me.
└(INF)┘(PN)

After careful consideration, the judges determined the winner to be her.
(PN)

Pronouns that serve as subjects or objects of infinitives are in the objective case.

We wanted him to pursue the matter.
(PN) └(INF)┘

The boss never desired the work load to overburden them.
└(INF)┘ (PN)

The question is whom to sue.
(PN) └(INF)┘

Sometimes the objective case is required when a pronoun is used in comparisons introduced by the words *than* and *as*.

We like the first option more than them.
(PN)
(Implied: We like the first option more than we like them.)

The boss confronted the loyal students as well as us.
(PN)
(Implied: The professor confronted the loyal students as well as confronted us.)

g. Use of who and whom/whoever and whomever

Who serves as subjects (s) of sentences and dependent clauses and as subject complements (sc).

Who is she? She is who?
(s)   (sc)

Who it is I think I know.
(sc—DEPENDENT CLAUSE)

We plan to specify who will represent our perspective in the debate.
                    (s—DEPENDENT CLAUSE)

A determination of who will load the pods aboard the aircraft is necessary.
                    (s—DEPENDENT CLAUSE)

We want people who we think are competent.
            (s—DEPENDENT CLAUSE)

Whoever also serves as subjects of dependent clauses.

The architect gave a photograph of the house to whoever wanted it.
                                        (s—DEPENDENT CL.)

Whoever needs a brochure is welcome to take one.
        (s—DEPENDENT CLAUSE)

Whom traditionally is the correct choice when the objective case is required.

For whom are you voting?
(PREP—OBJ)

Whom do you wish to answer the question?
(s OF INF)

Whom did she ask to the hearing?
(OBJ)

There are seventy-five respondents, of whom twenty-five are female.
                                (PREP—OBJ)

There is no telling whom the people of this district will elect.
                (OBJ—DEPENDENT CLAUSE)

The suspect, whom the witnesses saw leaving the scene of the crime, was
                    (OBJ—DEPENDENT CLAUSE)
arraigned.

Whomever, similarly, functions as the object of dependent clauses.

Whomever the voters elect will face enormous problems.
(OBJ—DEPENDENT CLAUSE)

Lend the money to whomever you want to have it.
                (OBJ—DEPENDENT CLAUSE)

h. The -self pronouns

The *-self* pronouns, including *myself, yourself, himself, herself, itself, ourselves, yourselves,* and *themselves,* serve in two capacities—as *intensifiers* and as *reflexives.* As intensifiers, they reinforce the message of the sentence, adding emphasis.

I myself would not care for another interview like that one.

As reflexives, -*self* pronouns allow subjects of sentences to act upon themselves.

He gave himself a lot of credit.

They were ashamed of themselves.

Often writers question whether or not the -*self* pronouns can replace nominative or objective case personal pronouns in sentences similar to the following. Generally speaking, the answer is no.

NOT:	Myself and my staff plan to be in New York.
BUT:	My staff and I plan to be in New York.
NOT:	People such as yourself are vulnerable.
BUT:	People such as you are vulnerable.

Sentences like the following are, however, becoming more acceptable simply because the grammatically correct alternative sounds awkward to the contemporary writer and speaker.

OK:	On behalf of Neil and myself, I would like to thank you.
CORRECT:	On behalf of Neil and me, I would like to thank you.

It is important to remember, though, that there are no such words as *hisself* and *theirself;* these words are often used incorrectly in place of *himself* and *themselves*.

5. Pronoun Agreement

Pronouns (pn.) agree with their antecedents (ant.) in *number.* Antecedents are nouns or other pronouns to which pronouns refer.

Sylvia Porter argues, in her article, that discrimination is the cause for unequal pay.
   └──(ANT.)──┘   (PN.)

Pronouns also must agree with their antecedents in *gender* (masculine, feminine, or neuter) and *person* (first, second, or third).

Each inductee in the Baseball Hall of Fame has his own plaque.
    (ANT.)   (PN.)

Before it reached the Eastern Seaboard, Hurricane Elroy fizzled.
  (PN.)   └──(ANT.)──┘

Difficulties occur for writers when the number of the antecedent is not obvious.

a. More than one antecedent joined by and

Pronouns whose antecedents are joined by *and* are generally plural.

Because of their achievements, Bill and Margaret were promoted.
    (PN.)   (ANT.)   (ANT.)

b. Antecedents joined by *or* or *nor*

When a pronoun's antecedents are joined by *or* or *nor,* the pronoun agrees with the closest antecedent.

Either Consolidated or United will make its bid today.
      (ANT.)   (ANT.)   (PN.)

Neither management nor the employees are excited about having their genes
      (ANT.)   (ANT.)   (PN.)
tested.

c. Indefinite pronouns used as antecedents

When the antecedent of a personal pronoun is an indefinite pronoun (e.g., *everyone*), a singular personal pronoun *(he, she, his, her)* is technically correct ("Everyone did his work"), but problems do arise. First, there is a gender problem. If you call "Everyone" either a "he" or a "she," your choice is gender-biased, except where you are clearly discussing either females or males.

Everyone in the women's professional association brought her own business card.

Either man will do his share.

Traditionally, the masculine singular pronoun has been used when the antecedent is an indefinite pronoun, such as *each* or *someone*. (Each of the employees pays for his own life insurance.) The so-called "generic he," however, produces or at least reinforces a male bias in language, and therefore its use should be avoided. One way to revise such sentences is to write them in the plural.

The employees pay for their own life insurance.

d. Collective nouns used as antecedents

When the antecedent of the pronoun is a collective noun, the pronoun can be singular or plural, depending on the meaning of the sentence. Collective nouns are nouns such as *group, team, class, audience,* and *personnel* that can be considered a single unit or a collection of parts functioning individually.

The group made its last decision.
    (ANT.)   (PN.)

When the house lights blinked, the audience returned to their seats.
                (ANT.)   (PN.)

6. Adjectives and Adverbs

Adjectives (adj.) modify nouns and pronouns; adverbs (adv.) modify verbs, adjectives, and other adverbs.

The nude mannequin stood in the hot window.
  (ADJ.)   (N)   (ADJ.) (N)

For several months, he had been ill.
  (ADJ.)   (N)   (PN.)   (ADJ.)

The tired lion lay quietly by the stream.
                 (V)   (ADV.)

The diplomat found herself in an extremely awkward position.
                                     (ADV.)   (ADJ.)

The detective acted very discreetly.
                  (ADV.) (ADV.)

Most errors involving the use of adjectives or adverbs occur because an adjective is used where an adverb is needed or an adverb is used where an adjective is needed.

While most adverbs end in the suffix *ly* and can often be recognized through their *ly* endings, many adjectives also end in *ly* (e.g., *lovely, lonely, stately, unsightly*). Conversely, many adverbs (e.g., *always, very, well, quite, then, too, often, now, soon, always*) do not end in *ly*. Finally, some words (e.g., *much, long,* and *fast*) are the same in both their adverbial and their adjectival forms.

To avoid mistaking an adjective for an adverb and vice-versa, writers should consult a dictionary. In addition, a familiarity with certain recurring problems is useful.

a. Some commonly misused adjectives

Three adjectives commonly mistaken for adverbs are *sure, good,* and *real.* These words are adjectives, not adverbs. Their adverbial forms are *surely, well,* and *really.* Because the adjectival and adverbial forms of these words are often misused in common speech, special care should be taken not to carry these errors over into writing.

INCORRECT:	The student sure did not intend to miss the deadline.
CORRECT:	The student surely did not intend to miss the deadline.
INCORRECT:	All of the professors hoped to do good on the evaluation.
CORRECT:	All of the professors hoped to do well on the evaluation.
INCORRECT:	The waiter was real sorry about spilling the soup.
CORRECT:	The waiter was really sorry about spilling the soup.

b. *Irregular adjectives and adverbs*

While most adjectives and adverbs form their comparative and superlative degrees through the addition of *er* and *est* or through the addition of *more* and *most* or *less* and *least,* some adjectives and adverbs form their comparative and superlative degrees irregularly—that is, through a change in the word itself. The following list charts the positive, comparative, and superlative degrees of some of the most common adjectives and adverbs.

POSITIVE	COMPARATIVE	SUPERLATIVE
bad	worse	worst
badly	worse	worst
far	farther	farthest
far	further	furthest
good	better	best
little	less	least
many	more	most
much	more	most
well	better	best

c. *Comparison of absolutes*

Some adjectives and adverbs such as *unique, perfect, square, impossible, round, complete,* and *supreme* cannot be compared. These words, called *absolutes,* cannot be compared because they are logically complete in their positive form. Either something is "perfect," or it isn't "perfect." It cannot, therefore, be logically "more perfect" or "most perfect." It is, however, possible to say "more nearly perfect" or "most nearly perfect."

7. Misplaced Modifiers

Modifiers such as *nearly, only,* and *almost* should be placed at the point in a sentence where their meaning is clearest. Sometimes sentences such as the following are illogical because of the faulty placement of these adverbs.

UNCLEAR:	The speaker almost talked the entire hour.
UNCLEAR:	The coach only wanted to congratulate the opposing player and leave.

The sense of these sentences would probably not be questioned if they were spoken. In writing, however, it is best to move the adverbs closer to what they modify.

CLEAR:	The speaker talked almost the entire hour.
CLEAR:	The coach wanted only to congratulate the opposing player and leave.

8. Dangling Modifiers

A *dangling modifier* is a phrase that common sense indicates does not logically modify another word in the sentence. Recurring types of phrases that tend to dangle include *prepositional phrases* and *verbal phrases*. The following sentences contain dangling modifiers.

> Before closing shop, the lights were turned off.
> (DANGLING PHRASE)
>
> Basted regularly, anyone can have a delicious turkey.
> (DANGLING PHRASE)
>
> To write a winning proposal, regular practice is required.
> (DANGLING PHRASE)
>
> While on the telephone, the ash tray caught fire.
> (DANGLING PHRASE)

In each of these sentences, the introductory phrase appears to modify the subject of the sentence. Common sense, however, tells us that (1) "lights" don't "close shop"; (2) people are not usually "basted"; (3) "regular practice" does not "write a winning proposal"; and (4) the flaming "ash tray" does not talk "on the telephone."

Thus the modifying phrases in the sentences above are called dangling modifiers—they dangle without purpose, sometimes rendering their sentences ridiculous.

A dangling modifier can be eliminated in two ways. First, furnish a word in the sentence for the modifier to modify.

> Before closing shop, I turned out the lights.
>
> Basted regularly, a turkey is likely to taste delicious.
>
> While on the telephone, John discovered that the ash tray caught fire.

Second, expand the modifier into a dependent clause that eliminates the confusion.

> For a person who wishes to write a winning proposal, regular practice is required.
>
> While John was on the telephone, the ash tray caught fire.

9. Parallelism

Parallelism means that items linked by coordinating conjunctions *(and, but, or, nor, for, yet)* or correlative conjunctions *(either . . . or; neither . . . nor; not only . . . but also; whether . . . or)* must be grammatically similar. For example, adjectives must be linked with adjectives, verbs with verbs, prepositional phrases with prepositional phrases, clauses with clauses, and so on.

INCORRECT:	The carpenter hammered the nail slow but confidently. (ADJ.) (CONJ.) (ADV.)
CORRECT:	The carpenter hammered the nail slowly but confi- dently. (ADV.) (CONJ.) (ADV.)
INCORRECT:	Jane is trustworthy, reliable, and knows her job well. (ADJ.) (ADJ.) (CONJ.) (V)
CORRECT:	Jane is trustworthy, reliable, and knowledgeable. (ADJ.) (ADJ.) (CONJ.) (ADJ.)
INCORRECT:	Football is a popular sport because it involves endurance, (N) skill, and the team plays as a unit. (N) ⌐(INDEPENDENT CLAUSE)⌐
CORRECT:	Football is a popular sport because it involves endurance, (N) skill, and teamwork. (N) (CONJ.) (N)
INCORRECT:	What the President says and his actions do not always ⌐(CLAUSE)⌐ (CONJ.) (N) correspond.
CORRECT:	What the President says and what he does do not ⌐(CLAUSE)⌐ (CONJ.) ⌐(CLAUSE)⌐ always correspond.

II. PUNCTUATION

1. Punctuating Compound Sentences and Avoiding Comma-Splices and Run-Ons

a. Comma-splices

A comma, by itself, cannot join two independent clauses (clauses that can stand alone as separate sentences). The result is a common error of sentence structure called a *comma-splice*.

INCORRECT:	Funding for the bomber was cut, the result was a loud uproar at the Pentagon.
CORRECT:	Funding for the bomber was cut, and the result was a loud uproar at the Pentagon.
OR:	Funding for the bomber was cut; the result was a loud uproar at the Pentagon.

b. Run-on sentences

Run-on sentences—sometimes called *fused sentences*—are compound sentences (sentences with two independent clauses) that do not contain proper punctuation between the independent clauses.

INCORRECT:	Television programs are mirrors of society but their reflections are often exaggerated.
CORRECT:	Television programs are mirrors of society, but their reflections are often exaggerated.
INCORRECT:	The government is spending millions of dollars each year to combat illegal immigration wouldn't it be cheaper just to open our borders and let people in?
CORRECT:	The government is spending millions of dollars each year to combat illegal immigration; wouldn't it be cheaper just to open our borders and let people in?

2. Commas

Keep commas to a minimum, but when you use them, follow these rules:

a. Commas and conjunctions

Use a comma before a conjunction to separate the main clauses in a compound sentence. Such conjunctions include *and, but, or, nor, for, so, yet.*

Three ideas were considered, but only one was adopted.
                                (CONJ.)

The Virginia land was ceded back in 1846 to ease the financial problems of the city of Alexandria, so the city of Washington now lies entirely in what was once Maryland.   (CONJ.)

b. Commas and introductory words

Use commas after certain introductory words, phrases, and clauses.

CONJUNCTIVE ADVERBS

Therefore, I favor mainstreaming as a means for improving education.
(CONJUNCTIVE ADV.)

LONG PREPOSITIONAL PHRASES

At various points in the discussion, the writer uses examples to demonstrate her
└──(LONG PREPOSITIONAL PHRASE)──┘
point.

VERBAL PHRASES

To fit, the suit has to be measured correctly.
(VERBAL)

Breaking the news of the new agreement, the president spoke of the hard work
└────────(INTRODUCTORY VERBAL PHRASE)────────┘
that the negotiators had performed.

INTRODUCTORY CLAUSES

When pregnant mothers drink excessively, they run the risk of causing fetal
└────────(INTRODUCTORY VERBAL CLAUSE)────────┘
alcohol syndrome.

c.   Commas and nonrestrictive modifiers

Use commas to set apart nonrestrictive modifiers (i.e., words, phrases, and clauses that describe nouns without limiting them). Restrictive clauses, as in the following sentence, are not set off:

Teachers who are receiving pay raises can look forward to a prosperous year.

The lack of commas means the clause *who are receiving pay raises* provides an important restriction on the noun *teachers,* here indicating that not all teachers are receiving pay raises. In the following sentence, however, the same clause becomes nonrestrictive (meaning that all teachers are receiving increases) and requires commas to set it apart from the rest of the sentence.

Teachers, who are receiving pay raises, can look forward to a prosperous year.

d.   Commas and series

Insert commas between a series of coordinated words, phrases, and clauses.

NOUNS

Damaged pipes, frayed wiring, and a weakened foundation are reasons the
    (N)   (N)   (N)
house will not sell.

PREPOSITIONAL PHRASES

Cameras were placed above the entrance, next to the counter, and in the vault.
        └─(PREP. PHRASE)─┘ └─(PREP. PHRASE)─┘   (PREP. PHRASE)

VERBAL PHRASES

The arrangement of floor area in the library was altered, allowing for easier
                                      └─(VERBAL PHRASE)──
access to the reference area and copy machines, providing more space for study
                                     ┘ └────────(VERBAL PHRASE)────────
carrels, and improving the location of the card catalog.
──────┘   └────────(VERBAL PHRASE)────────┘

COMPOUND VERBS

Citizens wrote to their representatives, presented public information forums, and
         (v)   (v)

staged protests outside the agency office.
  (v)

DEPENDENT CLAUSES

The article claimed that the candidate had had an affair with a campaign volunteer,
                              (DEPENDENT CLAUSE)

that the worker had subsequently tried to use the relationship with the candidate
                              (DEPENDENT CLAUSE)

to land a paid position with the campaign organization, and that when the candi-
                                            (DEPENDENT CLAUSE)

date tried to terminate the relationship the worker threatened blackmail.

e. Commas and dates and place names

Dates and place names are set apart by commas.

Eugene, Oregon, is the location of a UFO sighting.

January 15, 1999, is our target date.

3. Semicolons

a. Semicolons and long series

Use semicolons to set apart items in a long series.

The panel consisted of an ex-Army Colonel who had spent much of his career writing manuals, letters, and reports; a recent Ph.D. who wrote a book on language; and an editor with Mercury Aerospace who had also worked at IBM, Barrier Electronics, and Chip Services.

b. Semicolons and independent clauses

Use a semicolon (rather than a comma and coordinating conjunction) between two independent clauses to shift rhythm and gain emphasis.

The committee members argued forcefully; they wanted their proposal to pass.

c. Semicolons and conjunctive adverbs

Semicolons precede conjunctive adverbs such as *consequently, finally, furthermore, however, meanwhile, moreover, nevertheless, nonetheless, otherwise, then,* and *therefore* when they connect two independent clauses.

Downtown merchants created an association to lure businesses back to the urban center; however, they could not agree on the methods they should use.

4. Apostrophes

a. Apostrophes and possession

Use an apostrophe to show possession. Writers make words not ending in *s* possessive by adding *'s*.

The broker's advice made her friends rich.

Someone's head is going to roll.

The women's studies class will meet with the panel tomorrow.

Words ending in *s* are rendered possessive either with an *'s* or a sole apostrophe.

The business's reputation suffered.

The presidential cabinet met to discuss the crisis' effects.

Note: The key to determining whether to employ the *'s* or *'* is pronunciation; *'s* puts a "sez" on the end of a possessive. *Crisis's* would be pronounced awkwardly as kri-sis-sez. So a simple apostrophe at the end of the word would do.

A single apostrophe is used to make plural words ending in *s* possessive.

The educators' union drew up an agreement with the campus administration.

Two weeks' vacation is hardly enough.

b. Apostrophes and plurals

Use an apostrophe for plurals of letters, numerals, and abbreviations when clarity is at stake.

I tried to collect all of my IOU's.

The A's and S's on our printer look alike.

The 1040's and Publication 17's are in the filing cabinet.

c. Apostrophes and contractions

Use an apostrophe to show a contraction of two words into one: *can't, don't, haven't,* and so on. The word *it's* always is a contraction of *it is,* never the possessive pronoun *its:*

It's a shame the mouse lost its tail.

5. Colons

Colons furnish spotlights for things to come in sentences. Their uses are listed below.

a. Colons and explanatory items

Use a colon to introduce an explanatory item or items after a statement that tells what the items are in general. A grammatically complete sentence should precede the colon.

> The following is a list of people who have volunteered to canvas for the Heart Fund: Susan Joiner, John Dean, Jacob Horner.

b. Colons and explanatory words

Use a colon to introduce explanatory words and word groupings.

> The investors waited for one thing: dollar devaluation.

> He had one concern in life: making a lot of money.

Note: A sentence of explanation coming after a colon usually begins with a capital letter.

> The newspaper printed the following advice in its classified section: Let the buyer beware!

6. Dashes

Dashes can be used effectively for emphasis and effect.

a. Dashes and appositive phrases

Use dashes to set off a long appositive phrase that has commas within it, so that it is clearer where the appositive begins and ends. (Appositives are words and phrases that rename nouns.)

> The members of our group who were going to attend the march on Washington—Fred Mosely, Emily Smith, and Rosalyn Cohn—departed for the nation's capitol at 6 A.M.

b. Dashes rather than colons

Use a dash rather than a colon if you want to draw particular attention to a parenthetical word or phrase.

> The talk-show interviewer set an informal tone—the kind of tone that causes guests to relax and say too much.

7. Quotation Marks

a. Direct quotations

Use quotation marks to enclose a direct quotation.

> A customer stated, "Yobean is the best coffee I have ever drunk."

Note: Paraphrased statements are not set in quotes.

> A customer stated that Yobean is the best coffee she ever drank.

b. Reprinted material

Use quotation marks to enclose material taken directly from a printed source.

> According to the report, "Until 1983, the college had no coordinator of academic computing."

c. Titles of short works

Use quotation marks to refer to titles of short works, including articles, chapters within longer works, and lectures.

> I enjoyed your article in *Newsweek* titled "SDI or Suicide?"

d. Commas, periods, semicolons

Place commas and periods inside quotes, semicolons outside.

> The employee replied, "I would never vote for a union here at Westco"; after thinking it over for a moment, though, he added, ". . . almost never."

e. Question marks and exclamation points

Question marks and exclamation points can be inside or outside quotation marks. If just the quoted material is a question or exclamation, then the sentence punctuation is inside the quotes.

> The reporter inquired, "Do you expect lawsuits as a result of the tragedy?"

> In response, the executive exclaimed, "Of course!"

If the entire sentence is a question or an exclamation, then the end punctuation can be outside the quotes.

> Who said, "I cannot tell a lie"?

8. Hyphens

Hyphens are connectors to be used sparingly when nouns and modifiers must be joined. Their purpose is to aid clarity.

a. Hyphens and compound modifiers

Compound modifiers are often hyphenated when they appear in front of the words they modify and not hyphenated when they come afterwards.

The sugar-coated cereal captured 10 percent of the market.

Our most popular brand of cereal is sugar coated.

b.   Hyphens and compound nouns

Compound nouns may be hyphenated. New noun combinations, in particular, often start off as hyphenated combinations.

Our office's folder-gluer broke down.

Sometimes the hyphen disappears as combinations gain an identity of their own.

Policyholders will benefit from this new program.

When you are trying to determine if a particular combination is hyphenated, the best place to look is the dictionary.

III. MECHANICS

I.   Capitalization

"Proper" (meaning "one's own") names and titles are capitalized; general names and titles are not capitalized.

PROPER	GENERAL
Governor Christine Todd Whitman	the governor
Broadway	the street
Audubon Society	a society
Mercedes	the car

Note: In compound nouns, only the "proper" part is capitalized; for example, Angus cattle, Douglas fir, Chinese checkers, German shepherd.

Writers often have questions concerning the handling of the names and titles of (a) people, (b) places, (c) organizations, (d) temporal events and processes, and (e) written works.

a.   People

Proper names, traditionally capitalized, give writers few problems: Lauren Bacall, Humphrey Bogart. A title that precedes a name is capitalized: Chairperson Manfred L. Benedict.

Names derived from countries—Frenchman, American, Canadians—are generally capitalized. Further, it is standard practice to capitalize names of groups of people that derive from continents, races, religions, and tribes: Indian, Hispanic, Pygmy, Hindu. Classifications based on color, however, are usually, but not necessarily, written in lowercase: black, white.

b. Places

The names of geographical areas recognized as separate entities are capitalized (e.g., Europe, Iceland, South America, Antarctica). General designations, such as "the mountains," "the seashore," or "the continent" are not capitalized.

The names of empires, countries, territories, states, counties, and cities are capitalized, as well as their derivatives: Washington, Washingtonian.

Specific names of topographical features—rivers, oceans, islands, mountains, forests, and the like—are capitalized: Great Barrier Reef, Lake Michigan.

Places with proper names, such as buildings, dams, streets, avenues, parks, and squares, are also capitalized: World Trade Center, Disney World, Rodeo Drive.

c. Organizations

The names of government agencies, companies, institutions, associations, and conferences are generally capitalized.

Government Agencies: United States Supreme Court, Bureau of the Census.

Companies and Institutions: San Francisco State College, St. Charles' Hospital, Tyson's Corner Shopping Mall.

Associations and Conferences: Baltimore Orioles, League of Women Voters, Democratic Party.

d. Temporal events and processes

The names of days and the names of months are routinely capitalized, but the names of seasons are generally presented in lowercase: fall, spring.

The names of holidays—deriving both from proper nouns (Christmas) and common nouns (New Year's Eve)—are also capitalized.

The names of wars, battles, treaties, historical documents, legal cases, and other events in history are usually capitalized: World War II, Battle of Bull Run, Declaration of Independence, *Smith v. Alabama.*

e. Written works

Capitalize the titles of documents, books, and periodicals: The Stamp Act, *Structuring Paragraphs, Time.*

2. Abbreviations

Abbreviations are shortened forms of words that should be used judiciously.

a. *Types of abbreviations*

Some abbreviations refer to single words, others to more than one word. Single-word abbreviations generally consist of the most important letters from longer words and are followed by a period.

Inc.   (Incorporated)

Col.   (Colonel)

p.   (page)

Multi-word abbreviations, however, most often comprise the first letter or letters of all the words that are abbreviated.

C.P.A.   (certified public accountant)

R.F.D.   (rural free delivery)

Frequently used and familiar multi-word abbreviations appear without periods.

CIA   (Central Intelligence Agency)

RSVP   (Repondez s'il vous plait)

pc   (personal computer)

Multi-word abbreviations that form new words without periods are called acronyms.

MADD   (Mothers Against Drunk Drivers)

b. *Uses of abbreviations*

Abbreviated titles may appear after names.

Camilla E. Ramirez, C.E.O.

Chou N. Yang, Ph.D.

George H. Jones, Jr.

Most often, titles should not be abbreviated when they precede names, with the exceptions of Hon. (Honorable), Rev. (Reverend), and Mons. (Monsieur).

Latinate words and phrases are often abbreviated in text.

ca., circa (about, approximately)

etc., et cetera (and so forth)

P.S., post scriptum (postscript)

Certain designations of time are abbreviated.

A.M., ante meridiem—before noon (9 A.M.)

M., meridies—noon (12 M.)

Note: Because M. might be misinterpreted as midnight, it is usually better to write out noon, or midnight.

P.M., post meridiem—after noon (9 P.M., 12 P.M.)

Other important time indicators that are often abbreviated include *anno Domini* (A.D.) and "before Christ" (B.C.). Both are capitalized—A.D. appearing before the date (A.D. 1992), B.C. appearing after the date (55 B.C.).

In academic writing, abbreviations in the following situations are usually inappropriate:

First names (William, not Wm.)

Place names (Baltimore, not Balto.)

Names of days (Sunday, not Sun.)

Course names (English 101, not Eng. 101).

Names of organizations (Brothers, not Bros.; Company, not Co.)

In general, units of measurement (feet, not ft., inches, not in.), except in technical writing where the frequent mention of such units makes abbreviations appropriate.

c.   Abbreviation forms

The following is a listing of commonly used abbreviations; it is by no means comprehensive.

abbr.	abbreviated, abbreviation
abr.	abridged; abridgement
ac	alternating current
acct.	account
A.D.	*anno Domini*—in the year of our Lord
a.k.a.	also known as
a.m. (A.M.)	*ante meridiem*—before noon
anon.	anonymous
app.	appendix
Apr.	April
art.	article
Aug.	August
Ave.	avenue
b.	born; brother
B.A.	Bachelor of Arts
B.C.	before Christ
biog.	biography; biographer; biographical
bk.	book; block
B.S.	Bachelor of Science
c.	chapter (in law citations); *circa*
ca.	*circa*—approximately, about
Capt.	captain
cf.	compare, see

ch. (chap.)	chapter
COD	cash on delivery
col.	column
con. (cont.)	continued
copr.	copyright
cp.	compare
c.s.t.	central standard time
d.	died; daughter
dc	direct current
D.D.	Doctor of Divinity
D.D.S.	Doctor of Dental Surgery
Dec.	December
dept.	department
dict.	dictionary
dist.	district
div.	division; divorced
doz.	dozen
Dr.	doctor; drive
E.	east
ed.	edition; editor
e.d.t.	eastern daylight time
e.g.	*exempli gratia*—for example
engr.	engineer
esp.	especially
e.s.t.	eastern standard time
et al.	*et alii*—and others
etc.	*et cetera*—and so forth
et seq.	*et sequentes*—and the following
ex.	example
f. (ff.)	and following page, pages
Feb.	February
fig.	figure
Fri.	Friday
hdqrs.	headquarters
ibid.	*ibidem*—in the same place
i.e.	*id est*—that is
inf.	*infra*—below
inst.	institute; institution
Jan.	January
J.D.	Juris Doctor—Doctor of Law
Jr.	junior
l.	line; left
LL.B.	Bachelor of Laws
LL.D.	Doctor of Laws
loc. cit.	*loco citato*—in the place cited
Lt.	lieutenant
M. (MM.)	monsieur, messieurs
m. (M.)	*meridies*—noon
m.	married; male; measure
Maj.	major

Mar.	March
M.D.	Doctor of Medicine
memo	memorandum
mgr.	manager
misc.	miscellaneous
Mlle	mademoiselle
Mme	madam
Mmes	mesdames
Mon.	Monday
M.S.	Master of Science
MS, MSS	manuscript, manuscripts
m.s.t.	mountain standard time
n.	note, footnote; noun
N.	north
n.d.	no date
no.	number
non seq.	*non sequitur*—it does not follow
Nov.	November
Oct.	October
op. cit.	*opere citato*—in the work cited
p. (pp.)	page, pages
pass.	*passim*—throughout; passive
Ph.D.	Doctor of Philosophy
p.m. (P.M.)	*post meridiem*—after noon
Prof.	professor
pro tem.	*pro tempore*—for the time being
PS	*postscriptum*—postscript
p.s.t.	pacific standard time
pt.	part
Q.E.D.	*quod erat demonstrandum*—which was to be demonstrated
q.v.	*quod vide*—which see
Rd.	road
Rev.	reverend
R.N.	registered nurse
R.R.	railroad
S.	south
Sat.	Saturday
sec.	section
Sept.	September
ser.	series
Sr.	senior
St.	saint; street
Sun.	Sunday
sup.	*supra*—above
supp.	supplement
s.v.	*sub verbo*—under the word
Thurs.	Thursday
trans.	translator; translated; transitive
treas.	treasurer
Tues.	Tuesday

univ.	university
ut sup.	*ut supra*—as above
v.	versus; verb
viz	*videlicet*—namely
vol.	volume
W.	west
Wed.	Wednesday
yr.	year

d. State abbreviations

AK	Alaska	MT	Montana
AL	Alabama	NB	Nebraska
AR	Arkansas	NC	North Carolina
AZ	Arizona	ND	North Dakota
CA	California	NH	New Hampshire
CO	Colorado	NJ	New Jersey
CT	Connecticut	NM	New Mexico
DE	Delaware	NV	Nevada
FL	Florida	NY	New York
GA	Georgia	OH	Ohio
HI	Hawaii	OK	Oklahoma
ID	Idaho	OR	Oregon
IL	Illinois	PA	Pennsylvania
IN	Indiana	RI	Rhode Island
IA	Iowa	SC	South Carolina
KS	Kansas	SD	South Dakota
KY	Kentucky	TN	Tennessee
LA	Louisiana	TX	Texas
MA	Massachusetts	UT	Utah
MD	Maryland	VA	Virginia
ME	Maine	VT	Vermont
MI	Michigan	WA	Washington
MN	Minnesota	WI	Wisconsin
MO	Missouri	WV	West Virginia
MS	Mississippi	WY	Wyoming

3. Numbers

Rules governing the use of numbers in text can vary with the task. Writers generally want to know (1) when to spell them, (2) when to enter them as figures, and (3) what to do when a number begins a sentence.

a. Spelling numbers

In general writing, if the number can be expressed in one or two words, then it should be spelled (for example, twenty-one); otherwise, the number should appear as a figure. With units of measure, however, spell the number ("five feet long").

b. Numbers as figures in text

In the following cases, numerals are appropriate in general text:

Time of day: 9 P.M., 9:00 P.M.; but nine o'clock

Days and years: 30 August 1948; August 30, 1948

Addresses: 30 Fifth Avenue
              Route 1, Box 17A

Money (exact amounts that cannot be spelled out without awkwardness): $76.85; but twenty-five dollars

Direct references to texts: page 43; volume 3; Act I, scene ii

Decimals, percentages, fractions: 4.3 million; 70 percent; 2⅓ children per household

Divisions in enumerated text: (1) Call Carl, (2) Tell Mabel, (3) See Moe.

c. Numbers beginning a sentence

Spell out a number beginning a sentence. If it's more than two words, rephrase to avoid beginning the sentence with the number:

Seventy-five amoeba can fit on the head of a pin.

A total of 7,429 angels can fit on the head of a pin.

4. Italics (underlining)

Italic type is used by publishers and printers to set off particular words and phrases. In appearance, italics resemble handwritten script, and many typewriters and word processors come with italics capabilities so that the writer can employ them where needed. Those of us, however, who do not have machines with such capabilities, are left to underline where italics would normally be used.

The following is a listing of the kinds of words and phrases that are italicized or underlined.

a. Titles of long written works

Books: *World Book Encyclopedia*

Periodicals: *Time*

Newspapers: *The Washington Post*

b. Specialized words and titles

Scientific names (genus and species): *Orycteropus* (Aardvark)

Legal cases: *Craft v. Metromedia*

Transportation craft (sometimes): *Titanic, Orient Express, Airforce I, Challenger*

c. Letters as letters, words as words

Letters as Letters: *Aardvark* has three *A*'s in it.

Words as Words: The word *short* is longer than the word *long*.

5. Parentheses and Brackets

Use parentheses and brackets sparingly. If you must use them, follow these guidelines.

a. Parentheses

Parentheses surround words and phrases that are not essential but helpful. Parenthetical expressions include interruptions, examples, and explanations. Also, parentheses serve in numbered or lettered listings to set off the numbers or letters.

Enclose parenthetical expressions with parentheses.

INTERRUPTIONS	The lab assistant generously showed me how to switch on the terminal (I was too inexperienced to do it myself), and then he helped me access a software program.
EXAMPLES	The differences between the two countries (for example, their divergent opinions on human rights and dissimilar economic philosophies) stimulated suspicion between them that lasted for decades.
EXPLANATIONS	The Cumberland (MD) *Times* reports that the government agency is expecting severe cutbacks in funding.

Parentheses are used in enumerated texts. A parenthesis or two can replace the simple period in numbering lists of ideas or things.

This report will (1) furnish details about the production problems currently being experienced at our Frederick facility, (2) propose a three-point plan for overcoming those problems, and (3) present a detailed budget for that three-point plan.

When parentheses are used with commas, the commas are placed outside the parentheses.

Before he would sign the contract (Mom always said, "Don't sign anything!"), Baker had it perused by her lawyer.

When parentheses are used with periods, a parenthesis that ends a sentence is followed by the period.

> According to Jonathan Lipscomb, former manager of the Missouri Bluewings, "Communication is 90 percent of a manager's job" (*My Years in the Sport,* p. 165).

> Professor M. Kotelchuck discusses student morale and its relationship to frequent feedback ("The Importance of Evaluation." In M. Lamb [ed.], *A Guide to Higher Education.* [New York: Wiley, 1993]).

b. Brackets

Brackets serve as signals for editorial comments and corrections within texts.

Brackets sometimes enclose editorial explanations and clarifications.

> "For testifying before the House Committee, he [Ford] was granted immunity and allowed to relocate with a new identity."

Brackets also enclose the word *sic* (Latin for "in this manner"), which is used when writers want to signal that an error in original text was not made by them.

> The statement read: "The states [sic] attorney and the legislature have made this move legal. I hope the mayor and the council read this law."

IV. SPELLING

A misspelled word in a paragraph or essay can sometimes distract the reader from the writer's point and even give that reader the impression of carelessness or unreliability. In spite of the proliferation of computer spell checkers these days, writers still find that they still confront the same age-old problems.

1. Unfamiliar and Troublesome Words

Some of the reasons why spelling correctly is a formidable task are the same sounds in English are often spelled differently, words are often not spelled the way they sound, and mispronounced words do not sound the way they are spelled.

Some words that contain the same sound are spelled differently. Such words may contain suffixes like *-ar* and *-er, -ant* and *-ent, -ance* and *-ence, -able* and *-ible.*

> calendar/disaster
>
> descendant/eminent

reluctance/independence

irresistible/indispensable

Entire words, as well, may sound alike, but may be spelled differently. Such words are called homophones. Examples of homophones include *capitol/capital, principle/principal, discrete/discreet*. [The next section contains a full glossary of troublesome homophones.]

Further, words may not be spelled the way they sound. Such words as *nuisance, marriage,* and *maneuver* may pose problems because of the vowel combinations they contain. When the *-ui, -ia,* and *-eu* combinations are pronounced, one vowel sound predominates. So a writer may think their proper spellings are *nusance, marrige,* and *manuver.*

Also, letter combinations may have different sounds, depending on the words in which they appear. Consider the varying pronunciation of the *-ough* combination in the following words: *rough, bough, bought, through, though,* and *cough.*

Finally, mispronunciation or changes in pronunciation cause their share of misspellings. The dropping of sounds, such as the *c* in words like *acquire* or *acquaint,* can lead writers to spell them wrong. Other sound droppings that occur in words like *mathematics* and *temperature* can yield faulty spellings such as *mathmatics* and *temperture.*

Pronouncing the *-er* sound when saying words like *monstrous* and *disastrous* can result in versions such as *monsterous* and *disasterous.* And the hardening of the *-a* sound in pronunciations of the middle syllable of the word *separate* can lead the writer to write *seperate.*

The preceding discussion does little more than touch on problems facing spellers of English words. But to aid the writer/speller, there are a few rules for words containing the *-ie* and *-ei* combinations, for the doubling of consonants, and so forth. But there are always exceptions to the rules that complicate the situation.

So, to the person concerned with standard spelling, we offer the following advice. Use your spell checker when you can, but be aware that computer software programs cannot pick up misspellings when the misspellings are actual words—*an* for *and,* for example. Plus, you will not always have your trusty computer available, so supplement your technological aid by checking out any unfamiliar words in a reliable dictionary. Also, make a list of the words you commonly misspell. The following compilation of difficult words may help you make a start on your list.

absence	accumulate	address	annihilate
abundance	accustomed	adolescence	apparatus
accept	achieve	affiliate	apparent
acceptable	acknowledge	aggravate	apparition
accessible	acquaint	aggressive	appearance
accidentally	acquire	all right	appropriate
accommodate	across	a lot	arctic

argument	determine	interest	persuade
ascend	develop	interference	poison
asinine	diffident	irrelevant	pollute
assassination	disagree	irresistible	possession
assessment	disappear	irritable	potato
auxiliary	disappoint	judgment	precede
beginning	disastrous	knowledge	preference
belief	discipline	leisure	preferred
believe	discriminate	length	prevalent
breath	dispel	lenient	primitive
breathe	dissatisfied	license	privilege
bureaucracy	dominant	likelihod	procedure
business	duel	livelihood	proceed
calendar	dyeing	luxury	prominent
carriage	ecstasy	magnificent	pronunciation
category	eighth	maintenance	propaganda
cemetery	eligible	manageable	prophecy
certain	embarrass	maneuver	prophesy
changeable	eminent	manufacturer	publicly
changeover	environment	marriage	pursue
chief	equipped	memento	quandary
column	exaggerate	mischievous	quantity
commercial	exceed	missile	questionnaire
commitment	excellent	misspell	recede
committed	exercise	morale	receipt
comparative	exhaust	moccasin	receive
competent	existence	necessary	recognize
conceit	expedient	neighbor	recommend
conceive	familiar	ninth	referral
condemn	favorite	noticeable	referred
conscience	February	nuisance	relief
conscientious	fluorescent	obstacle	relieve
conscious	forcibly	occasion	remembrance
consistent	fulfill	occasionally	reminisce
convenience	gauge	occur	repetition
convenient	government	occurrence	resistance
courteous	grammar	omission	restaurant
criticism	guarantee	opportunity	rhythm
criticize	guard	optimistic	ridiculous
curiosity	harass	paid	roommate
deceive	humorous	parallel	sacrilegious
decide	hypocrisy	pasture	satellite
definite	incidentally	perceive	scarcity
definitely	incredible	permanent	seize
dependent	independence	permissible	separate
descend	indispensable	persevere	sergeant
descendant	inevitably	persistence	sherbet
desirable	innocuous	personnel	similar
desperate	inoculate	perspiration	sponsor

stationary	tendency	unnecessary	visible
stationery	tomato	used to	vitamin
superintendent	transferred	vacuum	warrant
supersede	twelfth	vengeance	weird
supposed to	tyranny	villain	wholly
suppress	unanimous		

2. Homophones and Commonly Confused Words

Homophones are words that have similar sounds but that are spelled differently. In addition, they have distinct meanings. The following is a glossary of homophones, and other commonly confused words.

ACCEPT/EXCEPT *Accept* is a verb meaning "to take" or "receive"; *except,* most commonly, is a preposition meaning "leaving out."

I *accept* the nomination.

Everyone, *except* Marge, has been eliminated.

ADAPT/ADOPT Both of these are verbs, but *to adapt* means "to change or adjust in order to suit new conditions" while *to adopt* means "to take up and make one's own, whether it be an idea, method or even a child."

Will the manatees *adapt* to the cooler temperatures?

United States families are *adopting* children from abroad.

ADVICE/ADVISE *Advice* and *advise* both involve someone giving wisdom to someone else, but *advice* is the actual message and *advise* is the act of giving that message.

The *advice* you have given to me I will always remember.

Maybe a lawyer can *advise* you in this matter.

AFFECT/EFFECT This combination gives writers the most difficulty. Most often, *affect* is used as a verb, and *effect* serves as a noun.

Her opinion will *affect* our decision.

The *effects* of the court's decision will not be felt for several months.

This is not to say that *affect* cannot be a noun or *effect* a verb. The word *affect,* as a noun, means "an emotion or feeling attached to an idea, object, place, and so forth"; *effect,* as a verb, means "to bring about."

Fred was plagued by a fearful *affect* as he approached his parents' old home.

The president *effected* many changes.

AGREE TO/AGREE WITH *To agree to* something means "to consent" to it; *to agree with* someone or something means to "be in accord with" that person or idea.

The citizens *agreed to* the new tax hike.

There were, however, a few parts of the new legislation that they did not *agree with*.

ALL READY/ALREADY   The two-word version means "completely prepared"; the one-word form, however, means "by or before the given or implied time."

Management was *all ready* for a strike.

They had *already* made interim plans.

ALL TOGETHER/ALTOGETHER   In this set, the two-word version means "in unison" or "gathered in one place"; the single-word form, on the other hand, means "wholly."

The team was *all together* on the strategy.

Reactions to the speech were *altogether* too harsh.

ALLUSION/ILLUSION   Sounding very much alike, these two words have quite different meanings. An *allusion* is an "indirect or casual reference"; an *illusion,* however, is "a false idea or conception."

The speaker's *allusion* to the political circumstances in that country was not missed by the listeners.

They had no *illusions* about the political ambitions of the new military dictator.

ALMOST/MOST   As a result of popular usage, *most* has become a sanctioned replacement for *almost,* when *almost* means "very nearly but not completely." Traditionally, however, *most* is the superlative adjective form of *many* and *much,* meaning "greatest in amount or number" or "a majority."

Almost all of the surveyed students favored intramural sports.

Most of our time was spent convincing the student government to support the program.

AMONG/BETWEEN   Both prepositions, *among* means "in the company of," "surrounded by," "included with" a group of more than two people or objects, and *between* means "connecting," "relating," or "separating" two people or objects.

You are *among* friends.

We will not let this episode come *between* us.

AMOUNT/NUMBER   *Amount* implies a quantity of something that cannot be counted; *number* indicates a quantity of items that can be counted.

The *amount* of work you put in on this paper will greatly determine the amount of satisfaction you will derive from the grade you receive.

The *number* of hours that my group has devoted to the project is staggering.

APPRAISE/APPRISE   The closeness of the sound of these two words often causes writers and speakers to confuse them. *Appraise* means to "set a price for" or to "determine the value of"; meanwhile, *apprise* means "to inform" or "to notify."

The realtor will *appraise* the value of my property.

She will then *apprise* the bank of her appraisal.

AS/LIKE   In formal writing, *like* is used as a preposition only, and *as* may be used both as a subordinating conjunction and a preposition.

Friends *like* me are difficult to find.

Morgan works hard, *as* a new member should.

Sheila was hired *as* a systems analyst.

ASSURE/ENSURE/INSURE   *To assure* means "to promise" that something will occur. *To ensure* and *insure,* on the other hand, have come to share the meaning "to make certain." Some writers prefer to use *insure* when the context is legal or financial and *ensure* when the context is personal.

They *assured* us that the book would be available tomorrow.

Urban Life *insured* the science building for $10.5 million.

To *ensure* our arrival at the appropriate time, we took the earlier plane.

A WHILE/AWHILE   Possessing similar meanings, *a while* is used after a preposition, and the adverb *awhile* is employed when no preposition is present.

The board will recess for *a while*.

Stay *awhile* while I check this out.

BORNE/BORN   These homophones present problems for many writers. *Borne* is the alternate past perfect form of the verb *to bear,* or "to carry." *To bear* can also mean "to give birth to"; hence the confusion with *born,* which is the adjective that means "brought into life or being."

The Public Relations Office has *borne* the responsibility for internal as well as external communications.

A new country was *born* out of the ashes of two dying nations.

BRING/TAKE   The distinction between these two words is ever so subtle and, in fact, dying in the language. Traditionally, *to bring* means "carrying or conducting to" and *to take* means "carrying or conducting away from a specified or implied place."

Ralph, will you *bring* a copy of the report with you to the meeting?

I am sorry, but I *took* it home and left it there.

CAPITAL/CAPITOL   *Capital* has many meanings and uses. In a sentence, it can mean everything from money to a seat of government. *Capitol,* on the other hand, does not appear in dictionaries anymore as a general noun. The Capitol is generally understood to be the building in which the U.S. Congress meets.

He tried to raise enough *capital* to expand his bicycle company.

She heads a lobbying organization that works on *Capitol* Hill.

CITE/SITE   Sound is the only characteristic these two words have in common. *To cite* has three frequently employed meanings, including "to summon to court," "to refer to in text," and "to quote." A *site*, on the other hand, means a "location."

The writers of the report *cited* over two hundred secondary sources.

We chose the *site* for our new plant.

COMPLEMENT/COMPLIMENT   Something that *complements* "completes" something else or brings it closer to perfection. A *compliment* points out the perfection by being a "statement of praise or admiration."

This new series of television ads will *complement* our total advertising campaign.

The president *complimented* us on our new series of television ads.

COMPRISE/COMPOSED OF   Although "is comprised of" is seen often these days, traditionally *comprise* is not used this way. *To comprise,* by itself, means "to include or contain." *Compose,* by contrast, has to change form to *composed of* before it can mean the same as *comprise.*

Our campaign *comprises* radio and television spots, full-page ads in major periodicals, and a mass mailing.

Our campaign is *composed of* radio and television spots, full-page ads in major periodicals, and a mass mailing.

CONTINUAL/CONTINUOUS   *Continual* means that something "recurs repeatedly"; *continuous* applies to something that "ranges uninterrupted in time or space."

Continual interruptions interfered with the class discussion.

Over the years the debate was *continuous.*

CONVINCE/PERSUADE   Americans do not distinguish between this duo as often as the British do. Traditionally, when one's opinion is changed, he or she is *convinced* by someone or something who has *persuaded* him or her to do so.

The public was *convinced* by the report's findings.

The report *persuaded* them that smoking is hazardous to health.

COUNCIL/COUNSEL   Similar to the distinction between *advice* and *advise,* the difference between *council* and *counsel* rests in their sentence function:

one is a noun, the other is a verb. A *council* is ordinarily a group of people assembled to make decisions or to *counsel* other people in particular matters.

George took his complaints to the Grievance *Council*.

They *counseled* him to seek legal redress.

DIFFERENT FROM/DIFFERENT THAN Both of these combinations mean to be "unlike." But *different from* is preferred, except when it leads to wordiness.

The new line of washers is *different from* those we have used before.

My roommate is a *different* person *than* he used to be.

DISCREET/DISCRETE *Discreet* means "careful about what one says"; *discrete*, on the other hand, means "separate and distinct."

Be *discreet* during your interview.

Two *discrete* considerations are opportunity and motive.

DISINTERESTED/UNINTERESTED To be *disinterested* means to be "impartial" or "unbiased"; to be *uninterested*, however, means to be "not interested."

The students and the administration sought a *disinterested* party to arbitrate the disagreement.

The first arbitrator who was approached about the job seemed *uninterested*.

DUAL/DUEL Often confused in spelling, *dual* means "two-part," and *duel*, its antiquated counterpart, refers to "formal combat between two participants." The latter's use today is limited.

The *dual* nature of the proposal caused us concern.

At the Medieval tournament, rival teams *dueled* for over three hours.

EMINENT/IMMINENT *Eminent* most commonly is employed as a describer for a person or group that is considered "high in achievement," "renown," or "outstanding." *Imminent*, however, means "likely to happen" or "impending."

The panel consisted of several *eminent* scientists.

A major storm is *imminent*.

ESPECIALLY/SPECIALLY Popular usage has merged the meanings of these two. *Especially*, traditionally, means "mainly" or "particularly," while *specially* means "in a special manner" or "for a special purpose."

The agency was stunned by the criticism, *especially* Senator Craig's.

Craig drafted a resolution *specially* aimed at resolving the problem.

EVERYDAY/EVERY DAY The one-word version is a modifier meaning "daily" or "ordinary." The two-word combination simply means "each day."

The chimpanzee's *everyday* routine was examined closely.

The researcher checked on their progress *every day*.

EXPLICIT/IMPLICIT Important to distinguish, *explicit* means "clearly stated and leaving nothing implied," and *implicit* means "suggested," "implied," or "to be understood, but not plainly stated."

The president *explicitly* stated her position.

Implicit in her statement were criticisms of the faculty's position.

FARTHER/FURTHER These words have also merged in meaning. For language purists, however, *farther* still means only "distant and remote," and *further* means "to a greater degree or extent."

To attend conferences, our faculty and students have to travel *farther* and more often each year.

We will look into this issue *further*.

FEWER/LESS Some people cringe when they enter a line at a grocery store express counter and read the sign announcing that this line is for customers with "10 Items or Less." They would prefer "10 Items or Fewer," citing the traditional distinctions between *fewer* and *less*. *Fewer*, to them, is a term used with separate quantities, and *less* is employed with portions of one quantified item.

I would have *fewer* headaches if I were not trying to go to school and support a family at the same time.

Less debate and more action is what we need.

HOPEFULLY This word, the mainstay of hedging politicians, is still best used to mean "in a hopeful manner." With the insistence of speakers and writers, however, it will be eventually accepted to mean "it is to be hoped."

(Still Wrong) *Hopefully*, we have made the changes in time.

(Accepted) We entered into the agreement *hopefully*.

IMPLY/INFER Two easily confused words, *to imply* means to "indicate indirectly," "hint," or "suggest," and *infer* means "to arrive at a decision based on known facts, observations, or evidence." As a result of popular usage, *infer*, these days, often is used synonymously with *imply*.

Over the phone, she *implied* that she would agree to lecture at our college next month.

I *infer* from your look that you disagree with the decision.

INCIDENCE/INCIDENTS *Incidence,* most commonly, is used to mean "extent of influence" or "the degree or range of occurrence or effect." *Incidents,* on the other hand, is the plural of incident, meaning more than one occurrence.

The *incidence* of bank failures these days is not great.

Three *incidents* involving bank failures in our state caused public outcry.

LEAD/LED Linked by sound, *lead* is the metal and *led* is the past tense form of the verb to lead.

The proposal to remove *lead* from all domestic gasoline was approved many years ago.

The speaker *led* us through a series of reasonings to his point.

LOSE/LOOSE *Lose* is a verb meaning "to mislay" or "to fail to keep or maintain"; *loose* is an adjective meaning "free" or "not confined."

Did he *lose* his book?

The cable connection is too *loose.*

PEOPLE/PERSONS Although the distinction between these two words is subtle, it is a viable difference. *People* refers to a general group; *persons* applies to a more limited collection.

The *people* of our state will not stand for more corporate tax breaks.

The *persons* involved in the class action suit were represented by Montague Associates.

PRACTICABLE/PRACTICAL A set of words that are finely distinguished, *practicable* means "feasible" or "capable of being put into action or practice," and *practical* means "realistic" or "useful."

We found that the solution to the problem was not *practicable* for the near future.

A *practical* alternative was to shut down three power plants for two weeks.

PRINCIPAL/PRINCIPLE *Principal* is an adjective meaning "first in rank in importance or authority"; *principle,* on the other hand, is a noun that connotes "a basic rule governing behavior" or "a regulation or tenet to be adhered to."

The country's *principal* product was oil.

One *principle* that should govern our choice in this matter is fairness.

STATIONARY/STATIONERY Common sources of spelling error, these two words have disparate meanings. *Stationary* is an adjective meaning "fixed" or "immovable." *Stationery,* however, is writing paper.

The room was outfitted with *stationary* cabinets but moveable partitions.

We wanted new student government *stationery,* so we consulted a graphic artist for new designs.

THAN/THEN *Than* introduces the second element of a comparison; *then* introduces a next occurrence in order.

She has been here longer *than* I have.

First the air conditioning failed, *then* the sprinkler system was activated.

THAT/WHICH One of the most frequent sources of confusion for writers, the *that/which* decision relies on the writer's knowing the difference between restrictive and nonrestrictive modifiers (see Handbook, p. 225). *That* is most often employed with restrictive clauses, and *which* is used with nonrestrictive clauses.

The booklet *that* contains the new schedule was sent out by the registrar's office on July 15.

The registrar's booklet, *which* contains the new schedule, was sent out on July 15.

THEIR/THERE/THEY'RE *Their* is the possessive of *they; they're* is the contraction for *they are. There,* on the other hand, is most often used as an adverb indicating a place or direction as well as in impersonal constructions such as "There are coffee stains on your report."

The colleges raised *their* prices.

They're trying to pressure us into doing the same thing.

We will be *there* in a few days.

TO/TOO/TWO *To* is a preposition that has countless meanings, including "in the direction of"; *too,* however, can be an intensifier or a synonym for "also." *Two* is the number.

He expressed his concern *to* the group.

They were *too* angry *to* listen.

Two members wanted a chance *to* speak, *too.*

V. GENDER-BIASED LANGUAGE

Gender-biased language is word usage that expresses a masculine bias. When a communicator chooses a gender-biased term, often that choice reflects not only a male preference but also a subordinate role for women.

Words and phrases that are gender-biased often contain the word *man.* Also, attempts to feminize a term can result in a sex-role stereotyping of women. So, to avoid gender-biased language, follow two rules.

1. Strive for Gender-Neutral Terms

When writing and speaking, avoid if possible words and phrases that contain the word *man*. This word, though historically linked in meaning with humankind in general, these days refers more specifically to males.

AVOID	USE
chairman	chairperson or chair
foreman	supervisor
insurance man	insurance agent
mailman	postal carrier
mankind	people or humans
man-made	manufactured or synthetic
manpower	personnel or staffing
salesman	salesperson or sales associate
to man	to operate or to staff
workman	worker or laborer

2. Avoid Feminized Words

Feminized words are words and phrases that transform a title into a special form that indicates the person holding the title is female. Some examples of feminized words include *authoress* and *woman doctor.*

To avoid using such feminized versions of titles, use the general title for both males and females. Apply the term *author* to all authors and *doctor* to all doctors, regardless of sex.

INDEX

Instructor's Manual
to Accompany

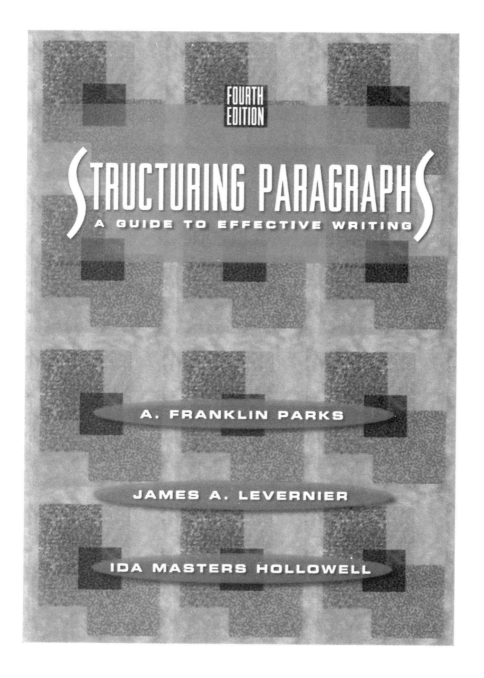

fourth edition

**INSTRUCTOR'S MANUAL
TO ACCOMPANY**

STRUCTURING
PARAGRAPHS

A Guide to Effective Writing

A. Franklin Parks

FROSTBURG STATE UNIVERSITY

James A. Levernier

UNIVERSITY OF ARKANSAS AT LITTLE ROCK

Ida Masters Hollowell

UNIVERSITY OF ARKANSAS AT LITTLE ROCK

ST. MARTIN'S PRESS • New York

Manufactured in the United States of America.
0 9 8 7 6
f e d c b a

For information, write:
St. Martin's Press
175 Fifth Avenue
New York, NY 10010

ISBN: 0-312-11516-4

CONTENTS

INTRODUCTION

The goal of *Structuring Paragraphs: A Guide to Effective Writing* is to teach the student to write general-to-specific paragraphs and then to graduate to the expository essay. Through mastering these forms of expression, the student learns the elements of effective writing.

The goals of this manual, in turn, follow from those of our text. We do not simply list answers to questions in the text, though we do give answers. We have also summarized each chapter for the instructor, made pedagogical suggestions, offered additional examples for duplication and classroom discussion, and thus served up more than the traditional "Answers-to-this-question-may-vary" manual, though there are exercises in the text for which we do not venture answers.

In the fourth edition we have added collaborative exercises and portfolio activities. The collaborative exercises enable students to develop their skills cooperatively, to provide one another with valuable peer evaluations, and to simulate the group writing environments that exist in the world of work. Further, in our classes we have found, like so many of our colleagues, that students benefit from viewing and reviewing their writing. So we encourage instructors using *Structuring Paragraphs* to require students to collect their paragraphs and essays in portfolios that they can examine and reexamine as the course progresses. This way, students gain greater insight into their own strengths and weaknesses, as well as the progress they have made.

While reviewers have commented, over the years, on the strengths of the organization of *Structuring Paragraphs,* some instructors employing the text have reported that they approach our chapters in a somewhat different order. For instance, some have indicated that they reverse Chapters 1 and 2 in order to get students composing earlier. Others have expressed a preference for teaching Chapter 6 (Coherence) immediately after Chapter 3 (Unity and Structure), so that these two important concepts are in students' minds before they proceed to the methods of development. We take great pride in the fact that *Structuring Paragraphs* is sufficiently flexible in its approach and organization to be adaptable to the different requirements of the hundreds of instructors who have used it. We encourage our adopters, therefore, to tailor its chapters and contents to their needs and those of their students.

Chapter 1: THE GENERAL-TO-SPECIFIC PARAGRAPH

Chapter 1 introduces the rationale of the text as a whole. The chapter explains that the general-to-specific expository paragraph is the best place to begin writing because it can be seen as an essay in miniature. Students, without being burdened by lengthy assignments, therefore, can practice the principles of good writing with the expectation of proceeding to the essay form that they will often use in college. These principles—topic formulation and limitation, unity, development, and coherence—are briefly listed in Chapter 1 and underlie subsequent chapters in this text.

To make clear the form that the student will learn first, Chapter 1 distinguishes the general-to-specific expository paragraph from other types of paragraphs, identifies its physical characteristics, and asserts that it consists of an introductory generalization and support. Although Chapters 3, 4, and 5 specifically treat the levels of generality and the most effective types of support for particular cases, the discussion here introduces the levels of generality with the outline of the paragraph on the television series *Roseanne* so that the student can see what the general-to-specific expository paragraph looks like and does.

As a prelude to this lesson, students in class might be assigned paragraphs without advance preparation in order for the instructor to explore their conceptions of the paragraph. These paragraphs can then be examined for basics of form such as their opening generalizations or their levels of support.

Answers to The General-to-Specific Paragraph, Exercise I, p. 5:

A.	General	C.	Specific	E.	General	G.	General
B.	Specific	D.	General	F.	Specific	H.	General

Answers to The General-to-Specific Paragraph, Exercise II, pp. 5–7:

A.		B.		C.		D.	
1.	GS	1.	GS	1.	GS	1.	GS
2.	1	2.	1	2.	1	2.	1
3.	1a	3.	1a	3.	1a	3.	1a
4.	2	4.	1b	4.	1b	4.	1b
5.	2a	5.	2	5.	2	5.	2
6.	3	6.	2a	6.	2a	6.	2a
7.	3a	7.	2b	7.	3	7.	2b
8.	3b	8.	3	8.	3a	8.	3
9.	3c	9.	3a			9.	3a
10.	3d	10.	3b			10.	3b

Chapter 2: HOW TO BEGIN WRITING PARAGRAPHS

In this chapter we begin the business of constructing paragraphs with creating a topic. Although a topic is assigned in most writing situations, we nonetheless encourage students to rely on experience for materials and authority when they write on topics of their own choosing.

This chapter reminds the student that the general-to-specific expository paragraph begins with a generalization, now identified as the topic sentence, from which the rest of the paragraph evolves. All the paragraphs taught in this text begin with topic sentences in order to encourage clarity and focus. Though we do not discuss paragraphs that have implied topic sentences or that have two or three opening sentences before they settle down to the topic, the instructor may want students to read or even write such paragraphs. If so, they can be introduced here, perhaps with exercises in determining the focus of particular paragraphs from their implications or opening sentences.

After introducing the topic sentence, we distinguish between its two components: the topic and the controlling idea, defined by what we call focusing words. Especially for basic writers, the instructor might parallel the distinction between topic and controlling the idea with that between subject and predicate, as the following sentence illustrates:

Subject (topic)	Predicate (controlling idea)
The (owner of the bakery)	is quite (successful).

The instructor can then use other less obvious examples, such as the following inverted sentence, in order to stress the diversity of topic sentences:

Predicate (controlling idea)	Subject (topic)
(Happy) is	the (person who has more than she needs).

Chapter 2 next describes and illustrates how the controlling idea limits the paragraph. A handy analogy between the topic sentence and a contract and a brief discussion of audience are also included in the chapter and pave the way for Chapter 3, on unity, by stressing the obligations of the writer to stick to the contract.

Answers to Selecting a Suitable Topic, Exercise I, p. 13:

Some suggested topics:

Hospitals (anxiety)
Excessive guilt (depression)
Working mothers (discrimination)
Flattery (enemies)
Public speaking (fears)
Flight attendants (jobs)

UFOs (movies)
Campaigning (politics)
Amusement parks (recreation)
Pressure (sex)
The Stanley Cup (sports)
Seinfeld (television)

Answers to The Topic Sentence and the Controlling Idea, Exercise I, pp. 14–15:

A. TOPIC: A student who works full-time and also runs a household
   FOCUSING WORDS: has busy evenings
B. TOPIC: A good wine is easily identified
   FOCUSING WORDS: by three traits
C. TOPIC: Drop/add policies at this school
   FOCUSING WORDS: too lenient
D. TOPIC: Planting a vegetable garden
   FOCUSING WORDS: many rewards
E. TOPIC: College registration
   FOCUSING WORDS: frustrating experience
F. TOPIC: The protective ozone layer
   FOCUSING WORDS: definite signs of deterioration
G. TOPIC: The crusade to save the great whales from extinction
   FOCUSING WORDS: a crucial ecological last stand
H. TOPIC: Purpose behind some television commercials
   FOCUSING WORDS: to annoy the viewer
I. TOPIC: Lives of some of Hollywood's greatest stars
   FOCUSING WORDS: self-destructive
J. TOPIC: A number of stand-up comics
   FOCUSING WORDS: self-deprecation the basis for successful careers

Answers to The Topic Sentence and the Controlling Idea, Exercise II, p. 15:

A. TOPIC SENTENCE: Designing a living room requires the special skills of an interior decorator.
   TOPIC SENTENCE: Designing a living room is not for the beginner.
B. TOPIC SENTENCE: Campus elections effectively teach students how the democratic process works.

	TOPIC SENTENCE:	The outcomes of campus elections are sometimes determined by the student press.
C.	TOPIC SENTENCE::	Television talk shows educate as well as entertain.
	TOPIC SENTENCE:	Each television talk show appeals to a different kind of audience.
D.	TOPIC SENTENCE:	There are many different kinds of diets, but few of them produce permanent weight loss.
	TOPIC SENTENCE:	Dieting without consulting a physician can seriously endanger the health of the dieter.
E.	TOPIC SENTENCE:	Single-sex colleges offer many advantages.
	TOPIC SENTENCE:	Many single-sex colleges have become coeducational institutions.
F.	TOPIC SENTENCE:	Cycling is an excellent way to relax.
	TOPIC SENTENCE:	Cycling is one answer to our nation's energy problems.
G.	TOPIC SENTENCE:	"The Far Side" offers a unique brand of humor.
	TOPIC SENTENCE:	The characters in the comic strip "The Far Side" resemble people I know.
H.	TOPIC SENTENCE:	Most secretaries are underpaid for the work that they are expected to do.
	TOPIC SENTENCE:	A good secretary has highly specialized skills.
I.	TOPIC SENTENCE:	The Information Superhighway promises to unveil a number of valuable information sources to the average citizen.
	TOPIC SENTENCE:	The Information Superhighway could change the way people do business.
J.	TOPIC SENTENCE:	Relics of the lost Mayan civilization often share certain characteristics.
	TOPIC SENTENCE:	Particular relics of the lost Mayan civilization reveal that the Maya had developed a sophisticated culture.
K.	TOPIC SENTENCE:	Vitamin E offers many benefits to the human body.
	TOPIC SENTENCE:	Vitamin E differs in distinctive ways from other healthful vitamins.

Answers to The Topic Sentence as Contract, Exercise I, pp. 18–19:

A. A home computer can be a valuable asset to any household.
B. Chronic depression manifests itself in a variety of different ways.
C. Television can be an important educational tool.

Answers to The Topic Sentence as Contract, Exercise II, p. 19:

A. Too specific.
   REWRITE: Raleigh, North Carolina, typifies the best in both old and new Southern architecture.
B. Satisfactory.
C. Too specific.
   REWRITE: George Washington's presidency established several precedents that helped to define the role of the president in the American political system.
D. Satisfactory.
E. Too specific.
   REWRITE: Feeding a family today costs a great deal more than it did twenty-five years ago.

F. Too vague.
   REWRITE: Ice skating is a far more exhilarating activity than roller skating.
G. Satisfactory.
H. Too vague.
   REWRITE: Communication between spouses is a crucial part of every successful marriage.

Answers to The Topic Sentence as Contract, Exercise III, p. 19:

A. SAMPLE PARAGRAPH:
   Commuting to school has its advantages and its disadvantages. Students who commute to college usually have more mobility than students who go away to college. Because they need transportation to get to and from campus, commuting students usually own cars, while students who live in dormitories normally cannot afford this luxury when they must pay for room and board. In addition, students who commute to college usually live at home, and they can use the money they save to buy and do things that resident students cannot afford. If they get into trouble or need a helping hand, students who commute to college often can turn to their parents or family. By contrast, most students who reside on campus must learn to fend for themselves, solving their own problems and meeting their own needs. But most commuting students will readily agree that, despite the advantages of commuting to college, nothing can compensate for the feeling of self-reliance that living on campus provides. The student who leaves home and family to attend college knows that he or she can adjust to new circumstances and build a new and productive life independent of past circumstances. As a result, the student who goes away to college approaches life with a sense of self-confidence often lacking in students who commute to a campus near where they grew up. And this sense of self-confidence carries over into later life, making them more secure in their professional and social activities.

Chapter 3: PARAGRAPH UNITY AND STRUCTURE

Chapter 3 examines how every sentence in a unified paragraph—or other piece of writing—supports the controlling idea. First, two versions of a paragraph on pilot error show the advantages of unity over disunity. After these preliminaries, Chapter 3 discusses primary and secondary support. Primary support directly reinforces the controlling idea of a paragraph; some texts refer to those sentences that function together to develop a controlling idea as *coordinated* sentences. Secondary supports, then, directly reinforce the primary supports and indirectly reinforce the paragraph's controlling idea. Other texts call the intermixed sequence of primary, secondary, and even tertiary supports a *subordinated* sequence.

Before determining what supports a topic sentence, however, a writer must amass the material or details. At this point the instructor may wish to review brainstorming techniques or methods for research, such as those performed by the student who wrote the sample paragraph on Washington, D.C.

Once material is accumulated, we emphasize the importance of careful planning. We start with the primary supports so that the beginning writer can plan the skeletal outline. After the primary supports are chosen, the search begins for secondary supports. Thus this chapter emphasizes a narrowing process—one that turns chaotic, unstructured information into outline form. Students who tend to organize hastily and get into trouble later because they do not plan will need some time with this chapter.

This technique of structuring raw material will help students organize essays later. For now, students practice supporting their points with adequate detail, forcing them to think about the levels of generality in a successful paragraph. But Chapter 3 does not include formal methods of development; it settles for any details in a paragraph, as long as they support the controlling idea. Chapters 4 and 5, on the other hand, introduce methods of development (such as examples, causes, and so forth) and aid the student in developing skill with rhetorical strategies.

Answers to What Is Paragraph Unity? Exercise I, p. 24:

A.   CONTROLLING IDEA: "gentle breaking" and "bronco busting"
      OUT OF UNITY: sentences 5, 6, and 7
B.   CONTROLLING IDEA: advance preparation
      OUT OF UNITY: sentences 10 and 11

Answers to What Is Paragraph Unity? Exercise II, pp. 24–25:

A.   CONTROLLING IDEA: appalling
      OUT OF UNITY: sentences 4, 7, and 8
B.   CONTROLLING IDEA: unusual parallels
      OUT OF UNITY: sentences 4, 5, and 9
C.   CONTROLLING IDEA: little resemblance to the myth
      OUT OF UNITY: none

Answers to Primary Supports, Exercise I, p. 30–31:

A.   PRIMARY SUPPORTS: sentences 1, 2, 6, and 7
B.   PRIMARY SUPPORTS: sentences 1 and 4

Answers to Primary Supports, Exercise II, pp. 31–32:

A.   PRIMARY SUPPORTS: all could be (discuss with the class)
B.   PRIMARY SUPPORTS: sentences 2, 4, 5, and 10

Answers to Primary Supports, Exercise III, p. 32:

Alternative answer for model:

TOPIC SENTENCE: Working students have special problems.
PRIMARY SUPPORT: Students with part-time or full-time jobs often have difficulty coordinating the hours they work with the hours they need to attend class and study.
PRIMARY SUPPORT: Spending long hours both at work and in school can easily lead to exhaustion and inefficient production.
PRIMARY SUPPORT: Students who work rarely can socialize with their fellow students and thus miss an important part of their education.

A.   TOPIC SENTENCE: Tragedies bring people together.
    PRIMARY SUPPORT: During times of tragedy, people have a special need to help one another.
    PRIMARY SUPPORT: Disasters such as floods, earthquakes, and tornadoes often force people to seek common shelter.

PRIMARY SUPPORT: The death of a loved one often unites the members of a family in a renewed respect for each other's needs and sorrows.

B. TOPIC SENTENCE: Hollywood has given us different kinds of classic movie monsters.

PRIMARY SUPPORT: During the early days of cinema, Hollywood introduced us to legendary monsters such as Dracula and Wolfman.

PRIMARY SUPPORT: As advances in aviation made interplanetary and even intergalactic travel seem a possibility, Hollywood created monsters such as the "alien."

PRIMARY SUPPORT: Still another type of monster popularized by Hollywood is the primordial monster perhaps best represented on the screen by King Kong and Godzilla.

C. TOPIC SENTENCE: Stress often reveals itself in a variety of forms.

PRIMARY SUPPORT: Many people respond to stress by eating either too much or too little.

PRIMARY SUPPORT: Other people find that their sleeping habits change when they are experiencing stress in their lives.

PRIMARY SUPPORT: Illnesses such as ulcers and migraine headaches have also been linked to stress.

D. TOPIC SENTENCE: Students who pay their own way through college value their education more than students who do not have to pay their own way.

PRIMARY SUPPORT: Most students who earn their tuition and living expenses are more aware of the cost of a college education than students whose parents pay their tuition and expenses.

PRIMARY SUPPORT: Since earning the money for a college education requires many sacrifices, students who pay their own way are more likely to take advantage of the opportunities a college education affords.

PRIMARY SUPPORT: Finally, the students who have worked their way through college are more inclined to express appreciation for the education they have received.

E. TOPIC SENTENCE: National health care reform would address a number of inequities in our society.

PRIMARY SUPPORT: Health care reform would result in a decrease in health care costs.

PRIMARY SUPPORT: Everyone would have the opportunity to enroll in a basic coverage plan.

PRIMARY SUPPORT: All U.S. citizens would be protected against the devastating costs of a major, long-term illness.

F. TOPIC SENTENCE: Many television commercials are an insult to human intelligence.

PRIMARY SUPPORT: Cleansers, cleaners, and detergents, for example, are said to have powers that no chemical cleaning agent can possibly possess.

PRIMARY SUPPORT: Similarly, cosmetic aids and toothpastes, when advertised on television, promise wealth and happiness to whoever uses them.

PRIMARY SUPPORT: The most insulting of all commercials, however, imply that one's human worth is determined by the shine of a dish, the freshness of a towel, or the appearance of a shirt collar.

G. TOPIC SENTENCE: Year-round schooling would present major challenges and benefits to local school districts.

PRIMARY SUPPORT: The cost of educating each student would rise significantly.

PRIMARY SUPPORT: Teachers would be able to cover more material.

PRIMARY SUPPORT: Having no long breaks from school, students would retain material much better.

Answers to Secondary Supports, Exercise I, pp. 38–39:

A. TOPIC: Students who need a part-time job
CONTROLLING IDEA: consider becoming a waiter or waitress
PRIMARY SUPPORTS: sentences 2, 5, and 6
SECONDARY SUPPORTS: sentences 3, 7, and 8
OUT OF UNITY: sentence 4

B. TOPIC: Pet owners who wish to keep their dogs fit and trim
CONTROLLING IDEA: reasons why overweight dogs tend to become obese
PRIMARY SUPPORTS: sentences 2, 4, 6, 8, and 10
SECONDARY SUPPORTS: sentences 3, 5, 7, 9, and 11
OUT OF UNITY: none

C. TOPIC: London
CONTROLLING IDEA: a city of historical splendor
PRIMARY SUPPORTS: sentences 2, 5, and 7
SECONDARY SUPPORTS: sentences 3, 4, 6, and 8
OUT OF UNITY: sentence 9

Answers to Secondary Supports, Exercise II, pp. 39–40:

A. TOPIC: A wooden pool cue
CONTROLLING IDEA: must be properly cared for
PRIMARY SUPPORTS: sentences 2, 4, and 7
SECONDARY SUPPORTS: sentences 3, 5, 6, 8, 9, and 10
OUT OF UNITY: none

B. TOPIC: Egyptian pyramids
CONTROLLING IDEA: three popular fallacies
PRIMARY SUPPORTS: sentences 2, 5, and 7
SECONDARY SUPPORTS: sentences 3, 4, 6, 8, and 9
OUT OF UNITY: none

C. TOPIC: The Zugspitze Mountain in southern Germany
CONTROLLING IDEA: an ideal place to visit for a wondrous view of the Bavarian Alps and their neighboring scenery
PRIMARY SUPPORTS: sentences 2, 4, 8, and 10
SECONDARY SUPPORTS: sentences 3, 5, 9, and 11
OUT OF UNITY: sentences 6 and 7

Answers to Secondary Supports, Exercise III, pp. 40–41:

A. **TOPIC SENTENCE:** Job applicants should always look their best for an interview.
PRIMARY SUPPORT 1: Job candidates should wear clothes that are pleasant and tasteful.
SECONDARY SUPPORT 1A: Depending on the type of interview, men should usually wear a tie and jacket, and women should wear a business-like dress or outfit.
SECONDARY SUPPORT 1B: Under no circumstances should a job candidate dress flamboyantly.

PRIMARY SUPPORT 2:	In addition, job candidates should make sure that they look clean and well groomed.
SECONDARY SUPPORT 2A:	Employers prefer to hire people who seem responsible and in control.
SECONDARY SUPPORT 2B:	A crumpled jacket or a scuffed pair of shoes may suggest that the job candidate will be equally unconcerned about details of performance on the job.
PRIMARY SUPPORT 3:	Above all, job candidates should appear cheerful, relaxed, and cooperative.
SECONDARY SUPPORT 3A:	Few employers want to hire someone who is ill-tempered or rude.
SECONDARY SUPPORT 3B:	Consequently, a candidate who looks tired or irritable is unlikely to receive a favorable rating during an interview.
B. **TOPIC SENTENCE:**	Americans are constantly being induced to spend their money.
PRIMARY SUPPORT 1:	Billboards and magazine ads bombard us with slogans that promise happiness and fulfillment if we buy this or that product.
SECONDARY SUPPORT 1A:	They tell us, for instance, that life will be more exciting if we "slam a Dew" or "catch the wave."
SECONDARY SUPPORT 1B:	They also tell us that the truly liberated woman smokes a particular cigarette because she "has come a long way" and that a certain smoke guarantees the user a masculine image.
PRIMARY SUPPORT 2:	Coupons and sales entice us to buy products and services that we often don't really need.
SECONDARY SUPPORT 2A:	As a result, we pamper our pets with chocolate treats and exotic perfumes, and we lavish expensive toys upon our children.
SECONDARY SUPPORT 2B:	While few of us may need a year's supply of frozen okra, a newspaper coupon for a 25 percent discount on a case of okra offers an irresistible buy.
PRIMARY SUPPORT 3:	Television commercials condition us to think that we can't live without the things they advertise.
SECONDARY SUPPORT 3A:	The right deodorants guarantee romance and excitement.
SECONDARY SUPPORT 3B:	Low-calorie foods promise to eliminate excess weight and make us more glamorous.
C. **TOPIC SENTENCE:**	People marry for a variety of reasons.
PRIMARY SUPPORT 1:	Some people marry for companionship.
SECONDARY SUPPORT 1A:	Few elderly people, for example, who have known companionship all of their lives are able to live alone after the death of a spouse.
SECONDARY SUPPORT 1B:	The need for companionship often draws these people together, and marriage is frequently the result.
PRIMARY SUPPORT 2:	Others marry because they want children.
SECONDARY SUPPORT 2A:	Many individuals feel that their lives are incomplete unless they have children to carry on their values and provide happiness for them in their old age.
SECONDARY SUPPORT 2B:	For them, the security of family life, together with the children it brings, is an important part of their identities.
PRIMARY SUPPORT 3:	But the majority of people marry because they are in love.

SECONDARY SUPPORT 3A:	In addition to the obvious advantages of companionship and children, marriage appeals to most people because it provides an opportunity for two people who love one another to spend their lives together.
SECONDARY SUPPORT 3B:	Although love may seem an old fashioned value to some, most people will not marry someone they do not love.

D. **TOPIC SENTENCE:** Anyone who enters the field of politics must be prepared to face the scrutiny of the public.

PRIMARY SUPPORT 1:	Because politicians are considered celebrities, the most trivial events of their personal lives attract public attention.
SECONDARY SUPPORT 1A:	Reporters and photographers are likely to follow them wherever they go—to the supermarket, to the bus depot, even on a fishing trip or to a restaurant.
SECONDARY SUPPORT 1B:	No matter where a politician travels or dines, he or she is always subject to the public eye and is likely to attract public attention.
PRIMARY SUPPORT 2:	Recently passed legislation requires candidates for public office to make their financial records public, and these records often become the subject of public controversy.
SECONDARY SUPPORT 2A:	To protect their reputations, governors and congressmen usually undergo routine financial audits.
SECONDARY SUPPORT 2B:	Such audits extend even to the office of the president, whose financial records are always a matter of public concern.
PRIMARY SUPPORT 3:	Even the families of politicians must sacrifice their privacy when one of their members enters politics.
SECONDARY SUPPORT 3A:	White House weddings, for example, are nationally televised, as are many activities that most American families enjoy in privacy.
SECONDARY SUPPORT 3B:	If their parents are involved in politics, even small children are subject to the prying lens of the camera and the anxious attentions of journalists.

E. **TOPIC SENTENCE:** Television has something for everyone.

PRIMARY SUPPORT 1:	Some programs are specially designed to provide entertainment and instruction for children of all ages.
SECONDARY SUPPORT 1A:	Such programs as *Sesame Street,* for example, teach children the basics of reading and writing while entertaining them with the antics of talking chickens and other fictional creations.
SECONDARY SUPPORT 1B:	Dramatic specials for children absorb the young viewers as they present and resolve realistic problems.
PRIMARY SUPPORT 2:	Lighthearted comedies and action-packed dramas cater to individuals who wish to escape from their everyday problems.
SECONDARY SUPPORT 2A:	Popular during the 1950s, shows like *I Love Lucy* and *Father Knows Best* rerun daily on television stations across the country and are still watched and enjoyed by the public.
SECONDARY SUPPORT 2B:	Detective programs like *NYPD Blue* and *Homicide* bring the drama of city streets into everyone's living room.
PRIMARY SUPPORT 3:	For the more discriminating viewer, television offers self-help programs, artistic productions, and carefully researched documentaries and specials.

SECONDARY SUPPORT 3A: For those interested in cooking, there is *The Frugal Gourmet,* and for those interested in gardening, there is *The Victory Garden.*

SECONDARY SUPPORT 3B: Each week, *Masterpiece Theatre* televises a famous work of literature, and programs like *The Undersea World of Jacques Cousteau* and *The National Geographic Specials* explain the mysteries of nature in terms that even the average viewer can understand and appreciate.

Chapter 4: METHODS OF DEVELOPMENT
Example, Cause and Effect, and Process Analysis

Three methods for developing paragraphs appear in Chapter 4: example, cause and effect, and process analysis. Three other methods will be presented in Chapter 5: definition, comparison and contrast, and classification. These six methods of development are distinguished from the forms of discourse (description, narration, exposition, argument, and sometimes persuasion). Chapters 4 and 5 deal exclusively with methods of development for exposition, the form used in most formal writing.

Whereas Chapter 3 is concerned with valid supporting evidence presented logically, Chapters 4 and 5 go further. They say, "Lay out your material not only logically but with a strategy that will best get your point across." Thus, the student should ask, "Can I make my point best by comparing or contrasting, or should I give examples, or does my topic call for process analysis?" and so on, seeking the most effective method.

The three methods presented in Chapter 4 are the easiest of the six methods for the instructor to present and for most students to use. Moreover, they are "musts" that all students should know. If lack of time during a course necessitates the omission of some of the methods of development, the cut should be made from those methods presented in Chapter 5. Of the three methods discussed in Chapter 4, example is presented first because it is generally considered the easiest and most basic of the methods for students to master. Cause and effect and process analysis are presented consecutively because both involve the use of analysis and both are fairly simple to use.

Answers to Example, Exercise I, p. 55:

(Examples numbered below provide primary support; those in parentheses provide secondary support.)

A. Some of the most popular programs on television today involve series that were first produced years ago.
   1. *The Andy Griffith Show* reruns appear on television sets across the country at all hours of the day or night.
   2. Episodes of *Star Trek* are as popular as they were years ago.
   3. *M*A*S*H* episodes are still being viewed by loyal fans who have seen the same programs many times.
B. Space exploration has given us many small miracles.
   1. Heat-resistant materials
   2. Weather forecasting accuracy
   3. Microcircuitry

C. Citizens who report sighting an unidentified flying object risk bringing ridicule upon themselves.
   1. Betty and Barney Hill
   2. Patrolman Schirmer
   3. Charles Hickson and Calvin Parker
D. Prejudice comes in many forms.
   1. Some people are prejudiced against members of another race with whom they have not associated intimately and whom they do not know (whites versus blacks in America or, particularly in earlier times, the English versus the Welsh).
   2. Some people will not eat certain foods because they are ignorant of the nutritional values and taste that these foods offer.
   3. Some people are prejudiced against certain products because they accept other people's adverse comments without any personal knowledge of the products' qualities.
E. Many new job opportunities are open today as a result of the development of the computer.
   1. Operators are needed to operate many different kinds of machines.
   2. A large sales force is employed nationally and internationally.
   3. Many persons have been hired by computer companies to write programs and create software.
   4. Experts are constantly being sought to design new and better technology.
F. Some people are their own worst enemies.
   1. The supercritical soul who expects perfection of everybody and drives people away
   2. The gossip
   3. The person who is always late
   4. The chronic borrower who never returns things
G. Americans have many patriotic songs.
   1. "Star-Spangled Banner"
   2. "America the Beautiful"
   3. "America"
   4. "Yankee Doodle"

D and F lend themselves to development by extended example, provided that the example is detailed, typical, and adequately supportive of the topic sentence.

Answers to Example, Exercise III, pp. 55–57:

A. Sentences 2, 4, 5, 6 and 7 introduce examples. Sentence 3 supports sentence 2.
B. Sentences 2 and 9 introduce examples. The other sentences develop these examples.
C. Sentences 2, 3, 4, 5, and 6 introduce examples, thus developing the paragraph with a series of primary supports. Sentence 7 reiterates the controlling idea.
D. Sentences 2 and 10 introduce examples. A series of secondary supports follows each sentence.
E. Sentences 2 and 5 introduce examples. Sentence 5 is followed by a lengthy series of secondary supports.
F. Sentences 2 and 3 furnish primary support. Sentence 3 introduces subsequent examples.

Most of the examples in these student papers are apt. Students should recognize, however, that secondary support for a primary support is usually desirable. In particular, paragraph C needs the addition of supporting examples.

Answers to Cause and Effect, Exercise I, p. 61:

A.   CAUSES: A logical treatment would include such reasons as increased crime in the schools, the inability of teachers to give sufficient time to individual students, and the distractions from study that occur regularly.

B.   CAUSES: Desire to fit into a fairly affluent society, no war to rebel against, the cyclical nature of political philosophies (the tendency for a conservative popular viewpoint to follow a liberal one, and vice versa).

C.   CAUSES: Some students are nervous and do not perform well on quizzes and exams. Some students do not learn the art of cramming and do not do well on tests although they have a good grasp of course material; exams do not always cover the crucial material in courses.

D.   EFFECTS*:   Students who are interested in biological phenomena or who enjoy pet ownership may have thought about this topic. When they read about the re-emergence of rabies as a major threat to wild animals, they will doubtlessly encounter statements by authorities concerning the causes, but they may have more personal experience with the effects. That is, they may have read in local newspapers about the increased incidence of rabid raccoons and skunks in their area. Or they may have heard from family and friends about infected bats and squirrels interacting with domesticated animals and infecting them. Perhaps the greatest effect is the concern that this epidemic creates whenever the writer experiences a stray dog and other animal in the wild.

E.   EFFECTS: According to the national press, the baseball strike of 1994 created a number of negative effects for professional baseball: the image of the owners and players was further tainted, and fan interest has migrated to other sports and activities.

F.   CAUSES: To keep out of jail, to keep acquaintances from knowing intimate details of their lives such as age or salary, to make other people feel good.

G.   EFFECTS: Increase in global temperatures, decrease in earth's capacity for producing vegetation, increased risk of loss of human life due to harmful solar radiation.

Answers to Cause and Effect, Exercise III, pp. 62–63:

A.   CAUSE: Causes are introduced in sentences 2, 4, 6, and 7. Each of sentences 3, 5, 8, 9, and 10 supports the primary support preceding it. Considering that human beings are subject to "nerves," the causes adduced in the paragraph are valid.

B.   CAUSE: The student writer intended to show the cause of the increasing importance of education to young people. However, the writer states only that education is necessary for persons entering medicine, engineering, and communications. Proficiency in these fields, as the writer alleges in sentence 3, is essential for human welfare. But the writer overlooks countless other professions that require college training and fails to mention other reasons for increased college enrollment.

C.   EFFECT: Sentence 1 expresses the controlling idea of the paragraph well. The writer gives two adverse effects of entering a hospital in sentence 3 (for which the reader is prepared in sentence 2) and in sentence 9. Sentence 10 recaps the topic sentence.

*OR CAUSES

D.   EFFECT: The effects of transferring are recounted in sentences 2, 7, and 10. Sentences 3, 4, 5, 6, 8, 9, 11, 12, and 13 provide secondary support for these effects. Though the writer includes a very personal set of effects in the paragraph, they do believably follow from the cause, which is the new experience of being at a university.

E.   EFFECT: The effects of using cocaine are stated in sentences 2, 5, and 8. Intervening sentences provide support for these sentences.

Answers to Cause and Effect, Exercise IV, p. 63:

SAMPLE PARAGRAPH: Adult Education

Adult education is booming in the United States today for a lot of reasons. Many people who want to work find themselves being turned down for lack of a passport in the form of a college degree even though they may actually be well qualified to handle the job being sought. Therefore, many go back to school. The rise in the cost of living has forced many families to have income from more than one member. This factor has caused many spouses to seek an education in order to qualify for jobs that will help keep up the family income and standard of living. A third cause for increased interest in adult education is the increasing desire of women for a career outside the home. If lack of an education stands in the way, they enroll in colleges and universities. Another cause of enrollment of a mother, father, or even grandmother or grandfather is the fact that colleges and universities are scattered thickly across the United States and beckon to the mature of mind. People who did not care to learn when they were eighteen or twenty find themselves wanting to explore new horizons, and a nearby college or university provides the way.

Answers to Process Analysis, Exercise I, p. 66:

A.   Washing (or waxing) a car requires more thought than people may realize.
   Steps:
   1.   Clearing papers or packages out of the car
   2.   Vacuuming the car
   3.   Gathering materials necessary for the job: a hose, soft cloths, a brush, polishing cloths, a washing compound to be used (if any), wax to be used (if any)
   4.   Washing the top of the car
   5.   Washing the painted parts of the car other than the top
   6.   Washing the tires
   7.   Washing the chrome
   8.   Washing the windows
   9.   Applying wax (optional)
   10.   Polishing

B.   Painting a room requires a good deal of planning.
   Steps:
   1.   Removing all small pieces of furniture from the room
   2.   Moving large pieces of furniture away from the wall
   3.   Covering all pieces of furniture left in the room
   4.   Laying drop cloths
   5.   Filling holes in the surface to be painted
   6.   Sanding rough spots
   7.   Washing any areas where grease has accumulated
   8.   Assembling ladders, paint, paint thinner, brushes

9. Dressing for the operation (including putting on a cap)
10. Actually applying paint.

C. From being seated to giving a tip, getting a meal in a restaurant has become a ritual.
   Steps:
   1. Being seated
   2. Waiting for a menu
   3. Considering menu and placing the meal order
   4. Placing the dessert order (optional)
   5. Paying the bill (if it is paid at the table)
   6. Leaving a tip

D. Growers of houseplants should learn how to repot a plant correctly.
   Steps:
   1. Covering work area to catch soil and other materials spilled
   2. Assembling plant, pot, trowel, potting medium (including soil, vermiculite, humus, and so on), broken pottery or small pebbles for the bottom of the pot, watering can
   3. Removing plant from old pot or container in which it was purchased
   4. Placing broken pottery or small pebbles in the bottom of the new pot to ensure drainage
   5. Mixing soil ingredients if these are not ready-mixed
   6. Filling pot about half full with the soil mixture, depending on the length of the plant roots
   7. Setting the plant in the pot
   8. Watering the roots
   9. Holding the plant with one hand while filling in soil around the plant with the other
   10. Packing soil gently around the plant
   11. Watering the plant
   12. Putting in extra soil where packing and watering have reduced soil level
   13. Putting the plant in a place sheltered from direct sunlight until it recovers from the operation
   14. Clearing away materials used

[Topic Sentences E, F, and G provide valuable opportunities for students to perform research or to apply learning they have acquired in other college courses.]

Answers to Process Analysis, Exercise III, pp. 66–69:

A.	PROCESS:	Some of the steps listed actually take place concurrently. Some are repeated from day to day. But here is a rough chronological sequence, from determination to break the smoking habit to setting up a schedule of exercise if reduction of smoking leads to weight gain.
B.	PROCESS:	Steps in the process are presented chronologically.
C.	PERSONAL EXPERIENCE:	This paragraph is a personal narrative rather than a strict process analysis. The steps the writer went through in becoming a vegetarian are not necessarily typical of those followed by all people who become vegetarians. Also, the writer presents background material that is not part of a process.
D.	PROCESS:	The steps are fully delineated with no extraneous information.

E.	PROCESS:	Steps are appropriate and complete.
F.	PROCESS:	Process is rendered clearly and in unified fashion.

Answers to Process Analysis, Exercise IV, p. 69:

SAMPLE PARAGRAPH: Making Fudge

Making successful old-fashioned fudge is an accomplishment that requires careful attention to detail. The fudge artist starts with a thick boiler to ensure against burning the sugar solution to be worked with. Into the boiler the cook tosses a lump of butter, perhaps a fifth of a stick. As this melts over low heat, two squares of bitter chocolate are added for melting and mixing with the butter. Next, two-thirds of a cup of milk is added and blended with the chocolate mixture. When the mixture boils to a smooth custard texture, two cups of white sugar are poured in. The sugar must be blended well with the other ingredients, and any crystals sticking to the boiler must be wiped off. A candy thermometer is then inserted. When the temperature reaches the "soft ball" stage on the thermometer, the boiler is removed from the heat and a teaspoon of vanilla added. After the mixture has cooled to under 120°, the thermometer is removed and the mixture is beaten with a large spoon. If the mixture thickens suddenly, cream should be added—perhaps several times—until the blend is shiny. Further beating will bring cooling and thickening of the candy until the experienced candy cook pours the fudge into a buttered dish, where it will soon be cut into blocks of candy. Only experience acquired from trial and error tells the fudge maker when the pouring-up time has come. This is the crucial moment, and no recipe can cover this important detail.

Chapter 5: FURTHER METHODS OF DEVELOPMENT
Definition, Comparison and Contrast, and Classification

Chapter 4 introduces the student to three methods of development: example, cause and effect, and process analysis. Chapter 5 introduces three other methods of development that students often find more difficult to use: definition, comparison and contrast, and classification. All three of these methods deal with the concept of "class." Definition involves putting something into a class and then differentiating it from other members of the class. Comparison and contrast involves a consideration of two items that are members of the same class. Classification involves assigning things to a class.

The treatment of the material in Chapter 5 depends in part on the time available to the instructor. If it is necessary to omit a method, definition is probably the best choice for elimination because it requires a good deal of time for students to be able to use it well. Comparison and contrast, however, probably should not be skipped since most students find it relatively approachable and since they will be required to compare and contrast on tests and assignments throughout their college careers.

A final section in Chapter 5 deals with using the methods of development to help students decide on controlling ideas for their paragraphs and choosing the particular method that is best suited for developing a paragraph on a particular controlling idea. This section of Chapter 5 provides a handy point at which to review the six methods of development, and it also provides a transition into Chapter 6, which deals with matters of style and coherence.

Answers to Definition, Exercise I, p. 76:

1. FORMAL DEFINITION. *Weeds* is the term to be defined, and the topic sentence itself provides a brief formal definition, *plants* being the class and *worthless* introducing the characteristic that differentiates weeds from other plants. The paragraph should establish the worthlessness to man of plants that he identifies as weeds. Thus, the paragraph itself is a definition.

2. FORMAL DEFINITION. *Microwave ovens* is the term to be defined, with *ovens* being the class and *microwave* introducing the differentiating characteristics. The definition here will provide clarification necessary to support the controlling idea.

3. FORMAL DEFINITION. *"Homemade" food* is to be defined, based on distinctions that traditionally separate it from other types of food. Then the paragraph should demonstrate that, despite the traditional conception, very often Mom's chocolate cake comes out of a box and her fried chicken out of the grocer's freezer.

4. FORMAL DEFINITION. *Video cassette rental stores* is the term to be defined. *Rental stores* is the class, and *video cassette* introduces the differentiating characteristics. The definition should function indirectly in a paragraph that develops the topic sentence.

5. FORMAL DEFINITION. *Vegetables* is the term to be defined; *cruciferous* indicates differentiating characteristics. The definition here will provide clarification necessary to support the controlling idea.

6. INFORMAL DEFINITION. Unless the writer is a psychiatrist or has advanced training with gifted children, the definition will have to be informal. The word *signs* in the topic sentence, however, indicates that the writer will point out certain characteristics of some gifted children. An extended definition would work well here, with the writer delineating in detail the characteristics of a single gifted child.

7. FORMAL DEFINITION. *Reggae* is the term to be defined based on distinctions between this form of contemporary music and other forms. The paragraph should then be devoted to demonstrating the impact of reggae on the current American music scene.

8. INFORMAL DEFINITION. The writer's imagination should function here to show how the school experience underlies and provides for future experiences the student will have.

Answers to Definition, Exercise II, pp. 76–78:

a. *Enabler* is the term to be defined. The definition is formal. *"A significant person in an addict's life"* is the class, with "who helps to maintain the addiction" expressing the differentiating characteristics. The rest of the paragraph serves to support the definition and also to back up the topic sentence.

b. *Sickle-cell anemia* is the term defined. The definition is formal. *Disease* is the class, and the specific characteristics of sickle-cell anemia are explained in the rest of sentence 1. The paragraph itself constitutes a definition, elaborating the brief definition given in the topic sentence. As in many definition paragraphs, the first sentence or first two sentences following the topic sentence restate the definition or, as here, simply provide one or two additional facts about the term.

c. *Black hole* is the term defined. Formal definition is used. *Remains of a star* is the class, and the rest of the topic sentence following this term explains the specific characteristics of a black hole. The paragraph itself constitutes a definition.
d. *Music* is the term defined. The definition is informal. The first sentence is not a formal definition because it does not identify a class. The paragraph has limited success in conveying what *music* means.
e. *Snow* is the term defined. The definition is informal. The only class evident in the topic sentence is *wolf*; the only differentiating characteristic is *in sheep's clothing*. The writer fairly successfully presents the implications of the term *snow*. A better paragraph might have resulted from a different method of development, such as a contrast between the beauty and charm of snow and its unfortunate side effects.

Answers to Definition, Exercise III, p. 78:

SAMPLE PARAGRAPH: Brunch

   Brunch is a typically American institution. The name itself illustrates a brief economy: Americans coin short terms to deal with things or customs that are part of their way of life. It is quicker to say "Come to brunch" than "Have a combination of breakfast and lunch with me." Brunch saves time for Americans in a hurry. And brunch can mean fewer calories. If one eats at ten-thirty or eleven o'clock, one may last until dinner and not put on at lunch further ounces that add up to extra pounds that Americans find unhealthy, not to mention unstylish. Brunch can be a doughnut and cup of coffee taken on an empty stomach during a break in office work. Or brunch can be toast or waffles with sausage and hot coffee served up to a half-dozen friends by someone who wants to meet some simple social obligations. But sometimes brunch saves neither time nor calories. Brunch has become high fashion. Brunch can mean silver trays loaded with ham, cheeses, and pastries served at a country club where the strong-willed nibble delicately to keep off pounds but where others completely lose their resolve and devour pastries and calories with typical American abandon.

Answers to Comparison and Contrast, Exercise I, p. 85:

A. **FORMAL COMPARISON**
    CLASS: Myths and stories of ancient peoples
    BASES: Use of a deity or deities, use of the supernatural, idealization of a people through story
B. **FORMAL CONTRAST**
    CLASS: Dangerous modes of transportation
    BASES: Frequency of accidents, number of fatalities, likelihood of injury
C. **FORMAL COMPARISON**
    CLASS: Sports involving kicking a ball
    BASES: The ball, the playing field, rules, scoring
D. **INFORMAL COMPARISON**
    CLASS: Indefinite, but something like "things that flow through space and time"
    BASES: Movement through space, movement in time, uncertainties in the course of movement, enlargement in some sense as the movement continues
E. **FORMAL CONTRAST**
    CLASS: Diapers
    BASES: Sanitary factors, convenience, cost, disposability (as pollutants in landfills)
F. **FORMAL CONTRAST**
    CLASS: Health care programs
    BASES: Amount the insured has to co-pay, extent of coverage, flexibility with regard to service providers

Answers to Comparison and Contrast, Exercise II, pp. 85–88:

A. **FORMAL CONTRAST**

CLASS:	Two prominent African tribes
BASES:	Extent of Westernization, attitude toward the supernatural
DEGREE OF SUCCESS:	The topic sentence mentions similarities, but it leaves the impression that the paragraph will be concerned with "a striking difference." For two-thirds of the paragraph, the reader is informed of likenesses while the "striking difference" receives somewhat scant attention. The paragraph would be greatly improved if reference to likenesses had been disposed of quickly in the topic sentence: "Although the Ibos and Yorubas, two prominent African tribes living in Nigeria, have both been influenced by their contacts with Western Christianity and education, one striking difference between them has impressed itself on the minds of visitors more than the similarities between the two cultures." The paragraph would then discuss differences in attitude toward the supernatural in more detail.

B. **FORMAL CONTRAST**

CLASS:	Forms of self-defense fighting
BASES:	Direction of action, kind of action, appearance to spectator, direction of movement, use of clawing and scratching, ease of learning
DEGREE OF SUCCESS:	The paragraph is at best fair although it makes some very good distinctions. A review of the bases reveals that direction of action is discussed in two places; the comments should be brought together. The writer would have produced a more closely knit paragraph by using three bases: techniques of fighting, ease of mastery, and appearance of the action to a spectator.

C. **FORMAL CONTRAST**

CLASS:	Rifles
BASES:	Weight, sensitivity to abuse, sights, scopes
DEGREE OF SUCCESS:	In this unsuccessful paragraph, the writer contrasts the two weapons with regard to weight, mentions only the target rifle with respect to sensitivity to abuse, mentions sights only for the target rifle, and finally treats scopes for both weapons. The necessity for filling in the gaps is obvious.

D. **FORMAL CONTRAST**

CLASS:	Films that depict Native Americans
BASES:	The view of European settlers, degree of aggressiveness of Native Americans, consideration of Native American cultures
DEGREE OF SUCCESS:	The message of the paragraph is compelling, but the bases could be better focused—say, on the stereotypes of Native Americans, as they are presented and countered in film.

E. **INFORMAL COMPARISON**

CLASS:	Roughly elements deadly to man
BASES:	Process of entrance, crippling effect
DEGREE OF SUCCESS:	The paragraph is moderately successful with insightful points of comparison, but it lacks any real concrete details to clarify generalizations.

F. **FORMAL CONTRAST**
CLASS: Meals (breakfast versus lunch and dinner)
BASIS: Foods served
DEGREE OF SUCCESS: This very good paragraph develops a contrast on one basis only. It says what everybody knows, but it makes the reader consider how completely breakfast foods are reserved for the first meal of the day. Thus, the paragraph makes the commonplace interesting.

Answers to Comparison and Contrast, Exercise III, p. 88:

SAMPLE PARAGRAPH: A Small College versus a Large University

Students attending a small college will have opportunities that differ markedly from those afforded by a large university. In the first place, greater academic variety is to be found at a large institution. There are more academic departments at a large university than are to be found at a small college. Thus, more major subjects are available for the choosing. Also, more courses will be offered. The variety of entertainment at a large institution is also greater than that offered at a smaller college. Sporting events are more publicized and more spectacular. Concerts by celebrated orchestras and soloists are features at large institutions while being rare at small schools. And noted speakers appear more often at larger institutions than at small colleges. On the other hand, the small college is more homelike than the large university. With fewer students and smaller classes, instructors at the small institution frequently come to know their students individually and have time to give each a certain amount of personal attention, which a lonely student at a very large institution usually finds lacking. Both the large university and the small college usually offer sound educational opportunities, but the advantages offered by the institutions differ a great deal.

Answers to Classification, Exercise I, pp. 92–93:

A. BASES: Secular or religious, patriotic or not, scope of observance (that is, by all the people or just a few), origin
B. BASES: Any characteristics that distinguish fairly sizable groups of drivers, such as driving record, courtesy, and so on
INFORMAL CLASSIFICATION: This topic sentence is perhaps best developed informally. We usually classify drivers according to whether their driving styles agree or conflict with our own. We identify, for example, "The driver who passes me and then slows down" and "The driver who stays in the passing lane but drives slowly." The student's individual reactions can be reflected here.
C. BASES: Official acceptance of pay, attitudes toward the game, response to fellow players and fans
D. BASES: Breed, origin, uses made of animals, suitability as pets
INFORMAL CLASSIFICATION: This topic sentence can be developed either formally or informally. If the classification reflects the student's personal, idiosyncratic reaction to dogs, the classification will be informal.
E. BASES: The background of the players, rules of the game, the nature of the prizes

INFORMAL CLASSIFICATION:	Certainly this paragraph would have to be developed from a personal standpoint since no exhaustive study would be available to validate the topic sentence. But, through observation and with ingenuity, the writer could establish classifications that would be not only plausible to the reader but humorous as well.
F. BASES:	Attitude to money, attitude to "specials of the week," attitude to the person who checks out the groceries, attitude to children
INFORMAL CLASSIFICATION:	This topic sentence is perhaps best developed informally. A paragraph developed through informal classification of this topic will reflect the student's personal reaction to shoppers at the checkout counter. Whether the writer has actually been a checker or not, he or she will have observed shoppers who have two dozen coupons but have not sorted them into usable and unusable ones and do the sorting while other shoppers wait. And there are shoppers who do their complaining about prices to checkers who can do nothing about the situation and who must listen patiently.

Answers to Classification, Exercise II, pp. 93–95:

A. FORMAL CLASSIFICATION

BASIS:	Participation of the plant in capturing an insect
DEGREE OF SUCCESS:	The paragraph comes off well considering that only one basis is used. Its detail is good. Further bases for classification might have included locations in which the plants are found, ease of growth in captivity, and so on.

B. FORMAL CLASSIFICATION

BASES:	German, Latin, and other origins of the English language
DEGREE OF SUCCESS:	The topic sentence establishes the three classifications into which English words can be placed according to their originating language. The remainder of the paragraph does the work suggested by the topic sentence—that is, it assigns particular words to each of the three classifications. The third classification is broader and perhaps less satisfying than the other two.

C. FORMAL CLASSIFICATION

BASES:	Voting laws, lack of interest in a specific party, feelings of alienation
DEGREE OF SUCCESS:	In this successful paragraph, the three bases are introduced as primary supporting statements. After each come secondary details that back up the three primary statements.

D. FORMAL CLASSIFICATION

BASES:	Success of the Crusades, chivalric behavior of the participating Christians, cultural exchange between East and West
DEGREE OF SUCCESS:	The writer successfully classifies the fallacies regarding the Crusades into types. There is no overlap in bases.

E. **FORMAL CLASSIFICATION**

BASES: Precautions that make theft difficult, new devices that discourage theft, measures to secure items in a car, methods to help identify a car

DEGREE OF SUCCESS: This paragraph is good but not spectacular. For example, the steps an owner can take to avoid tempting a potential thief with items might immediately follow the precautions for locking and parking the car. The first basis would reasonably include ways in which an owner can prevent or discourage theft. The other two bases could follow as given.

F. **INFORMAL CLASSIFICATION**

BASES: Fabrics, colors

DEGREE OF SUCCESS: Although the subject is interesting and the topic sentence raises expectation of an interesting paragraph, this classification is unsuccessful because it does not achieve its purpose. First of all, it muddles fabrics and colors. The color and fabric of typical costumes of each class of society are not consistently treated. Secondly, the symbolism of the clothing is lost in the muddle.

Answers to Classification, Exercise III, p. 95:

SAMPLE PARAGRAPH: Thieves

Thieves are people who take things that don't belong to them, and they are not all the kind that climb into windows to purloin valuables or snatch a purse on the street; some who are always with us are less spectacular. Students turn into thieves when they steal answers to test questions from papers being written by other students. Some people borrow books, fail to return them, and become what might be called "thieves after the fact." People in advertising occasionally steal ideas and use them to further promotional schemes of their own. A politician steals the thunder of another politician by having a spy on his opponent's campaign staff. By finding out in advance what his opponent is scheduled to say or do, he can say or do it first. Some people even steal recipes from friends who want to keep secret the special dishes that have helped to make their dinners popular among colleagues from the office. There are many kinds of thieves quite aside from the types who go to jail.

Answers to Using Methods of Development, Exercise I, p. 98:

A. Cause and effect, specifically cause
B. Comparison and contrast, specifically contrast
C. Example
D. Definition
E. Process (or classification)
F. Example
G. Definition
H. Classification

Answers to Using Methods of Development, Exercise II, pp. 98–101:

A. COMPARISON AND CONTRAST (SPECIFICALLY, CONTRAST): The paragraph is extremely well done, treating both the chauvinist and the nonsexist on the same bases.

B. CLASSIFICATION: Students should easily recognize the problem with this pat classification of individuals into good-average-failing categories. Students don't fall so neatly into these classes. The paper could be improved if more or different bases for classification were used. Example, however, might prove more effective as a method of development. Without trying to classify all students in these three narrow categories, the writer might mention that the three types are observable on all campuses and give an example of each type.

C. COMPARISON AND CONTRAST (SPECIFICALLY, CONTRAST): The paragraph is well done. The three bases are introduced by "first of all," "second," and "finally," and the writer discusses the two terms being compared under each.

D. CLASSIFICATION: It would be impossible to classify laughs and do an inclusive job. But even the informal classification used in this paragraph might include another type. The paragraph is, however, imaginative.

E. DEFINITION: *Autism* is the term that is successfully defined in the paragraph through an examination of characteristics, possible causes, and potentially effective treatments.

F. PROCESS: This paragraph is obviously thoroughly developed.

G. CAUSE AND EFFECT (SPECIFICALLY, EFFECT): This paragraph focuses on the effects of Attention Deficit Disorder on those who suffer from this neurological disorder. While the paragraph could have been slanted more toward definition, the writer chose an approach and stuck with it.

H. EXAMPLE: This paragraph fully illustrates its point.

I. CLASSIFICATION: In this simple but interesting paragraph, the writer presents three classes of anglers based on the anglers' methods of locating fish. More detail about each of the three classes would make the paragraph more interesting, but it is technically well done.

Chapter 6: ACHIEVING COHERENCE

In Chapter 6 we show students how to achieve coherence through three general means: order, transitional devices, and combining sentences. Obviously, a paragraph needs a principle of order underlying it, governing the flow of details, making that flow congenial to the mind of the reader who expects order. Transitional devices, or guideposts that point backward to where the writer has been and forward to where the writer is going, are also essential to the reader's understanding of the paragraph as a whole. And finally, well-integrated sentences that demonstrate, through subordination and co-ordination, the relationship between more and less important ideas, are also vital to coherence.

Time, space, and importance are three ordering principles that can govern the arrangement of supporting details. While temporal and spatial order may at first seem more appropriate for narration and description than for exposition, many expository paragraphs are subtly ordered in these ways. Perhaps the key ordering principle for college students is importance. Here we stress ordering for effect, that is ordering supports from the least to the most important so that the reader finishes on the writer's most significant point.

Under transitional devices we include several techniques for achieving smooth transition. Transitional words and phrases signal the reader to recall what has gone before and to proceed to what lies ahead. Similarly, key words and phrases, when repeated in exact or synonymous form, signal the reader to remember the topic of the paragraph and perhaps its controlling idea. Paradoxically, eliminating repetition of concepts can also aid coherence, as can substituting pronouns for frequently repeated nouns.

Next, we use sentence combining to demonstrate the advantages, in some cases, of subordinated and coordinated sentences over choppy, single subject-verb constructions. This section thoroughly presents neither the method of sentence combining that aims to improve sentence maturity and fluidity nor the embedding process. Instead, the chapter reminds students that expression on the sentence level finds many forms, some clearer and more exact than others. The instructor may wish to supplement this chapter with other sentence-combining activities and focus intently on sentence-writing techniques and habits.

Two final ways of increasing coherence are grammatical, through consistent verb tenses and pronoun persons. Besides aiming to correct frequent shifts in tense and person, this section also reviews the principles for forming simple verb tenses and for using pronouns correctly. Here the instructor may also want to spend some time on related grammatical matters, referring when appropriate to "A Concise Guide to Editing Sentences," located at the end of the text.

Answers to Time Order, Exercise I, pp. 108–109:

4, 9, 5, 1, 3, 2, 7, 6, 8

Answers to Transitional Words and Phrases, Exercise I, pp. 119–120:

A. 1. a. But
   2. c. Consequently
   3. b. Therefore
B. 1. b. First
   2. a. Consequently
   3. c. Further
   4. a. In addition
   5. b. Finally
   6. c. In particular

Answers to Transitional Words and Phrases, Exercise II, pp. 120–121:

A. *Suggested answers:*
   EXAMPLE: For instance
   ADDITION: In addition
   RESULT: Consequently
   ADDITION: What is more
   CONCLUSION: In conclusion

B.   *Suggested answers:*
    EXAMPLE: First of all
    COMPARISON: Likewise
    ADDITION: Second
    ADDITION: Finally

Answers to Transitional Words and Phrases, Exercise III, pp. 121–122:

A.   *Suggested answers:*
for example
Adjacent to
And
Therefore
B.   *Suggested answers:*
therefore
First
then
In addition
further
C.   *Suggested answers:*
In the first place
for instance
What is more
Second
therefore
Finally
however

Answers to Pronouns, Exercise I, p. 125:

A.   their   their   its
    they   their   it
    it   they
B.   those   them   his or her
    They   they
    themselves it

Answers to Pronouns, Exercise II, pp. 125–126:

A.   *This* (sentence 4): broad reference
    This (sentence 7): broad reference
B.   *they* (sentence 3): ambiguous reference
    them (sentence 3): ambiguous reference
    they (sentence 3): ambiguous reference
    their (sentence 3): ambiguous reference
    this (sentence 4): broad reference
    that (sentence 6): broad reference
    they (sentence 7): ambiguous reference
    that (sentence 8): broad reference

Answers to Repetition of Key Words and Phrases, Exercise I, p. 127:

A.   Lamaze, a word that sounds exotic, actually refers to something quite practical: a method of prepared childbirth. Lamaze classes teach the expectant mother and her "coach" methods of coping with the birth process. The mother, first of all, learns breathing and hand-motion techniques to aid her during labor. These techniques often enable the mother to undergo "natural childbirth," or childbirth without anesthesia. In addition, Lamaze classes instruct the mother in how to deal with such problems as "back labor" or even an emergency delivery. The "coach" is also trained to oversee the mother's breathing techniques, to time her contractions, and generally to offer moral support to her efforts. Lamaze classes, which are intended for women in their last months of pregnancy (and for their coaches), are usually taught by registered nurses with Lamaze certification.

B.   One of the major causes of our city's traffic problems is Main Street. To begin with, the street is not wide enough to handle the flow of traffic that plagues midtown. The midtown area has expanded vastly in the last few years, and the number of vehicles traveling through it has grown. Furthermore, there is an inadequate number of traffic lights on Main Street. For example, the very busy intersection at Second Avenue, where traffic flowing onto Main Street is always backed up, is greatly in need of a traffic light. There is also an urgent need to improve the condition of the street itself. There are numerous potholes that slow vehicles down, impeding the flow of traffic even further.

Answers to Repetition of Key Words and Phrases, Exercise II, pp. 127–128:

A.   Television furnishes an effective means of advertising. One of the reasons for its effectiveness is simply that millions of Americans view television every day. It is estimated that the average American family watches television four hours a day. Second, television is more effective than, say, radio because television can appeal to the prospective buyer through both ear and eye. Viewers who can see the product that is being sold are more likely to buy it. And, finally, television advertising in the last twenty years has become so sophisticated that television advertisers have been able to determine what kinds of audiences watch at specific times of the day. They can now air commercials that appeal specifically to the audience watching at any given time, and the result is, of course, that their pitches are more successful than when they promote their products randomly.

B.   Getting a dog creates several duties for the owner. First of all, feeding the new pet regularly is necessary to its well-being. A puppy needs to be fed twice a day, as opposed to an adult dog, who needs feeding only once a day. Second, a healthy dog requires regular exercise. Taking it for daily walks or allowing it to run for lengthy periods of time increases its chances for good health and a sound muscular structure. Exercise also helps the dog to release the tension that builds up while it is confined. Finally, the dog must be protected from disease and health problems and therefore requires occasional trips to the veterinarian's office. It should be inoculated against distemper and rabies, as well as tested for worms and skin ailments.

Answers to Combining Sentences, Exercise I, pp. 132–133:

1. The thirsty, disappointed tourists crowded into the bars.
    Cool and dark, the bars offered relief from the beach.

2. In the lodge, the hot, blazing fire quickly thaws the skiers. Next to the crackling fire, an ex-skier uncomfortably props his cast.

3. Early in the morning, the excited and quite awkward beginners appear for their lessons.

    Racquetball, an easy game to play, is a difficult game to master.

    Among the skills that distinguish a pro from an amateur are judging angles, placing shots, and serving effectively.

    Because the novice player often does not anticipate the ball's angle off the wall, the novice wastes much energy by running to catch up with the ball that he missed.

4. Watching television, America's favorite pastime, is shared by young and old.

    Many programs shown on television reflect Americans' lifestyles of today, their interests, and their ethics.

    Shows such as *Getting Fit* and *In Motion* are targeted at people who are into fitness and who also like to mingle viewing and exercise.

5. Tornadoes, intense low pressure areas found in severe thunderstorms, are only a few hundred feet in diameter.

    Measuring devices cannot measure the speed of the winds in tornadoes since the devices are broken when tornadoes hit them.

    When a tornado first touches down on a mountain top, it may skip along the mountain peaks, leaving the valleys in between untouched.

    A tornado leaves behind a trail of destruction and devastation: houses leveled, buildings torn to shreds, trees uprooted and blown down, people killed and injured.

Answers to Combining Sentences, Exercise II, pp. 133–134:

A. *Possible answer:*

   Blood pressure is the force of the flow of blood against the walls of the arteries. Created by the pumping action of the heart, this pressure rises with each contraction and then falls as the heart relaxes. The blood that is pumped goes throughout the body and returns to the heart by way of a system of vessels. The movement of blood is rapid; in fact, a drop of blood usually requires less than one minute to complete the trip from and to the heart.

B. *Possible answer:*

   In a span of three hundred years (1600–1900), white newcomers to the United States uprooted and conquered more than half a million Indians. Naive and friendly, the Indians did not foresee the threat the newcomers posed. Soon, however, it became apparent that too many whites were beginning to arrive. Friction developed over land, and hatred and fear grew up among the settlers, who regarded the Indians as savages. By the time the United States won its independence in 1783, most of the tribes along the Atlantic coast had been dispossessed of their land.

C. *Possible answer:*

   Land is one of the best investments that people can make. They can do whatever they choose with their land: they can build the house of their dreams on it, they can use the land as a weekend camping resort, or they can cultivate or landscape it. Best of all, a piece of land can be a place where the owners can put down roots; it can be "home." When people own their own land, they can relax and do almost anything there without fear of reprisal. Since its value is on the rise, land bought today will surely double in value in the next ten years. Thus, land is an investment that can satisfy everyone and that should never be passed up.

D. *Possible answer:*

A method of testing for fetal abnormalities called transabdominal amniocentesis has been developed. This method involves drawing amniotic fluid, located in the uterus, from the mother for study. Requirements for this process are antiseptic solution; sterile towels; syringe and needle, needed for inserting the local anesthetic; and a four-inch spinal needle, employed to penetrate the walls of the uterine cavity. First of all, the uterus is probed to locate the unobstructed area anterior to the fetal shoulder. Then the selected site for needle entry is prepared with antiseptic solution. A local anesthetic may be introduced at this point but is not always needed. Next, the puncture needle is inserted into the cavity, and the fluid that is removed is tested. This procedure, which tells whether or not the fetus is normal or has any congenital abnormalities, takes only a short time.

Answers to Consistent Verb Tense, Exercise I, p. 136:

A. Driving erratically is a characteristic of some drivers. They weave all over the road as if unaware of their actions. On a four-lane road, these drivers usually drive in two lanes because they are unable to stay in one. On a two-land road, on the other hand, they drive down the center of the road, not only because they are unable to stay in one lane, but also because they are afraid of hitting the curb at the side of the road. When a car approaches from the opposite direction, they move into their own lane slowly, scaring the other driver half to death. Therefore, careful drivers should be on the alert for erratic drivers who do not always stay in the proper lane.

Answers to Consistent Verb Tense, Exercise II, p. 136:

A. After living in a women's dorm for a little more than one semester, I have noticed that when women come to college they immediately become fanatics. No matter what they look like, fat or thin, the calorie count of every food item around campus becomes imprinted on their brains. I am not sure why this fanaticism develops. One possible reason is that living with so many other women makes one realize that her own figure may be less than perfect. Another strong possibility is that calorie counting is an activity that everybody does. Whatever the reason, however, fanaticism about dieting is apparent in every women's dorm on campus.

Answers to Consistent Pronoun Person, Exercise I, p. 140:

A. Final exams are psychologically difficult for students, and, with few exceptions, students hate them. They know that finals can make or break their grades, regardless of how well they have done previously in the semester. So students usually cram relentlessly; they bury themselves in notes, texts, and supplementary readings with the hope that something will sink in. Soon, though, the pressure begins taking its toll: the students may become discouraged, frustrated, short-tempered, and fatigued. Regardless of whether students have one or all of these symptoms, they are sure to have the disease: "finalitis."

B. I enjoy using my creative abilities when I teach elementary school. I prefer making my own teaching materials, such as educational games, learning centers, drill cards, and exercises. So when funds for professionally made textbooks and workbooks are low and materials are difficult to obtain, my students never suffer. And I find that my materials are better anyway. I also enjoy creating my own bulletin-board materials. Why should I go out and buy snowflakes or Thanksgiving scenes or letters made by a machine when I can make them myself? My students appreciate the items on the bulletin board more when they realize the effort that I have put into them. And I find that my creative efforts help students to discover the rewards of using their own creative abilities. It is not difficult to imagine the satisfaction they feel when they see something they made—a map or a picture—up on the bulletin board. No professionally made materials can instill that sense of accomplishment and pride.

Answers to Consistent Pronoun Person, Exercise II, p. 141:

A.   Cashiers are expected to handle any situation that may arise in the course of a day's work without becoming disgruntled or unpleasant. For instance, when a customer buys something, he expects it to be in working order, and if it is not, he becomes upset. Generally, when the disappointed buyer returns a broken item, he takes out his feelings on the first person he sees. And that person is usually the cashier. Sometimes the dissatisfied customer can be violent, cursing loudly and even threatening physical harm if his demands are not immediately met. The cashier must keep his cool through it all and wait until the emotion has subsided; then he can deal with the problem in an efficient and appropriate fashion. After the merchandise has been returned and a refund has been made, the customer feels embarrassed. All of the apologies in the world, however, cannot make the job of a cashier any easier.

B.   A home garden offers an inexpensive and nutritious alternative to paying exorbitant prices for supermarket produce. Green beans, for instance, cost as much as a dollar a pound in the supermarket, but one can grow a year's supply of beans on a small plot of land for only a few cents and a little effort. Apples and oranges, too, can be expensive, especially during off-season months. But if the climate is right, the gardener can plant a fruit tree in his backyard, store the fruit in a cellar or garage, and enjoy fresh fruit all year round at a fraction of the price he would pay for it in a grocery store. In addition to beans and fruit, one can grow tomatoes, squash, peas, potatoes, beets, lettuce, and other types of produce in his garden. The savings to his pocketbook can prove phenomenal: if properly planted and tended, a ten-foot-square plot of land can produce several hundred dollars' worth of produce.

Chapter 7: FROM PARAGRAPH TO ESSAY

Chapter 7 applies what students have learned about the paragraph to the standard short essay with an introduction, three body paragraphs, and a conclusion. This 1-3-1 form, though perhaps overly formal and formulaic, introduces most of what students need to know to approach with confidence any longer form of writing. Of special note are the sections about writing introductions and conclusions since these paragraphs can significantly enrich a student's short essay.

This chapter presents two methods for creating a short essay. The first method is a step-by-step procedure that turns a general-to-specific expository paragraph of the kind presented in this book into a 1-3-1 essay. The instructor must stress that this process is not recommended for every essay. (In fact, it is simply a pedagogical tool to teach students the relationship between the two forms and to ease them carefully from one stage in writing to the next.) The second method, starting from scratch, is the one that students should consistently use since it enables them to move from selecting and narrowing a topic to writing the thesis to organizing the essay, creating the body paragraphs, and supplying the introduction and conclusion.

Answers to The 1-3-1 Essay, Exercise 1, pp. 147–148:

THESIS SENTENCE: This high suicide rate is influenced by a number of factors.

DIVISIONS: Psychological states, sociological conditions, ineffective means of prevention.

CONCLUSION: The final paragraph reviews the three divisions in the essay, concluding that increased awareness and knowledge of these factors may help prevent suicide.

Answers to Paragraph into Essay, Exercise 1, pp. 160–162:

INTRODUCTION:

Over the past decade winters have been getting worse, inspiring scientists to formulate theories about an emerging "Little Ice Age." As a result of the subzero temperatures and increased snowfall in many parts of the country, people have become wiser. They have insulated their homes more thoroughly, begun conserving precious fuel, and learned to dress more sensibly for the cold. They have found, for one thing, that *winter temperatures need not be uncomfortable if one learns to dress properly* [thesis]. They have discovered the benefits of *layering, wearing hats and vests,* and *donning warm gloves and socks* [divisions].

CONCLUSION:

A little practical attention to the type of clothing worn on a cold, snowy day can overcome the effects of the weather [thesis restated]. After layering clothing, covering the sources of body heat, and protecting the extremities, one is ready for a sleigh ride or a snowball fight or a bus ride to work [divisions reiterated].

Answers to Writing an Essay from Scratch, Exercise 1, p. 171:

A. Music
    1. A split major in music and business
    2. High school band
    3. "Tuning in" while driving
    4. Dorm stereos
    5. Instruments and personalities of musicians
B. Health
    1. Nutra Sweet
    2. Smoking and pregnancy
    3. Birth control pills
    4. Swimming as exercise
    5. "All-nighters"
    6. Caffeine
C. Fashions
    1. Style of dress and personality of wearer
    2. Comfortable styles
    3. Jogging attire
    4. Trend-setters in fashion
    5. Proper dress for job interviews
    6. Teenage clothing
D. Drugs
    1. Drinking age
    2. Generic drugs

      3.   "Growing your own"
      4.   Nasal sprays and decongestant tablets
      5.   Prozac
      6.   Miracle drugs

E.   Films
      1.   Sex and violence
      2.   Rating procedures
      3.   "Home Box Office"
      4.   Clint Eastwood (or a favorite film star)
      5.   The "credits"
      6.   Home movies

F.   Automobiles
      1.   Stereotypical cars of the 1950s
      2.   A car at college
      3.   Battery-powered automobiles
      4.   State inspections
      5.   Car salesmen I've known
      6.   "Fender-benders"

G.   Education
      1.   Learning the hard way
      2.   Cost versus worth
      3.   Back to basics
      4.   Liberal or practical?
      5.   Teaching at its best
      6.   Training a Labrador

H.   Computers
      1.   Types of software
      2.   Uses in the home
      3.   Word processing
      4.   Advice to prospective buyers
      5.   Uses for the student
      6.   Cost of various types of home computers

Answers to Writing an Essay from Scratch, Exercise II, pp. 171–172:

A.   Good thesis statement
B.   Too narrowly focused
C.   Good thesis statement
D.   Too broadly focused
E.   Too narrowly focused
F.   Good thesis statement
G.   Good thesis statement
H.   Too narrowly focused
I.   Too narrowly focused
J.   Too narrowly focused
K.   Good thesis statement
L.   Too narrowly focused
M.   Too narrowly focused
N.   Too broadly focused

O. Good thesis statement but mechanical
P. Good thesis statement
Q. Too broadly focused
R. Too broadly focused
S. Good thesis statement
T. Too narrowly focused

Answers to Writing an Essay from Scratch, Exercise III, p. 172:

A. THESIS 1: Privatizing schools is a way of offering education to students more economically.
   THESIS 2: In some areas privatizing schools has worked, in others it has not.
B. THESIS 1: What we refer to as a blizzard is actually a combination of many phenomena.
   THESIS 2: Being marooned by a blizzard can be pleasant.
C. THESIS 1: Effective communication between adults and teenagers can lower the rate of teenage pregnancies.
   THESIS 2: There are many tragic effects of a teenage pregnancy.
D. THESIS 1: Intramural sports are vital to the life of a college or university.
   THESIS 2: There are several important points to remember when setting up an intramural program.
E. THESIS 1: An embarrassing accident for a child can be more serious for an adult.
   THESIS 2: Embarrassment generally results from one of the following situations.
F. THESIS 1: Men and women often fail to communicate due to a phenomenon called "genderspeak."
   THESIS 2: Genderspeak often affects the way men and women interact in the workplace.
G. THESIS 1: Health clubs are a perfect place for a woman who wants to get back in shape after a pregnancy.
   THESIS 2: Health clubs attract certain types of people.
H. THESIS 1: People who have made important contributions to civilization have often done so as a result of a life-changing experience.
   THESIS 2: [Student choice] can be a life-changing experience.

Answers to Writing an Essay from Scratch, Exercise IV, pp. 172–173:

A. THESIS SENTENCE: Having to take basic courses in order to graduate from college can often be very frustrating.
   1. English composition for the science major
      a. Little attention paid to writing in high school
      b. Has to make up grammar from four years of high school in one semester
      c. Has to write more fluently for English instructors than for science instructors
   2. Basic speech for the naturally timid
      a. The fear of getting up in front of people to speak
      b. Stammering when up there so all the preparations are forgotten
      c. The nausea and the critique afterward
   3. Biology for the humanities major
      a. Dissection is nauseating

        b.   All those facts to memorize
        c.   Many objective tests and few essays

B. **THESIS SENTENCE:** Babysitting is a good job for a teenager to consider.
   1. Flexible hours
      a.   No strict schedule as with other part-time jobs
      b.   Freedom to select hours if enough customers
      c.   Can schedule around school activities and social events
   2. Extra money
      a.   Hourly rate
      b.   Other benefits
      c.   Special jobs
   3. Generally easy work
      a.   Children usually asleep
      b.   Get paid for watching television or doing homework
      c.   When attention to children is required, job still is fun: can play with them and enjoy their antics

C. **THESIS SENTENCE:** Living in the country is better than living in the city.
   1. Noise levels
      a.   City—high: traffic, industry, construction
      b.   Country—low: wind rustling leaves, occasional thunderstorm, small animals
   2. Pollution levels
      a.   City—high: industry, automobiles, haze as health hazard
      b.   Country—low: fresh air with clarity and beauty
   3. Pace of life
      a.   City people: high-keyed, impatient, impersonal due to rushed schedules and frustration from delays
      b.   Country people: low-keyed, patient, personal, friendly

Answers to Writing an Essay from Scratch, Exercise V, p. 173:

A. **THESIS SENTENCE:** Having to take basic courses in order to graduate from college can often be very frustrating.
    TOPIC SENTENCE 1: For the science major, English Composition may be very frustrating.
    TOPIC SENTENCE 2: Basic speech can also cause a college student anxiety, particularly a timid student.

B. **THESIS SENTENCE:** Babysitting is a good job for a teenager to consider.
    TOPIC SENTENCE 1: One advantage of babysitting is flexible hours.
    TOPIC SENTENCE 2: While allowing the teenager virtually to determine his or her own schedule, babysitting is, at the same time, quite profitable.
    TOPIC SENTENCE 3: Finally, not only does babysitting easily fit into the babysitter's schedule and provide extra spending money, but it is generally easy work.

C. **THESIS SENTENCE:** Living in the country is better than living in the city.
    TOPIC SENTENCE 1: For one thing, the country gives one a break from the incredible noise of the city.
    TOPIC SENTENCE 2: Second, there is not only less noise but also less pollution in the country.
    TOPIC SENTENCE 3: And finally, to accompany the quiet and clean air, the slow pace of life in the country is preferable to the pressure of the city.

Answers to Writing an Essay from Scratch, Exercise VI, p. 173:

B. *Sample Essay:*

When one is a teenager and in need of extra money, there are only a few alternatives. One can beg for it, cozy up to a rich uncle, work at McDonald's, or babysit. In fact, *babysitting is a good job for a teenager to consider,* regardless of sex. Babysitting usually entails a flexible schedule, good pay, and easy work.

One advantage of babysitting is flexible hours. Since babysitters are so much in demand these days, one can be selective when accepting jobs; the sitter can, in essence, plan the job around activities without sacrificing any needed income. What is more, since there is no set schedule week after week as there is for one working in a fast-food restaurant or a department store, the babysitter can even permit certain interruptions in the schedule, say for a date or a trip, without penalty. If the sitter normally babysits on Wednesday night but on a particular Wednesday wants to go to a basketball game, he or she can go, knowing that with advance notice an employer will not mind and that he or she can make up the time lost on Sunday by sitting for someone else.

While allowing the teenager to determine his or her own schedule, babysitting is, at the same time, quite profitable. The standard rate per hour varies with geographical location, but usually one charges two dollars per hour for one child and adds fifty cents for each additional child. In addition, if the period to be worked is long enough, meals and snacks are included. Occasionally, a sitter will be asked to do something special such as take the child to a movie or the zoo. The cost of the sitter's ticket is generally covered by the parent. There are, in addition, "dream sits" that involve travel and hotel stays. For instance, a friend of mine was once hired to accompany a family on their three-month stay in Europe. Her job was to take care of the children in the family when the parents needed her; her remuneration was all expenses paid!

Finally, not only does babysitting easily fit into the babysitter's schedule and provide extra spending money, but it is generally easy work. The children, in most cases, are asleep when the sitter arrives at the home in the evening, or they are at least close to being ready for bed. Once they are nestled and snug in their beds, the babysitter can relax with a book, study, or watch television. A smart babysitter makes good use of the time, working on homework and projects, so that free time can be used for socializing and hobbies. But even when the children are awake, babysitting is a joy. One can play with them, read to them, or even take a walk with them. Their waking periods furnish important opportunities for the babysitter to get to know the children. And the sitter too benefits from the experience, learning much to store away for future years when he or she may have children to raise.

There are, therefore, many advantages to consider before giving up babysitting to take on a job in a restaurant or store. The sitter should remember the flexible schedule, the money, and the relative ease that comes with babysitting. If the sitter recalls these factors, chances are he or she will stay a babysitter.

Chapter 8: ANSWERING DISCUSSION QUESTIONS ON QUIZZES AND EXAMINATIONS

Chapter 8 is intended to show students how they can go about writing carefully organized and effective answers to essay examination questions that they might be required to answer in the other college courses they are taking or are likely to be taking in the future. It thus allows the student to make practical and immediate use of the skills discussed in the preceding seven chapters of the book, and it shows them exactly how those skills can be used to enhance their effectiveness and success as writers and students.

In this chapter, an effort is made to guide the student, in a simple and direct fashion, through the process involved in successfully responding to an essay examination question. In the first step of this process, we show the student how to recognize the essay examination question when it appears on an examination and how to distinguish between a question that calls for an essay response and one that calls for a different kind of answer (i.e., true/false, identification, or multiple-choice questions). In the next step of the process, we show the student how to evaluate the nature of the question at hand and determine what the question specifically asks the student to accomplish in an answer.

After providing the student with instruction in these preliminary steps, we instruct the student in how to sort through and analyze facts and information recalled from such sources as lectures, notes, and texts and how to begin ordering this information with a view toward answering a given question. At this point in the chapter, the student is shown how to decide whether or not to answer a question with a single-paragraph or a multi-paragraph essay response. The final section of the chapter reviews the actual writing of the answer to an essay examination question in terms of the principles of unity, development, and coherence discussed in the preceding chapters of the book.

Use of this chapter by the instructor will depend partly upon the amount of time remaining in the course. Some instructors might find it useful to put students through the actual process of answering an essay examination question by first discussing and then asking questions on materials covered in a reader. Other instructors might find it useful simply to have students answer or rewrite answers to questions given them on essay examinations from courses they have already taken or are in the process of taking.

Answers to How to Recognize a Discussion Question, Exercise, p. 176:

A. ESSAY ANSWER. The question calls for causal analysis.
B. A true/false question.
C. ESSAY ANSWER. The question calls for a definition of both "pidgin" and "creole" and for a comparison of these two terms.
D. An identification question.
E. A multiple-choice question.
F. ESSAY ANSWER. The question calls for classification.
G. ESSAY ANSWER. The question calls for process analysis.
H. ESSAY ANSWER. The question calls for a contrast

Answers to Responding to a Discussion Question, Exercise, p. 181:

A. Classification
B. Process
C. Cause/Effect
D. Comparison/Contrast
E. Definition
F. Example

Answers to Responding to a Discussion Question, Exercise I, p. 189:

A. This question calls for a discussion. A formal definition of subatomic particle should be followed by a discussion that includes examples, locations, and functions.

B. This question indicates that a discussion is necessary. Students must provide a series of effects that demonstrate the impact of Jung on psychotherapy.

C. This question calls for a fairly lengthy discussion of the steps in the life cycle of the butterfly. Process analysis is obviously indicated.

D. This question calls for a discussion answer. The writer is asked to contrast the ideologies of the two political parties.

E. An informal classification is required. Students are called upon to demonstrate how the experiences of the Cherokee people can be classified as a "Trail of Tears."

F. The writer needs to discuss in detail a principal effect of the development of the nuclear bomb.

Chapter 9: REVISING PARAGRAPHS AND ESSAYS

This chapter focuses on revision, an important step in the writing process that is difficult to engender in the beginning writer. Despite encouragement, coaxing, and threatening, most students just will not write and rewrite as carefully as they should. We encourage the student to revise a paper both during the drafting process and when the graded paper comes back from the instructor. When word processing is available, we integrate revising on the computer into this part of the course as well.

For improvements between the first and final drafts, we supply "A Checklist for Major Revisions" that covers the major points in the text, including unity, development, and coherence. Then, for the final step in the student's own revision process, we furnish "A Style and Usage Checklist" to aid him or her in the refining of a paragraph or essay. The usage section of the "Checklist," in turn, refers students to sections of the appended "Concise Guide to Editing Sentences" for supplemental help with problems of grammar, punctuation, mechanics, spelling, and gender-biased language. In addition, we include exercises that ask the student to revise rough drafts into final drafts. For the student looking over a graded paper, we supply a guide to correction symbols and abbreviations often used by instructors.

Finally, for the instructor who wants to tackle revision in a class discussion, we have furnished some sample annotated papers along with their revised versions.

Answer to Step One: Major Considerations and Step Two: Style and Usage, Exercise I, pp. 198–199 ["A" only]:

A. There are four basic ways to reduce the risk of heart attack. The most important is to limit the amount of saturated fat and cholesterol in one's diet. Cooking should be done with polyunsaturated fats, and eggs and whole-milk dairy products should be limited. Second, one should keep trim. Heart disease is less likely among men and women who maintain a reasonable weight and who diet if necessary. Third, one should exercise regularly. People who have sedentary jobs and who do not exercise are much more susceptible to heart attacks than are people whose jobs require physical activity or who engage in sports or jog. Finally, one should never smoke. Smoking is a major cause of heart and lung disease and contributes to many heart attacks. In these four ways, one can maintain a strong heart and reduce the risk of heart attack.

Answer to Step One: Major Considerations and Step Two: Style and Usage, Exercise II, pp. 199–200 ["C" only]:

C. Striving too hard for success can be a terrible mistake. By setting an extremely difficult or impossible goal and then concentrating on nothing but that goal, an individual misses other important aspects of life. The boy who plays on the school football team just to win misses the enjoyment of the game. He feels only the pressure to win, and he fails to appreciate friendships with other players and the satisfaction of doing his best even if his team loses. Like the boy who plays football only to win, the student who studies only for grades sacrifices happiness for success. Such a student never enjoys school and never appreciates an education. Similarly, adults who seek only economic success often discover too late that money is not happiness. For the sake of money, they neglect their families and even hurt friends and colleagues who get in their way. Success is indeed important, but so are other things in life.

Answers to Step One: Major Considerations and Step Two: Style and Usage, Exercise IV, pp. 200–201:

A. The traditional American funeral has been called a social function at which the deceased is the guest of honor. Approximately 22,500 funeral establishments in the United States compete to bury two million bodies a year. Next to buying a house or a car, purchasing a funeral is the largest single investment a person is likely to make. The average funeral costs more than two thousand dollars, and the funeral industry itself is a thriving multimillion-dollar business. Perhaps people should think twice before they decide to bury their dead as the funeral industry tells us the dead should be buried. Knowing the facts about such costly funeral items and services as caskets, embalming, and graveyard plots can be an advantage should one ever have to confront a funeral director and purchase these things for a loved one.

The casket is the single most expensive item on the funeral bill. Attractiveness, protection, and comfort are the selling points that funeral directors emphasize when they market a casket. In an attempt to cater to and encourage the American mania for luxury items, manufacturers have produced caskets of glass, steel, wood, cement, marble, rubber, and even plastic. Whatever the decision, one should remember that the deceased will not enjoy the purchase and that friends will only have an hour to admire the casket before it is lowered into the ground, encased in two thousand pounds of concrete and covered with half a ton of dirt.

Embalming is also costly, but it is not as essential as most people think. Contrary to popular belief, embalming is not required by law unless the deceased succumbed to a contagious disease. Too horrible to describe in detail, embalming is a process most people might consider doing without. Technically, embalming is simply the replacement of bodily fluids with a liquid preservative, but the actual methods of embalming severely mutilate the body through incisions and manipulations. Each year, more people feel that embalming is a senseless waste of money, an expensive luxury that can raise the price of a funeral by as much as two hundred dollars.

The final item on the funeral bill is the cemetery plot, and it too can prove costly. Spending on location, a cemetery plot can cost from one to several hundred dollars. In addition, many states require a vault to hold the casket when it is placed in the ground. These expensive vaults add to the cost of the plot. Cemetery plots can be purchased through the funeral director or from the cemetery. The cost of a plot depends on the social status of the cemetery and the location of the grave within the cemetery. Exclusive cemeteries that cater to the wealthy resemble spacious parks, and the plots there are quite expensive. Older, less exclusive cemeteries often sell plots for much lower prices.

Until people decide what they want for their dead, American funerals will continue to be mysterious and expensive rites. According to Mary Hartman, "There should be a new field of funeral people who are much less funereal. . . . The way they do it now is just much too serious. It should be sillier or something . . . maybe they should play games."

Answers to Revising a Graded Paper, Exercise I, p. 204:

Before students begin revising their own paragraphs, the instructor might wish to reproduce and analyze one or more of the following paragraphs:

A. Honeybees can communicate with others of their kind through signals that sometimes are very complex. According to scientists, they have a /amb complicated language, and they communicate with an elaborate system of signals, transferring a message through the patterns of a dance. A bee that has found a flower garden ripe with honey can describe its location by the /amb shape of a dance it performs when back at the hive. It can do a round
dev/ dance or a sickle-shaped dance another is a tail-wagging dance. It also /ro
agr/ communicate a certain amount of information by the amount of energy it puts into the dance. [And the number of times it performs a pattern.] [frag]
agr/ They can indicate direction with the angle formed by a line in the dance | dev
pattern and a vertical line pointing straight upwards.

Revision:
Honeybees can communicate with others of their kind through signals that sometimes are very complex. According to scientists, honeybees have a complicated language, and they communicate with an elaborate system of signals, transferring a message through the patterns of a dance. A bee that has found a flower garden ripe with honey can describe the location of the garden by the shape of a dance it performs when back at the hive. It can, for example, perform a round dance, a sickle-shaped dance, or a tail-wagging dance, each of which conveys a different message to the other bees. Furthermore, the number of times that the bee performs a particular pattern indicates how much honey is available in the garden. By using various angular motions in their dance patterns, bees can also indicate direction. A vertical motion tells the other bees that they should fly upwards, and an angular motion in a specific direction tells the other bees to fly in that direction.

B. There are evidence to suggest that ancient civilizations were visited by /agr
people from outer space. According to an ancient Inca tradition, the Incas were visited by a man from the sky. This man was called Viracocha. [Later [dev] he was identified as a god and called Quetzalcoatl.] Some people believe trans that ancient pictures in various parts of Europe depict prehistoric astro-
trans nauts. The figures wear a sort of headgear with pronged projections that /vag
suggest antennae. Other figures sketched or carved on rocks in the Sa-
sp/ hara Dessert, Sweden, and which are in other places show human figures not//
apparently floating in the air. These figures could easily be creatures from outer space. [Waiting for their parachutes to open.] Near Nazca in South [frag]

1c/ America is what appears to be a gigantic airfield. In the opinion of certain
historians and anthropologists, this airfield was laid out by visitors from
1c/ Øuter Ƶpace who also laid out other gigantic markings. [Hoping the men [dang]
1c/ from Øuter Ƶpace would one day return,] the system of markings was
kept up by later generations of Indians and is still alive today. Pictures
carved on stones in Central America show what may be machines that traveled through space. In fact, Central and South American folklore contain /agr
many stories of ancient visitors from the sky. Thus, when the early Europeans arrived on the shores of Central America, the natives thought that the
amb/ ships in which they came were giant space vehicles. [Fulfilling prophecys /sp
[frag] made centuries earlier.]

Revision:
There is evidence to suggest that ancient civilizations were visited by people
from outer space. According to an ancient tradition, the Incas of South
America were visited by a man from the sky. Originally called Viracocha,
this strange visitor from the heavens was identified as a god whose name
was Quetzalcoatl. Ancient Europeans also have left evidence of extrater-
restrial visitations. According to certain anthropologists, ancient pictures
on the walls of caves in various parts of Europe depict prehistorical astronauts. The figures in these pictures wear what appears to be a headgear
with pronged projections suggesting antennae. Other figures sketched or
carved on rocks in the Sahara Desert and other parts of the world show
human figures apparently floating in the air. These figures could easily be
creatures from outer space who are in the air waiting for their parachutes
to open. Near Nazca in South America is what appears to be a gigantic
airfield. In the opinion of certain historians and anthropologists, this airfield was laid out by visitors from outer space who also laid out other
gigantic markings. Hoping that the men from outer space would one day
return, later generations of Indians maintained the system of markings.
Finally, pictures carved on stones in Central America show what may be
machines that traveled through space. In fact, Central and South American
folklore contains many stories of ancient visitors from the sky. Thus, when
the early Europeans arrived on the shores of Central America, the natives
thought that their ships were space vehicles that fulfilled prophecies made
centuries earlier.

C. Many of the students who are graduated from American Ħigh Ƶchools /1c
need to return to school and start all over in order to learn the three /wdy
basics—reading, writing, and arithmetic, as a popular old song puts it.
1c/ Tests show that many Ħigh Ƶchool graduates are extremely slow readers,
and that their comprehension of what they do read is equally poor. [Not
[dang] having been trained in writing,] their essays and correspondence show
lack of organization and coherence. It is sad but true that college fresh-/cliché
sp/ men no longer no their multiplication tables, and, with a few exceptions,
are not fully qualified to take college courses in math. This is why the sale /amb
sp/ of small calculaters is up. Unable to calculate with simple figures, eight,- / ‿een
dev | year-old students across the entire nation punch their little pocket-sized
brains for answers. All in all, it appears that man is [regressing back to an [wdy]
sp/ earlier stage] of intelligenȝe. He can spend his time watching the television screen [having entrusted his brain to a computer.]   [dang]

Revision:

Many of the students who are graduated from U.S. high schools need to return to school and learn the three basics—reading, writing, and arithmetic, as a popular old song puts it. Tests show that many high school graduates read extremely poorly and that their comprehension is equally poor. Not having been trained in writing, they produce essays and correspondence that lack organization and coherence. Studies also show that college freshmen no longer know their multiplication tables and, with few exceptions, are not fully qualified to take college courses in mathematics. For this reason, the sales of small calculators are up. Unable to calculate with simple figures, eighteen-year-old students across the nation must punch their little pocket-sized brains for answers to basic math problems. All in all, it appears that people are regressing in intellectual development. Having entrusted their brain to a computer, they can spend their time watching the television screen.